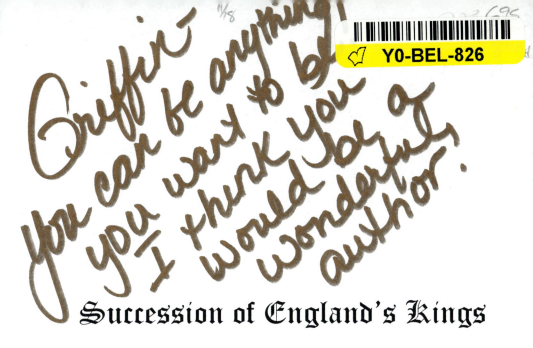

Griffin—
You can be anything
you want to be!
I think you
would be a
wonderful
author.

Succession of England's Kings

Saxons to Stuarts

KELLI KLAMPE

Kelli Rea
Klampe
& Bear
Bear

DEDICATION

This book is dedicated to the many people who have stood by and given me encouragement through my many many hours of research for my Novels. Thank you!

To Brandi, Maygen and Tristin who are the greatest children a Mother could ever hope for! You are my drive to do something better always, and though live can be a struggle, you have been there not only as my children, but as motivation and best friends. I love you so much beyond words! You are all of my heart, my greatest accomplishment and my inspiration to accomplish on paper what at times seemed impossible. I love you with every breath, and this was written every word with you at heart.

CONTENTS

ACKNOWLEDGMENTS

First and Foremost I need to acknowledge Jennifer Denman Musick for contributing the chapter of the Tudors, and the Biographies of Richard II and John 'Lackland' Her expertise and help in this book was invaluable.

Also I need to Thank Javaneh Fennell for contributing the Biographies of Alexander the Great, King Alfred, Richard III, Edward IV, Henry III and Edward I. Javaneh was instrumental in the completion of this book.

To list all the people that have stood by me, encouraged me and made my writing possible it would be impossible to list them all. Thank you all and thank you, Eva, Wes, Stephanie M, James and Carmine, Dawn & Dan

I would also like to thank Bob and Colleen for praying for me every night. Everyone who had faith and believed I had it in me.

Thank You, you have all been invaluable. And to my family and children of course that have waited patiently for this. Brandi, Tristin, Maygen. And my parents.

I would like to thank the University of Leicester for the use of their timelines and photographs. The extensive research they did on the remains of Richard III that inspired me to delve into the succession of England's Kings.

Also I would like to thank Google Books for the mass amount of work they have done resurrecting historical manuscripts for public use. Without them I would not have been able to do such extensive research.

And thank you God for blessing me with all the people above,
And everything you have and have not placed in my life.

Timeline of England's Kings and Queens-

800-Present

The House of Wessex- The Anglo-Saxon Kings 800-1066

802-839 Egbert- King of Wessex

839-852 Ethelstan (Ruled Kent, Essex, Eastex and Sussex)

839-858 Ethelwolf (Ruled Kingdom of Westsax only until 839)

858-860 Ethelbald

860-866 Ethelbert

866-871 Ethelred

871-901 Alfred 'Alfred the Great'

901-924 Edward 'Edward the Elder'

924-939 Ethelstan

939-946 Edmund I

946-955 Edred

955-959 Edwy

959-975 Edward II 'The Martyr'

979-1013 Edmund II 'Ironside'

1016-1035 Canute 'The Great'

1035-1040 Harold 'Harefoot'

1035-1042 Hardicanute

1042-1066 Edward III 'The Confessor'

1066 Harold II

1066 Edgar

The Norman Kings 1066-1087

1066-1087 William I 'The Conqueror'

1087-1100 William II 'William Rufus'

1100-1135 Henry I 'Beauclere'

1135-1154 Stephen and Matilda

The House of Plantagenet   1087-1399

1154-1189 Henry II 'Curtmantle'

1189-1199 Richard I 'Lionheart' The Crusades

1199-1216 John'Lackland'

1216-1272 Henry III

1272-1307 Edward I 'Longshanks'

1307-1327 Edward II

1327-1377 Edward III

1377-1399 Richard II

Lancaster and York1399-1484

1413-1422 Henry V

1422-1461 Henry VI

1461-1483 Edward IV

1483 Edward V- disappeared from the Tower under Richard III

1483-1485 Richard III

The Tudors   1485-1603

1485-1509 Henry VII

1509-1547 Henry VIII

1547-1553 Edward VI

 Lady Jane Grey was named heir and reigned for 9 days 1553

1553 1558 Mary I

1558-1603 Elizabeth I

The Stuarts 1603-1714

1603-1625 James I

1625-1649 Charles I

1649-1660 Commonwealth Of England (Oliver Cromwell)

1660-1685 Charles II

1685-1688 James II (Overthrown by daughter)

1689-1702 William and Mary II

1702-1714 Anne

The Hanoverians   1714-1901

1714-1727 George I

1727-1760 George II

1760-1820 George III

1820-1830 George IV

1830-1837 William I

1837-1901 Victoria

The Windsor's 1901-Present

1901-1910 Edward

1910-1936 George V

1936- Edward VIII(Abdicated)

1936-1952 George VI

1952- Elizabeth II

Chapter One

THE DEVELOPMENT OF ENGLAND'S MONARCHY

Authors Note:

I need to point out that I have, throughout this book, used the original writings and biographies of some of our first recorded historians. Those whom most of the authors of our history books used to write their theories of the past. I thought it appropriate to compile a book using those original accounts and allow readers and historians to form their own opinions. Since most of those manuscripts are written in Old English I have tried to modernize them while keeping them as original and as accurate as possible. You will see that there are some grammifical errors in keeping with the originality of those authors documents.

We have several historians that have given us good accounts of early historical events. Those such as Asser's: King Alfred the Great. An early history written in the mid-8th century and preserved for us today. The Saxon Chronicles is another invaluable historical document that gives great detail of the earliest centuries, even mentioning in a few places the line of John the Baptist. (Yes I have read it) While it is a tedious piece of history for most to read cover to cover, it does have some fascinating accounts; some I have included in the following pages of this book.

After the Roman Empire, England was oppressed by its own weight and divided into Eastern and Western portions. During England's intestine wars, the country was over flowing with barbarous Kingdoms. The Island of England in that time was so torn and shaken. The rulers which governed Britain in that time was Ecuisthe, the Roman General, under Honorius and Valantinian the 3rd. They declared war on Britain to gain control of the Island against Attila, King of the Huns.

The Huns, who appeared on the borders of Eastern Europe, after A.D. 350, continued to migrate in a generally westward direction, pushing the peoples they encountered further west into the path of Roman citizens. Some of these, mainly Germanic, tribes eventually set out from Europe into northern Roman-controlled Africa.

The poor Britain's, were led by Attila and other Kings that ruled over the dominions of England. They were at that time, so utterly destitute of martial discipline that they easily became prey to the Scots- who were not subject to the Roman rule. If the rule of the Roman's was bad, the Scots ruler ship was even worse. The Scot's treated them more intolerably and tyrannically than the Romans had ever done.

Britain's fought alongside the English Saxons, who came to their relief in the Year 409 (Bede) 'But these Saxons used the poor Britain's worst of all, and expelled the whole race of them out of that part of the Island now called England.'

Though the Saxons had their wills of the Britain's, they were before the Heptarchy at a continual variance among themselves, and it is almost as impossible to give a completely accurate account of the succession of their Kings as it would be to try to give a history of the Succession of their Kings, as it is of Britain's before Julius Cesar'

I wanted to include a few Kings, prior to the Saxons that helped bring control and the Monarchy of Britain into a controllable existence that was generally accepted by the people.

King Alexander the Great. (July 356 BC- June 323 BC)

Alexander III, known as Alexander the Great, was born in July 356 BC to Philip II of Macedon and Olympias of Epirus in Pella, Macedon. He was a legend from birth with rumors surrounding his conception and delivery. He was said to be the son of Zeus and that the Greek gods attended his birth but it would be the expansion of his kingdom for which he would truly gain his fame. Being the much adored heir, Alexander was tutored by Aristotle until the age of 16 when he was old enough to discontinue education. At the age of 21, his father was assassinated making him the new King of Macedonia. Alexander's father left him with a stable kingdom and a strong military. This encouraged him to pursue his dream of having a kingdom that reached all corners of the Earth.

Ambitious and brave, Alexander squashed his enemies in

Macedon and set his sights on the Persian Empire. He would add Pharaoh of Egypt, King of Persia and King of Asia to his titles along with three wives, the most famous being Roxana of Bactria. Roxana would give him a son to temporarily carry on his legacy. He accomplished his greatest conquests by the age of 25. He powered his way through Asia Minor, Syria and Egypt with his extremely loyal army. Not once did he face defeat up through Egypt. Alexander the Great would establish more than 70 cities over three continents. He expanded the routes of trade and commerce in his new territories and sympathized with his new subjects by adopting some policies of their lands. Although he was a fierce and driven leader, he cared about his subjects.

The rumors about his birth inspired Alexander's military pursuits. He was considered a military genius and was often reckless due to his belief that he was immortal and indestructible. He led is army over 11,000 miles, countless battles and faced some of the greatest armies of the world. In return his army was undeniably loyal, to the point of only refusing to follow him once into battle. This allowed Alexander to conquer the Persian Empire and create one of the largest, most expansive empires the ancient world had ever seen.

In 323 BC, the great king would throw a grand banquet complete with copious amounts of wine. He would shortly develop a fever and die in Babylon. Possibly believing he was the son of a god and immortal, Alexander did not leave an heir and his empire went into turmoil. After his death, Roxana gave birth to Alexander IV, solving the succession crisis for a moment. She would be attributed with killing Alexander's second wife and possibly the third. She would be protected for a time by her mother-in-law, Olympias, along with her son. Eventually, Roxana would also be assassinated along with her young son, thus ending the blood line and empire of Alexander the Great. His lands would be broken up and distributed amongst his generals. To this day, Alexander III is regarded as one of the greatest political and military minds of history with many kings and emperors attempting to emulate him. ~ Contributed by, Javaneh Fennell

Julius Cesar led two expeditions against Britain. In 55 BC and also in 54 BC.

> "Britons dye themselves with woad and as a result their
> Appearance in battle is all the more daunting" –
> Julius Cesar, the Gallic Wars, 47 BC

Cesar's first invasion set sail across the Channel on August 26th, 55 BC His Roman ships landed somewhere near Dover in deep waters. Four days later a storm struck and scattered approximately 500 Calvary on the ships that Cesar brought across the channel. Without his Calvary support, Cesar was severely outnumbered, ambushed and he soon returned to Gaul. However, he was able to capture several British hostages.

On July 6th, 54 BC – Julius Cesar landed again on Britain's shores. This time with 800 Ships, 30,000 men and 2,000 Calvary. The Britain's were reportedly intimidated by the size of the invasion, unprepared yet ready to defend. The Romans won a series of battles. After the capture of the Chieftain Cassivellaunus, rallied the British Chieftains in an uprising against Cesar. It had little success and Cassivellaunas begged for peace. It has been said Cesar agreed only because he had no intention of remaining in Britain over the winter. Rome now occupied their own territories in Britain.

However, Julius Cesar was murdered in 44BC and it was nearly 100 years before the Romans made Britain a Roman Province. In 40 AD England was once again invaded under the Emperor Claudius. Britain remained under Roman control until 410 AD.

By the year 500 Britain had revolved into a more resistant country. Divided into kingdoms that consisted of Kent, North Umbria, Mercia, Essex, Sussex and Wessex. Christianity was more prominent in Britain. Many Kingdoms welcomed this new religion.

Javaneh Fennell graciously contributed to this book the Biography of Alexander the Great:

710-800~ Mercian's and West Saxons-
Murder, Marriage and Revenge:
In the early 700's Britain was still divided, although the Christian religion had been introduced and many of the people had embraced it, it was still a tumultuous and unlawful time. Several Kings had

helped spread the Christian Doctrine and several had became Saints. Despite the Christian faith uniting Britain as a whole, Britain was still fighting great battles with in itself. Of the Kingdoms that divided Britain.

King Offa (773-796) ruled Kent, Sussex and East Anglia. King **Cynewulf (757-786)** was during that time the King of Wessex.

In 786, Cynewulf was murdered at Marten by Cynehard. Here is the historical account of that event according to the **Saxon Chronicles.**

"Cynehard learned that the King with a small army was at Merton, and in the company of a woman. And there he surprised him and surrounded the chamber from the outside before the men were aware of him. And then the King perceived this and went to the door and bravely defended himself. Then he got sight of the Etheling (Cynehard) so he rushed out upon him and sorely wounded him; and they were all striking at the King until they had slain him. And the King's thegns discovered the treachery through the woman's cries.

(As I mentioned earlier, I have modernized all the historical quotes as little as possible throughout this book. As you can see now in the above and below articles. While trying to keep them as original as possible yet easy to understand. I understand some may be difficult to understand, especially some of the names. It was a difficult decision where to draw the lines between original document and a readable document in our time. I tried to stay original, yet readable. Toward the end of the book and in specific documents I stayed original, only correcting the spellings, and letter differences from Old English to Modern Time.)

The Chronicle of Florence records the incident as follows:

"When Cynewulf, King of Wessex was taking measures for expelling Cynehard from rulership he at that time went to visit a woman, bringing with him only a few attendants to a vill called in English Merton. The Etheling, (Cynehard) learning of this with his retainers he hastened to the spot with great glee. On his arrival, finding all the world asleep, he found the chamber in which the King lay, they quietly surrounded on all sides, although nearby the kings followers slept. The King being alarmed opened the chamber-door, and fought stoutly in resistance to his assailants. After a while, getting sight of the etheling, he rushed forth to attack him, and gave him a severe wound. Seeing this, the whole band of the eltheling's soldiers fell on the King, wounded and slew him.

The woman, uttering cries of terror and grief, filled the chamber with her lamentations. The few troops who were in attendance on the king ran to the spot, and found their master, whom they had just before left alive, lying dead. At this they were in a rage of fury, and drawing their swords they made a desperate rush on his murderers.

The Etheling endeavored to pacify them, promising to each a large sum of money, besides sparing their lives, if they would withdrawal; they, however, reject his offers, and continue the combat till they all perished, except one British hostage, who was desperately wounded.

When morning came and the news of the King's death got abroad, his ealdorman Osric, who was much attached to him, and Wifertham his most faithful thane, hastened to the spot with all the force the king had left behind the day before: but they find all the gates barred. While they are trying to burst them open, the Etheling boldly approached them, promising them that he will cheerfully heap them in gold, silver and honor's, whatever they desired, if they will only raise him to the royal throne, he suggested also, that there are many of their relations on his side, who are ready to follow him to the death.

The royal troops reject his offers, and earnestly entreat their kinsman to desert their lord and depart home in safety with all dispatch. But, the eltheling's party replied: -- "What you offer us, we proposed to your comrades who fell with the King; but as they would not attend our summons, neither will we allow yours on the present occasion." On receiving this answer, the royal troops advanced, forced opened the doors, leveled the barricades, and put the Etheling and all his followers, in number eighty-four, to the sword except only his little son, who was severely wounded.

Etheling was an Old English, Saxon word was meant nobility, or person of Royal Blood.

The Murder of King Cynewulf by Cynehard in 786:
The King's corpse was conveyed to Winchester for interment; the Eltheling's was buried in the monastery at Axminster."

Now, Egbert who had been in exile with King Charles,

(Charlemagne) did not succeed quite yet to the throne. King Offa gave his support to Beorhtric (aka Brihtric) his son-in-law, whose marriage to Offa's daughter caused conflict between the two Kings.

Offa had made allies with Beortric, King of Wessex by giving his daughter Eadburga to him in marriage rather than to the King of the Franks, Charlemagne. King Offa may have hoped to unite all the Kingdoms of Brittan and thought that could be accomplished by marriage.

King Charles, (Charlemagne) had asked Offa for the hand of his daughter Eadburga to his son and successor Charles. This Offa countered: requesting that he would give his daughter's hand in marriage on the condition that Charlemagne give his daughter Bertha to his son Egfrid. 'His most beloved.' This was not acceptable terms to Charlemagne. Upon the Kings denial of his Son's hand in marriage, Offa denied the request of his daughters- this causing turmoil between the two Kings.

The offended Charlemagne cut off all communications between the Channel. Charlemagne's temper seems to have been very affected by this denial.

Offa then made allies with Beortric, King of Wessex by giving his daughter Eadburga to him in marriage rather than to the King of the Franks, Charlemagne. King Offa may have hoped to unite all the Kingdoms of Brittan and thought that could be accomplished by marriage within the Kingdoms.

King Offa offered his other daughter to King Ethelbert, 'The most glorious and holy King of the East-Angles, whose eminent virtues rendered him acceptable to Christ, the true King, and who was courteous to all men, who lost at once both his kingdom and his life, being beheaded by the detestable commands of Offa, the mighty King of Mercia, at the infamous suggestion of his own wife the Queen; but though iniquitously slain and deprived of his Kingdom, the King and martyr entered the courts of the blessed spirits, while angels rejoiced in triumph."

King Ethelbert was the King of East Anglia. It is recorded that he married King Offa's daughter, Etheldritha. Ethelbert had heard of the beauty and virtues of this princess, the youngest daughter of King Offa. King Ethelbert's friend and confident Earl Oswald strongly urged him to demand her hand. Although the young King had vowed to devote his life to the Service of God and his Kingdom he resolved to marry. A council was held and all the Nobles of the East Anglia were present, as well as those of King Offa and his Queen, Lanorine, whom, according to some histories was the only one to object of the marriage.

In a book, 'The Queens of England before the Normans" written in 1859, there is written a story of this account. I should mention that it is debated how accurate this account is. I think there is 'some' truth to it, though embellished. However, there are not many accounts written on the subject of King Ethelbert's death and marriage. If the marriage actually took place, or who was behind the actual murder of the young King. Historians are split on the marriage taking place before his death.

King Ethelbert's wedding and death:

"When Ethelbert's proposal was thus accepted- it was settled that the marriage should take place at the same time as that of her sister Elfeda and Ethelred, King of Northumbria (d. 796). The nuptial ceremony for both the Royal couples was arranged to be performed at the ancient Mercian palace of Sutton Wallis, near Hereford.

"Our kindred all within the halle,
The wedding feast arraye;
When the song shall sound, and the dance goe rounds,
And the musicke merrills plays,"

On the day previous to that event, the young King of East Angles departed on his journey towards Mercia, full of hope and expectation, attended by a retinue of his own nobility. In conformity with his usual custom prior to commencing his journey, he heard mass with his habitual attention and devotion. Late in the evening Ethelbert arrived in the neighborhood of Sutton, where instead of entering the town, he ordered his tents to be pitched- that he might stay the night in open country. Some East Anglian nobles, however, were deputed to proceed to the Palace of Offa, and announce his arrival, with the cause of his coming, and at the same time were instructed to present to the Mercian King some rich gifts prepared by Ethelbert, his future son-in-law. They were most graciously received, and Offa signified his happiness with the East Anglea's suit.

Ethelbert, after a night harassed with frightful dreams, which seemed to forebode some impending calamity, rent forward his chariots and pack horses laden with rich baggage, well-stored chests, and provisions; and accompanied by an immense number of men on foot and horseback, followed himself, with a magnificent band of Knights, arranged in due order. The approach of this cavalcade was soon rumored through the town, and reached the Palace of King Offa.

Amongst others who were attracted to behold the sight was Etheldritha, his bride to be, from a window of the lofty palace of her Father she beheld the young King Ethelbert and his Knights entering the court-yard. She marked with a woman's interest the splendid spectacle, and then hastened to her mother to speak to her of the manly beauty of Ethelbert, of the stately nobles, the valiant Knights and the wondrous splendor of his retinue. The Queen listened to her daughter's enthusiasm, and her malice and envy was even more enraged.

The Queen had openly opposed the marriage from the first, disliking Ethelbert for his religious devotion; being an unbeliever herself, Christian observances were hateful in her eyes. She had been deeply mortified that her daughter should have been unable to form foreign alliances, and had even persecuted the Archbishop of Litchfield and other bishops, because, in policy, as ruinous to Mercia; and now nothing could exceed her vexation when she found that she was likely to be foiled in her last expectation.

Meanwhile Offa, delighted to receive Ethelbert, his daughter's bridegroom. He bestowed on him a paternal embrace, accompanied with the words, "Welcome, my son! Welcome my son-in-law, welcome! You shall henceforth be regarded my favorite child!" The Queen stood aloof, beholding the joy of the meeting with a scowling brow, and resolving in her mind how to make Ethelbert feel the effects of her resentment.

Unsuspicious of her designs, Offa afterward repaired to his wife, to ascertain when it would be convenient to her that her daughter's marriage should be celebrated. It was then that the Queen spoke as follows.

"The subject is one which requires very grave consideration. You are well aware that the pretty princes of East Angles have long desired to obtain dominion over the Mercians. You have full knowledge of hereditary enmities, and the mutual injuries inflicted upon each other by both these kingdoms; and now I am greatly deceived, if ambition rather pretext, friendship the cloak, which have served the purpose of the keen spy, who would judge for himself the weakness that accompanies your advanced years, and the best means of insuring your destruction. You should regard your guest, not as a lover, but as a hostile commander; for it is the later capacity he has appeared before you, accompanied by numbers of soldiers, large enough for an army- too large for the purpose of peace.

Suppose he marries your daughter, and that such is the sole cause of his coming, then by right of that marriage he will regard himself as your heir, and entitled to succeed you on the throne. As an impatient heir, he will daily wish for your death; and all that you now peacefully enjoy, he will constantly seek for, and as sedulously struggle to acquire. You prepared a rod to chastisement for yourself; you knit together the whip which you will hereafter be beaten, if you give to one like this, pretentions to be your successor. Make him your son-in-law, your life is in peril, and your own crown in danger; or if life be long spared to you, it must be passed amid the terrors of fear; you exchange the independence of a free King in your own dominions for the trembling timidity of an Eastern slave.

Suppose on the other hand, that you now reject his alliance, and that you allow him, justly offended with the treatment he has experienced, to withdraw from your Kingdom, there can be no doubt that you expose yourself to danger as that which you desire to escape. He knows the roads to your Kingdom- he requires no spy to tell him what parts of it are most accessible for his troops- how it can best be assailed, or what are the points on which you will rely for your defenses. He has seen and has noted your age and your infirmity; and all he has to do is to make a pretext for hostilities, the affront to which you have subjected him, and on the instant he proclaims war, he begins the destruction of your Kingdom, and deprives you of life.

There is but one of two modes of escaping from the danger and perplexity entailed upon you by the coming of this guest; either he will in a short time cause your death, or you now must cause his- in my mind a just and fitting punishment for his presumption."

When Queen Quendrida finished speaking, King Offa sighed deeply, and after considering for a few moments, answered her thus:-

16

" Your discourse has, in sooth, convinced me that I am reduced to a dangerous and pitiable plight; for I plainly see that on this side there is imminent peril, and on the other irretrievable infamy. Far, far, however, be from me the detestable crime that you suggest; a crime which, if once committed, would bring eternal opprobrium upon me and my successors"

He quit her presence, and soon after rejoined his royal guest with an appearance of tranquility which covered the real anguish which preyed upon his mind.

I wanted to pause a moment in this story. I am not suggesting that this is a completely accurate account of the events leading up to King Ethelbert's death. This however, has been recorded as a version, one that seems somewhat plausible. An only version recorded explaining a motive for the horrific, unexpected and seemingly unprovoked acts that are soon to follow. This does give the reader, possibly one explanation. Although there are accounts, such as this that the evil Queen Quendrida, took matters into her own hands, without the Kings knowledge. Many historians do not believe that the Queen would have had the power to cause the young King's death and there-fore the order had to have come from Offa himself. Many historians believe this theory because of Offa's actions of retribution and 'that he lived the rest of his days trying to repent'.

The ending of the story goes as follows:

A magnificent banquet was served, with costly wine, accompanied by music, singing and dancing. The two Princes sat down together to the entertainment, the day passed away in joy and merriment. But Queen Quendrida, with 'murder in her smile' meantime had prepared a tragic ending to the scene.

Queen Quendrida had erected in the young Kings room a throne that was decorated with magnificent tapestries. In this room under the floorboards was the opening of a deep well. The Queen made open the well and placed over it the Throne.

The Queen asked Ethelbert to come and 'speak to his betrothed' which he readily agreed to. His companions not accompanying him to this private meeting. His bride to be of course not being there, the Queen asked the anxious bride-groom to sit while they waited for her arrival. When he did the throne gave way, plunging him into the well where her accomplices waited. They muffled the young Kings screams with "pillows, bedding, hanging and tapestry until he was dead."

"To complete the deed, the scarcely lifeless body was decapitated. By order of the relentless Queen"

That this act was perpetrated without the knowledge of Offa, even this storyteller agreed was unlikely- since it is certain that after this horrible crime Offa immediately invaded East Anglia, and annexed it to his own dominions, which would give motive to the deed.

Of his Bride Etheldritha, it is assumed that she was also a victim of this crime. She immediately abandoned her Mother and Father's court. And moved to the Monastery of Croyland, in Lincolnshire. It is said that having discovered the treachery done by her parents, Etheldritha warned the Nobles that had accompanied Ethelbert so that they were able to safely make an escape.

She is also to have when she realized what had been done, "in her consternation and despair, filled the air with lamentations, and even in the extremity of her anguish was led to curse the authors of her being, and prophetically to denounce the vengeance of heaven which was about to punish them for their awful crime. To her mother she declared in words, as if inspired, that her only son Egfrid would not live three years longer, and that she herself should die in a few months, overcome with misery and despair to that she had caused."

Etheldrida received the habit of a nun, preferring 'to be a surf in the house of the Lord, than to dwell as a queen in the palace of sinners'

Offa, after the murder, either from remorse or disgust, avoided his Queen, commanding that she remove herself from court to one of the 'most remote and solitary places of Mercia, to be placed there in confinement.

"She had with her in her solitude the instruments of her doom; for these heaps of accumulated gold and silver that she had taken from the Castle, induced robbers to attack the mansion in which she dwelt, for the sake of so splendid and booty; and the Queen, being seized by the robbers, who little heeded her dignity, was flung into a deep well, where bruised and maimed like her ill-fated victim, she expired in torment. This Lady Macbeth of her time is said to have been called by the Saxon name of 'Leog', signifying "A Queen to be feared"

The Saxon Chronicle also records the event without the significant detail as follows-

A.D. 798. This year Offa, King of Mercia, commanded that King Ethelbert should be beheaded; and Osred who had been king of the Northumbrians returning home after his exile was apprehended and slain, on the eighteenth day before the clands of October. His body is deposited at Tinemouth. Ethelred this year, took unto himself a new wife whose name was Elfeda.

Desirous of re-establishing his character, either with God or that of the world, and to appease his remorse, or quiet the souls of the murdered King- Offa paid great court to the clergy, and assumed the monkish devotion of his time. He even undertook a pilgrimage to Rome, to obtain absolution from the hands of the supreme Pontiff.

He was ordered to erect a Cathedral over the remains of Ethelbert. On his return the Cathedral of Hereford was erected. And the Abbey of St. Alban's as well as the Abbey at Bath. King Offa also enriched the church at Westminster. He made rich gifts to Canterbury, and other places far out of his Kingdom. King Offa, his children and Queen all perished miserably. Offa's line became distinct. He was succeeded for a short time by his son-in-law Beorhtric (Brihtric).

Cathedral at Hereford, erected in the memory of King Ethelbert

The remains of the young King have been rumored to possess great powers. There are different versions of what happened to his body, as numerous as the cause of his death. Miracles have been recorded beside the grave of the young murdered King.

Ethelbert's body was buried in secret in a hidden spot. It is said that a fountain and a column of light, brighter than the noon-time sun rose from the spot towards the heavens revealing where the body had been secretly hidden. Three days after his burial, a Nobleman, Brithfrid, an attendant of Ethelbert's had a vision where those miraculous fountains could be found, directing him to proceed thither and remove the body of his master to the Lady Chapel of the Church at Fernley. These directions he forthwith proceeded to comply with, and after exhuming the body of Ethelbert set off with it, accompanied by a long procession towards Fernley. On the way, the head of the King fell from the bier and rolled upon the ground to the feet of a blind man, who upon picking it up, instantly regained his sight.

So many miracles had been reported around the burial site of King Ethelbert that Offa sent two Bishops to enquire into the validity of them. Those two dignified Bishops arrived just in time to witness a noble Welshman who was cured of Palsy beside Ethelbert's grave. Sending an account to King Offa, he with fear and a contrite heart immediately sent presents to the Shrine and intended to build the Church in the more enduring material of stone. He however died and this project was completed by Milfrid, Ethelbert's viceroy. The Church was dedicated to Mary and Ethelbert.

Beorhtric, as I said earlier succeeded King Offa in the year 792. Married to Offa's daughter Eadburgh. The Queen is said to have the same wickedness inherited from her Mother.

There is a story in Asser's book of Alfred, which many historian deems to be genuine work of that time. Its authenticity has been affirmed by two scholars, Plummer and Stevenson. "The work which bears Asser's name cannot be later than 974, and the attempt to treat it as forgery of the eleventh or twelfth century must be regarded as having broken down. I may add that I started with a strong prejudice against the authenticity of Asser, so that my conclusions have at any rate been impartially arrived at" -Stevenson 1904

From Asser's writings on King Beorhtric and Eadburgh:

"And because I think it is not known to many, this custom first arose in Wessex.... It seems right to explain... as I have heard it from my Lord Alfred, the truth teller, King of the Anglo-Saxons, who often told me about it, as he had heard it from many men of truth who related the fact, or I should rather say, expressly preserved the remembrance of it.

There was in Mercia in recent times a certain valiant King, who was dreaded by all the neighboring King. His name was Offa, and it was he who had the great dike made from sea to sea between Wales and Mercia. His daughter, named Eadburh, was married to Beorhtric, King of the West Saxons. The moment she had possessed herself the King's good will, and practically the whole power of the realm, she began to live tyrannically, and after the manner of her Father.

Every man whom Beorhtric loved she would execrate, and would do all things hateful to God and man, accusing to the King all whom she could. Thus depriving them insidiously either of life or of power. And if she could not obtain the King's consent, she used to take them off by poison, as is ascertained to have been the case with a certain young man beloved by the King, whom she poisoned, seeing that she could not accuse him to the King.

It is said, moreover, that King Beorhtric unwittingly tasted of the poison, though the Queen had intended to give it not to him, but to the young man; the King however, was beforehand with him, (and they both drank) and so both perished.

King Beorhtric therefore being dead, the Queen, since she could no longer remain among the Saxons, sailed beyond sea with countless treasures, and came to Charles, King of the Franks (Charlemagne). As she stood before the dais, bringing many gifts to the King, (It is assumed that Charlemagne at this time-still remembered that her hand in marriage had been denied to him for his Son by Offa years before.)

The King said to her- "Choose, Eadburh, between me and my Son, who stands beside me on this dais.' She without deliberation, foolishly replied: 'If I am to have my choice, I chose your son, because he is younger than you.'

At which Charlemagne smiled and answered: 'if you had chosen me, you would have had my son: but since you have chosen him, you shall have neither me nor him.'

However he gave her a large convent of nuns, in which, having laid aside her secular habit, and assumed the dress worn by nuns, and she discharged the office of Abbess for a few years. As she is said to have lived irrationally in her own country, so she appears to have acted much more so among a foreign people; for, being finally caught in illicit intercourse with a man of her own nation, she was expelled from the Monastery by orders of King Charles. Henceforward, she lived a life of shame in poverty and misery until her death; so that at last, accompanied only by a slave, as I have heard from many that have saw her, she begged her bread daily at Pavia, 'And so wretchedly died'

Chapter Two

THE SAXONS 800-1066

Egbert, King of Wessex 802-839, in the year 802 King Egbert finally came out of exile from King Charles' Court, having spent thirteen years with the infamous Charlemagne, it is fair to say in that time Egbert acquired skills not only in arms and war- but those qualities of a great leader.

At an invitation to return to his Kingdom by friends and Nobles Egbert returned and was named King of Britain's empty Throne.

One of first and most memorable acts done by the new King was to call a 'witenagemot' in Winchester. This was an Anglo-Saxon advisory council of the Kings that usually consisted of several Ealdormen, Nobles and Bishops.

With the consent of the people, Egbert bestowed the name of England, on his United Kingdoms. The name of the 'Angles' had been considered to be the identifying name of the collective Kingdoms and actually remained so for several years. Some historians debate that Egbert only named his Kingdom Wessex that of 'England'.

There is however, no doubt that this is when the name England was first officially proclaimed and ultimate became the predominant name of this illustrious country. Despite that the new name of England did not take on catch on in the full effect for the people for some time to come. The Britons continued to call their neighbors Saxons, although England was now officially in existence. It would also be some time before the name 'Englishmen' would come into existence.

The first few years of Egbert's reign was one of tranquility, it seems the warring had subsided for a time and all was well in the Kingdom.

In many historical accounts; Saxon Chronicles, William of Huntington, Malmsbury and the Venerable Bede, We find the same recorded account of the first major battle, and Victory, in the Battle of Ellandune in Wiltshire.

Unfortunately while the accounts of the battles are all very similar, the dates all vary. Malmsbury has this battle dated in 806 (unlikely) I do believe this battle was actually in late 822 or 823.

The Battle of Ellandune: about 822/3

Beomwulf caused a great rebellion among the Kingdom. It is generally believed there were Civil Wars for about two years that finally came to a head in Wiltshire. Beomwulf, who is described as- the unworthy heir of Offa, and also as a usurper- an Ealdorman of his late brother. Bede writes:

Egbert, King of the West-Saxons and Beornulf, King of the Mercian's fought at Wilton (aka Wiltshire). Egbert got the victory, and there was great slaughter made. He then sent from the army, his son Ethelwolph, and Eathelstan his bishop. Also Wulfherd, his Ealdorman into Kent with large force, and they drove Baldred the King Northwards over the Thames. The men of Kent, Surrey, South Saxons and East-Saxons submitted to him with great happiness.

Having formerly being Kin. The same year the people sought the alliance and protection of King Egbert for protection from the Mercian's; fearing dread. This same year the East-Angles slew Bernulf- King of Mercia.

Egbert was called the "First of the Saxon Monarchs" although the Kingdom of the Mercian's, or now England, was not complete. That happened after many battles that occurred throughout and past his monarchy. It is commonly agreed that England was more established towards the end of King Egbert's reign than ever before. Because of this, Egbert is recognized in history for giving 'birth' so to speak to England.

Not only did King Egbert bestow England with its name, he laid the seeds for its future Kings to establish and grow into what England is today. England was by the year 828 under the rule of one man for the first time in its history. England at last had found peace, greatness and flourished.

Unfortunately, this peace did not last for long. In 835 England would experience invasion, spoil, slaughter and desolation. The last five years of Egbert's reign was one of war and misery protecting and trying to regain the peaceful tranquility England was quickly losing.

"Egbert in full height of glory, having now enjoyed his conquest seven peaceful years. His victorious army long since disbanded, and the exercise of arms perhaps laid aside, England was unprepared against a sudden storm of Danes from the sea, whose landing in the 32nd year of his reign, wasted Shepey in Kent. Egbert the next year gathering an army, for he had heard of their arrival in 35 ships, gave them battle by the river Carr in Dorsetshire; the event whereof was that the Danes kept their ground, and encamped where the field was fought. Two Saxon leaders, Dudda and Osmund, and two Bishops some say, were there slain."

This was the only time in Egbert's reign that he was overthrown and suffered a great defeat. Of these invasions against Egbert the British history is not silent. And we learn the following year Egbert found victory once again.

"The victor Egbert, as one who had done enough, seasonably now, after prosperous success in 836 with glory ended his days, and was buried at Winchester"

King Egbert died sometime in August 839AD at the battle of Hengston, in Cornwall- "after a reign of thirty years and seven months, he departed this life, and was buried in Winchester, leaving an ample field of Glory for his Son, and declaring that he must be happy, if he was careful not to destroy the indolence natural to his race, A Kingdom which he himself had consolidated with such consummate industry"

King Ethelwolf (839-858)

Ethelwolph 'Athulf' - (839-858) Ethelwolph succeeded his father in the Kingdom of Westsax, but not those of Kent, Sussex and Eastsax and Essex. These had being given to his younger son Ethelstan. Ethelwolph and Ethelstan ruled jointly the two Kingdoms as allies and fought many battles together.

They had even a more difficult struggle than their Father had with the invading Danes. They had now spread their attacks throughout the southern and eastern coast of England. A succession of constant battles were fought, hundreds of ships had landed at the mouth of the Thames and conquered Canterbury and London.

They finally defeated them in 851 at Aclea (Ockley,) in Surrey, the battle described below. Ethelwolph died in 858 and four of his sons succeeded him in succession.

His eldest sons, Ethelbald and Ethelbert ruling only a short time alongside **Ethelstan (839-852)** their Uncle.

Ethelwolph succeeded his younger brother and inherited the thrones of Kent, Sussex, Eastsax and Essex (Eastsax has also been called Surry) in 852 once again England was under the rule of one

King.

It should be noted that the Saxon Chronicles plainly state that both Kingdoms had been left to Ethelstan alone, by his father King Egbert. However, both Ethelwolph and Ethelstan ruled Kingdoms together. We know this from the many accounts of the Battles against the Danes that were recorded.

It is possible that the Kingdoms were divided, given the state of the country at the time. Ethelwolph is described by Malmsbury as a 'man of mild nature, not inclined to war, or delighted with much dominion'. It is quite possible this is true and King Egbert, as always, was thinking as a Monarch for the great of England rather than that of a Father and hereditary rights and gave the Kingdom to only Ethelstan.

However, you could argue that the Kingdom was equally divided due to the invasion of the Danes. We know that both son's had been helping their father defend the Kingdom from the invaders. So it would be reasonable to believe that King Egbert did in fact divide the Kingdom's, thinking- 'For the good of the Kingdom' and that perhaps both sons would have their hands full with the Danes. By making each of them ruler to 'defend their own Kingdom' it might have given piece of mind to King Egbert that the Danes would have less chance of a victory over England.

Obviously it can be argued either way, and since both brothers ruled together and Ethelwolph succeeded his brother it is a moot point. At this time it seems the succession varied between sons and brothers.

In 851 'The Pagans, with 350 ships, came to the mouth of the river Thames, and laid waste to Canterbury, that is by the chief city of Kent, and London and put to flight Beorhtulf, King of the Mercian's, who was with all his army had come up to war against them. After the same pagan army advanced into Surrey, a district situated on the south bank of the river Thames, and to eastward of Kent;

Ethelwolph and his son Ethelbald fought a long contested battle with the whole of that army at a place called Ockley, which means Oak's Field. After both sides had fought fiercely and courageously for a long time, the greater part of the pagan army was utterly routed and put to the sword, so much so that we have heard that there were never so many of them slain in that region in one day either before or after, the Christians gained a splendid victory, and remained masters of the field of carnage.

In 852 Beortwulf, King of the Mercian's died and was succeeded by Burhred. In 853 King Burhred sent messengers to King Ethelwolph requesting his assistance in bringing the Western Dominions who were in rebellion against him under control. The Western Dominions being located between Mercia and the Western Sea.

King Ethelred quickly set his army in motion and entered the territory of the Britain's in the company with King Burhred. They were victorious and 'laid waste to the people'.

The Saxon Chronicles tells us that in 855 King Ethelwolph 'with great honor departed for Rome. Taking with him his favorite son Alfred and remained there a year. At the end of that period he returned to his own country, bringing with him a wife, Judith, daughter of King Charles, (Charlemagne) King of the Franks.

However, during the short time that King Ethelwolph was absent, a scandalous transaction, and contrary to all Christian behavior, occurred at Selwood.

King Ethelbald and Elhstan, Bishop of Sherborne, and Eanwulf-ealdorman of Somersetshire, are reported to have conspired to prevent King Ethelwolph from ever resuming his Kingdom when he returned from Rome.

"This piece of mischief, unheard of in any former age, is by very many attributed to, considered to have been concocted by, the bishop and the ealdorman only; but many say that the King's (Ethelbald) haughtiness alone caused it. We have heard from certain persons, the King was very offensive, both in that respect and in many other pieces of forwardness and the issue of the affair proves this."

"But God did not permit it, nor would the Saxon nobles consent thereunto; for in order that there might not accrue to Saxony the irremediable danger of a civil war, growing fiercer and more cruel day by day."

This dispute between King Ethelwolph and his son Ethelbald, as with any family dispute, has also divided historians.

In the previous chapter I quoted Asser in an account of King Beortric and his Queen Eadburga, who destroyed many noblemen's lives and ultimately murdered her husband the King. Since this time it was a general rule that no wife would be named Queen and placed on a throne next to her husband. King Ethelwolph, broke this rule by placing his new wife Judith on the throne next to him and declaring her Queen. No man resented this more than his son Ethelbald.

"He let Judith, daughter of King Charles, whom he had received in marriage from her Father, to sit beside him on the throne of state as long as she lived, without any controversy or opposition on the part of his nobles, although this was done in contradiction to a preposterous custom of that nation: for the West-Saxon nation does not allow a queen to sit by the King's side, or even endure to call her the Queen, but only the King's consort. The origin of this arose on the account of a certain forward and evil queen of that nation."

Rather than quarrel with his son and cause a civil war, he chose to divide the Kingdom. Ruling jointly with his son. Ethelwolph refused to let the difficulties between himself and his children disrupt the peacefulness of England. I believe peace was sole motive for splitting his Kingdom with his son- to avoid war and to keep the peace in England. A peace that three generations had been fighting to obtain.

"This partition was an unjust one; for malignity was so far successful that the Western portion, which was better, was allotted to the Son. The Eastern, which was worse, fell to the Father...- He however "*with incredible forbearance, dreading "a worse civil war' calmly gave way to the Son-* And though all this arose on the account of his foreign wife, he held her in the highest estimation and used to place her on the throne near himself; contrary to the West Saxon custom."

Ethelwolph by his will in 856 divided his Kingdoms between his *two* eldest sons.

Ethelbald (858-860) Ethelbald only ruled for two years, those years spent battling the Danes. He gave the Kingdom of the West Saxons to his younger brother **Ethelbert (860-866)**

There were two other sons of Egbert still living, Ethelred and Alfred that would eventually inherit their Fathers Crown. Unlike some of the future Kings of England they seemed to have been a tight family. One without any inner turmoil and all defended the Kingdom and fought battles together. There does not seem to be any controversy or jealousy over the Crown.

Kingdom of the West Saxons.

Throughout the 9th Century there were many battles fought by English King's to establishing territories and to protect them from invaders.

Malmsbury writes of King Ethelbert " It is related that this King was personally engaged in hostel conflict against the enemy nine times in one year with various success indeed, but for the most part the victor, besides sudden attacks in which his skill in warfare, and that of his brother Ethelred, they quickly defeated those straggling depredators. In these several actions the Danes lost nine Earls and one King besides common people innumerable."

Ethelred (866-871) Ethelred succeeded his brother Ethelbert, inheriting the whole of the West Saxons, and of the Kingdoms of Kent, the Eastern, Southern and Middle Angles.

Alfred 'The Great' (871-901), after the death of Ethelred, by universal applause, the famous and youngest son of Ethelwolph succeeded to the Throne of England.

Alfred, Asser writes, was no ordinary man. In his childhood he had visited Rome and been hallowed as King by Pope Leo IV, though the ceremony could have no weight in England.

During Ethelred's reign he had very little time for learning. He had fought nobly by his brother's side in the battles of the day, and after he succeeded him he fought nobly as King at the head of his people.

In 878 the Danish under King Guthrum beat down all resistance in England. Alfred was no longer able to keep in the open country took refuge, with a few chosen warriors, on the little Island of Athelney, in Somerset. He gathered an army quickly and after a few weeks defeated Guthrum at Edington, in Wiltshire.

"Now the King was pierced with many nails of tribulation, though established in the royal sway; for from the twentieth year of his age to the present year, which is his forty -fifth," he has been constantly afflicted with most severe attacks of an unknown disease, so that there is not a single hour in which he is not either suffering from that malady, or nigh to despair by reason of the gloom which is occasioned by his fear of it. Moreover the constant invasions of foreign nations, by which he was continually harassed by land and sea, without any interval of quiet, constituted a sufficient cause of disturbance. "

Alfred signed a treaty after this with Elfred in Chippenham where afterwards they were baptized in a body at Aller. By this treaty Elfred retained no more than Wessex, with its dependencies, Sussex and Kent, and the Western half of Mercia. The remainder of England was surrendered to the Danes, and became known as Danelaw, because Danish and not Saxon law prevailed. The English people never again had to struggle for its very existence as a political body. In 866 however, after a successful was Alfred acquired London and the surrounding area in a new treaty from Guthrum.

Alfred the Great- 849 AD- 26 October 899

The only English king to ever be styled as "the great", Alfred the Great united England and established law, order and education in a country previously divided. Known mainly for his intellect, Alfred was nonetheless a courageous leader. He helped his brother defeat the Danes, succeeded his brother and defeated the Danes again. The Danes would continue to try to conquer Wessex. To stop the ruthless Danes, he built a navy to keep the coast safe from attacks. He also reestablished his army and organized them into an impenetrable defense to maintain unity of his lands and protect his people.

Alfred was known for his military accomplishments but he was better known for his kindness and intellect. He was a just king, organizing law of the land in written and formulated code so his subjects had clear rules and punishments for any and all crimes. Establishing the Law Code, he would appoint literate and well educated men to be judges as he felt they would be capable of fully investigating a crime. If he felt they could not accomplish this, Alfred would submerge himself into the facts and dictate a decision. Not only was he a great lawmaker but he was also well known for his excellent relations with his foreign counterparts. He held great relations with Jerusalem and Ireland. He famously made peace with the Danish king, Guthrum, and even preceded over Guthrum's baptism. This opened the doors for a treaty to be made with the Danes and secure peace among his lands.

Above all else, Alfred is better known for his push to better education. At the age of 30 he learned Latin and assisted in translating religious books and documents from Latin to Anglo-Saxon. He aimed to help his subjects have better access to educational tools because he felt that England could not succeed and be prosperous without it. Several schools and colleges in Great Britain, and even the United States, are named in his honor. Alfred would offer education to all free men in his land and encouraged children of his subjects to be educated as well. This differed from most kingdoms at the time who wanted to suppress the people and keep them uneducated.

The details of Alfred's death are unknown. He suffered from illnesses throughout his life and this may have attributed to his death. He was originally buried in Old Minster in Winchester the New Minster. From there his remains would be lost and still have not been found or identified to date as of late 2014. He was succeeded by his son Edward. His favorable image and reorganization of law, military and education earned him the deserving title of Alfred the Great, King of Wessex.

~ Javaneh Fennell

I need to add a note that through the Saxons and Norman's part of this book I have included, and used as reference many of the writing s that Alfred had hired Asser and other historians to write and 'record histories with the object of imparting knowledge."

It is Asser that I have read and referred to several times in this book. The Chronicle, as it was called in its earliest history, teaches not of the history of England but of "the deeds and words of men who had ruled the English nation from the earliest of times. So that these things may not be forgotten." He had "bade his men to bring together all that was known of the history of his people since the day when they first landed as pirates."

These books are the earliest and the most accurate accounts of the past that have been preserved, quoted and transcribed to teach the world the History of England.

In 901 Alfred died. He had already fortified London as an

outpost against the Danes and left to his son Edward, a small but strong and consolidated Kingdom. The Danes on the other side were not united. A century earlier a Mercian or a Northumbrian had preferred independence to submission of a West Saxon King. Now they preferred a West Saxon King to a Danish master, especially as the old royal houses were extinct, and there was no one but the West Saxon King to lead them against the Danes.

The people welcomed their new King Edward.

Edward 'The Elder'' (901- 294) Edward was not like his Father. He was not a legislator nor was he a scholar, but unlike his Father he was a Great Warrior. In a series of campaigns he subdued the Danish parts of England as far north as the Humber.

He was aided by his brother in law, Ethelred, and afterward Ethelred's death by his own sister. Ethelflaed, the Lady of the Mercians, one of the few warrior women of the world.

Ethelflaed, Lady of the Mercians:

Step by step the brother and sister won their way, not contending themselves which victories in the open country. They secured in each district as they advanced by the erection of fortifications. Some of these fortifications 'burhs' Were placed in desolate roman the strongholds, such as Chester. Others were raised like that of Warwick, on the mountain's piled up in past times by a still earlier race. Others again, like that of Strafford, were placed where no fortress had been before.

This year by the permission of God went Ethelfleda, lady of Mercia, with all the Mercian to Tamworth; and built the fort there in the fore-part of the summer; and before Lammas that at Stafford: in the next year [914] that at Eddesbury, in the beginning of the summer; and late in the autumn, that at Warwick. Then in the following year [915] was built, after mid-winter, that at Chirbury and that at Warburton; and the same year before mid-winter that at Runkorn.

After his sister's death, Edward took into his own hands the government of Mercia. From that time all of Southern and Central England was united under him. In 922 the Welsh King acknowledged Edwards supremacy.

In the middle of the 9th century the picts and the intruding Scots had been amalgamated under Keneth MacAlpin, the King of the Scots. The new Kingdom had since been wielded together by the attacks of Danes.

It is said that in 925 the new King of the Scots, Constantine, together with other northern rulers, chose Edward "to father and lord'. It is likely that this statement only covers some act of alliance formed by the English King with the Scots King and other lesser rulers.

Nothing was more natural than that the Scottish King, Constantine, should wish to align with the English King, Edward, against his enemies. It is also natural that Edward would want to align with Constantine against his enemies. However, what the precise form of that agreement is uncertain. I do believe that there was such an agreement made for the first time between the newly formed government of Scotland and that of England.

Ethelstan, (924-939) after the death of Alfred and of his brother, Ethelstan was elected by the nobles, of whom it was said 'there was nothing noble about him.' It is said that Ethelstan was of 'illegitimate' birth.

He was, like his brother and sister a great warrior. He drove the Welsh out of the half of Exeter, which seemed to be and ongoing battle. Great rulers sought him out seeking his alliance.

One of Ethelstan's sisters was given to Charles the Simple, the

King of Western Frank's, another sister had married Hugh the Great, Duke of the French- and the 'Lord in Power.' Their son becoming the First King in modern France.

Ethelstan did not have a great relationship with the Scots, whatever agreement if any that had been made by his brother was no longer in existence.

> "Ethelstan's greatness drew upon him the jealousy of the King of Scot's and all of the Northern King's"

I believe that it is fair to say that this battle was more of a personal one, not one of land or revenge. In 973 he defeated the Scot's King in the great Battle of Brunanburh.

After dying without issue in 940, his younger brother Edmund who had fought with him at that battle succeeded him.

Edmund (939-946) Edmund succeeded Ethelstan without any opposition. He fought a general uprising of the Danes at Mercia as well as those in the North. It is said that he was a great statesman as well as a warrior.

The relationship with the Scot's also seems to have been repaired now, though there is very little written to be certain. It does seem that they joined together to fight the Danes. I have to say, that is also appears as though the Scot's joined the Danes to fight the English when they had disagreements.

Edmund, and the great statesman he was, had given to Malcolm, the Scot's King- the Kingdom of Strathclyd. On the conditions of an alliance. The Scot's King entered into a position of dependent alliance with England. The dominate powers of the British Isle was to be that of Scot's and English. Edmund figured that it was worthwhile to align with the Scot's and protect the Isle with allies against the Danes rather fight the Danes and the Scot's, preventing the Scot's to switch sides at their convenience.

This seems to have worked and gives much credit to the statesmanship abilities displayed by Edmund. Up until now war had been the primary solution to problems. Edmund introduced leadership through negotiations.

Edmund did not live long enough to see this alliance succeed. In 946 an outlaw who had taken his seat at a feast in his hall slew him as he was attempting to drag him out by his hair.

Edred (946-955) – Edred is recorded as being 'sickly', that does not seem to have stopped him from conquering the Danes and aligning the Kingdom of Northumberland. Northumberland was given to an English Ealdormen Oswulf, was given the title of Earl. The first recorded entry of 'Earl'. Also I must make a note that this is the first time recorded that an Ealdorman or now 'Earl' was actually given a county to govern.

Edred had finally completed the work that Alfred had begun. England was now completely under one ruler. Even the fight with the Danes, for the most part, was gone.

I think that it should be noted here that the lines of succession at this time were not much different as they are today. All four of Egbert's sons succeeded him in order,
1. Ethelbald 2. Ethelbert 3. Ethelred 4. Alfred
Alfred's oldest son succeeded him 1. Edward
Edward's sons succeeded him in order.
Ethelstan, Edmund and Edred

Edmunds son's succeeded him, Edwig and Edgar, so it would seem that the line of succession does not necessarily go towards the eldest son and his sons, but the line of succession is hereditary in the line that all four of Egbert's sons succeeded him. And then those of Edmunds.

In today's line of succession the hereditary rights would have been- Egbert to his eldest son Ethelbald, then to Ethelbald's eldest son, and if not an heir to Ethelbert and then to Ethelbert's son and so on.

Edwy, (955-959) aka: Edwig, was the eldest son and succeeded his Father into a somewhat peaceful England for the first time. Edwy was 'hardly fifteen years old' when he inherited the Crown. He gave great offense to the Ealdormen and Earls at his coronation feast.

'By leaving to amuse himself with a young kinswoman. Elfgifu, in her mother's room. Edwy was dragged back to his feast by two ecclesiastics, one of them being Dunstan.'

However- being a 'vicious Prince', the Mercian's and the

Northumbrians supported Edgar, his younger brother and crowned him King in the life of Edwy. - This statement is debated by historians and I am positive made and 'repeated' through history by either a Bishop or a friend of the Church, Dunstan more than likely. As you read further, you may understand that perhaps the 'Bad and Viscous Prince' was really not as bad as he was young and in love.

Dunstan: Dunstan was a childhood friend of Edwy and Edgar having grown up in King Edmunds court. He was never a warrior and had been driven off by other children at a young age. "He preferred words, books and God to that of war.' Edmund had made him a Monk and Edwy gave Dunstan the authority of restoring the Monastery's which had nearly become extinct from all the Danish plundering.

Edwy's marriage- Dunstan had restored the Monastery's and also started to restore the order of the Church. Wanting to set up a pure standard of morality, the Church had made rules against the marriage of even distant relations. Edwy offended against these rules by marrying his Kinswoman Elfgifu, we met her on the night of his coronation.

I believe that these two had an actual true love for each other. However, love mattered not to the church when the rules are broken. A quarrel arose between the two childhood friends, Dunstan and the young King. Dunstan perhaps was thinking that he as a 'Monk' representing the Church, and having a personal friendship with Edwy engaged the King in 'quite a quarrel' based on familiarity. The young King in his defense would not back down and was greatly offended by Dunstan's objection towards his new bride. Edwy overruled Dunstan as King and he was driven out and banished.

Unfortunate for all involved, this incident could not have happened at a worse time. The Ealdormen and other great men were also in quite a quarrel themselves. They then took sides between the King and the Church. The Ealdormen of the North and Central England revolted siding the marriage was illegal on the side of the Church and crowned Edwy's brother King Edgar- He was to be King of all England above the Thames.

Edwy's wife was then seized and she was carried 'beyond the sea', their marriage being declared 'to close of kin' by the Church. Edwy soon died, as a novelist I am going to assume of a broken heart, however history says it was "very suspicious' There are assumptions that Edgar, his brother whom some have said was a 'vicious prince' had ordered his murder.

Edgar (959-975) Edgar after the death of Edwy became King of the Whole Nation. He was known as the peaceful King. Having the advantage of ruling with the Church on his side. Not long after his accession, Dunstan was welcomed back and made Archbishop of Canterbury. Everything was to be done to raise the standard of morality and knowledge.

Edgar established a hierarchy in England that gave the people needed protection. It was the people who served the neighboring 'Earl' or Chieftains, by promising to work so many days a month in their service. This essentially made them 'bonded' to their Lords service. They were different from a slave and a farmer. Like a slave they were bonded to the land and could not leave as they wished, however unlike a slave they could not be sold. Unlike a Farmer, they could not be turned out as long as they fulfilled their obligation to their Lord. The neighboring Lord was now free to be at the King's command while his property was being cultivated and cared for. He also provided justice for those in his care, settling disputes and acting as judge. This is the first time that the King of England was no longer the head of the whole people. Where this may have lost some freedom, it unified the Kingdom.

Edgar died in 975 leaving two boys, Edward and Ethelred.

Edward 'The Martyr" (975-979), Edgar's had named Edward his successor, a quarrel broke out between the Earl's. Some declaring for Edward and others for the succession of Ethelred.

The political quarrel was that of an Ecclesiastic quarrel. The supporters of Edward were the friends of the Secular Clergy; the supporters of Edward were the friends of the Monks. Dunstan with his usual moderation, gave his voice for the Eldest son, and Edward was chosen and crowned King. Not only had there been a strong party opposed to him, he had dissatisfied his step-mother. Whose validity of her marriage to King Edgar was and is still in question. She wanted her Son, Ethelred to succeed. He was the younger of the two boys and his legitimacy was called into question. There was no legitimate cause to her claim that Ethelred should succeed.

Edward only reigned for four year when he was murdered near Corfe, it was commonly supposed that he had been murdered by his step mother~

Ethelred II 'The unready' (979-1013/1014-1016) Ethelred was only a boy of ten when his step brother was murdered and he ascended to King.

The epithet the unready is generally assumed due to be his age. It is often mistranslated of a word which properly means the Rede-less, or the man without counsel. He was entirely without the qualities befitting a King. Dunstan being the only guiding hand of counsel he had.

Ethelred's father had kept the Chieftains in subordination to himself because he was a successful leader. Edgar had kept them in subordination because he treated them with respect. Ethelred could neither lead nor show them respect. He was constantly quarrelling with then when he should have been trying to keep peace.

He was only 15 years old and had tried to reduce the power the Earls and the Chieftains. Completely undoing what his father had successfully done to free up his Earls so that they could serve him as needed for war or whatever may be needed. In 985 he drove out Elfric, the Earl of the Mercians. In 988 Dunstan died, and Ethelred no longer had a wise adviser by his side who could try to maintain a semblance of peace by reasoning with the teenage King.

Danes and Norwegians had been appearing in England in mass numbers, settling in England peacefully since 984. In 991 Brihtnoth, the Earl of the East Saxons was attacked and defeated by them at Malden.

Being a boy, without council, Ethelred could only think to buy them off with 10,000. Which today would be more than 5 million dollars.

To keep them from their destruction. It was not necessarily a bad thing to do given the circumstances. One of the greatest Kings of the German's, Henry the Fowler, had paid money for a truce to barbarians. Ethelred's own Grandfather, Edmund had given the Scot's King Malcolm- the Kingdom of Strathclyd for peace and an alliance against the Danes.

What went wrong with Ethelred's plan was he had no back-up plan. Henry, who after he had paid off the barbarians that he was unable to fight at the time, he immediately strengthened his army strong enough to destroy them when they came again.

Ethelred failed to do anything, perhaps because of lack of counsel or age, or a combination of both, he was foolish enough to believe it they wouldn't come again. Whatever the reason, he was never ready or made any preparations of defense for the future. So when in 994 Olaf was driven from the Kingship of Norway, and Swyne had been driven from the Kingship of Denmark, joined forces and embarked on London- the King was unprepared and once again unable to defend his Kingdom.

The London citizens fought better than the King and claimed victory. 'They went thence, and wrought the greatest evil that ever any army could so, in burning, and harrying, and in man-slaying, as in Essex and in Kent, and in Sussex, and in Hampshire. And at last they took their horses and rode as far as they could, and did unspeakable evil" they were known as the "Army".

Ethelred paid them 16,000. Olaf sailed away and was killed by his enemies. However he never permanently got rid of Swyne who regained his Kingdom of Denmark in 1000.

In 1002 Ethelred was a widower and married Emma the sister of the most powerful overlord in France the Duke of the Normans, Richard II. It was the beginning of a connection with Normandy which never ceased till a Norman Duke made himself by conquest, King of England.

In England, the relations between the King and his Earls was grave, the Kingdom as a whole had no unity. The King could not control the Earls. The Earls could not control the King. England as a nation in the true sense of the word hardly existed. It was only natural that the men who during these times of trouble were ruling their own districts- like little Kings, would think more of keeping up their own. It was an independent power at home, their individual districts, rather than of the common interests of all of England.

With his Kingdom falling into ruin to the Danes. The Earls unwilling to come to his service in the defense of the country. Ethelred knowing he had no power over them and unable to fight the Danes. He was also unable to buy them off again, thought that he only had one option. He decided to murder them.

Massacre of the Danes: St Brice's Day:

"The day before St. Brice's Day, secret letters were sent by Ethelred to every city, commanding the English at an appointed hour to destroy the Danes by fire and sword. The day selected for it was Sunday, the festival of St. Brice. Neither age nor sex was spared-men, women, and children being mercilessly slaughtered.

Amongst those who perished was Gunilda, sister of Sweyn, the Danish monarch, who had been given as a hostage for the treaty of peace concluded between her brother and the perfidious Ethelred. Having embraced Christianity, and married Palling, a Saxon courtier, she had settled in this country. This noble lady beheld her husband and child massacred before her eyes: she herself was killed by strokes from a lance. In the agony of her grief for the loved ones who were falling around her, her words to the Saxon murderers were, "God will punish you, and my brother will avenge my death."

According to the Saxon Chronicles:
" The King ordered all the Danish men, who were in England to be slain on St Brice's mass-day., because it was made known to the King that they would beguile him of his life and afterwards all his witan, and that of his Kingdom"

I think this is very important, in the Saxon Chronicles it was written Danish-Men. There are many historical and some contemporary accounts of St Brice's day that states- only the men. I believe that those are mistaken from this source. Huntington and many other reliable historians of the time clearly state, men, women and children.

The Account of the Danish Massacre from the Chronicle of Huntington:

In the year 1002, Emma, the flower of Normandy, came to England, and was crowned and received the title Queen. After her arrival the King was so elated with pride that he committed a breach of faith by giving clandestine orders that all the Danes who were living peacefully in England should be treacherously massacred in one and the same day; on the feast of St. Brice. I have heard in my youth some very old persons give an account of this flagrant outrage.

They said that the King sent with secrecy into every town letters, according to which the English suddenly rose on the Danes, everywhere on the same day and at the same hour, and either put them to the sword, or seizing them unawares, burnt them on the spot.

Henry of Huntington does not relate the motives given in the Saxon Chronicles for Ethelred that the Danes were conspiring to murder the King and his 'witan'. It may be that he did not believe that story, as he conveys that the massacre was "A wanton and unjustifiable cruelty"

However I also find it hard to believe that having just married Emma, who was of Danish decent. Richard II his new wife's brother and the alliance that he gained with this marriage- the reason for the marriage was to gain an ally. I just seem to find Huntington's account that it was done in 'pride'. While Ethelred was not a statesman he was not stupid. I doubt he would have offended the one hope he had to regain any type of order and do something that would light a fire underneath the greatest threat to his Kingdom.

If Ethelred really believed however, that this massacre would truly remove the Danes from England 'forever' as he did when he paid them of 10,000 the first time- perhaps we should look into the mental health of this Monarch.

The Revenge of Swyne and the Danes:

In 1003 Huntington writes, "The fury of the Danes was inflamed like fire that could only be distinguished with blood" Revenging his sisters murder Swyne invaded England with a vengeance. "Overspreading the country like a swarm of locusts, some of them came to Exeter, which they stormed and sacked, carrying off all the booty, and leaving nothing but ashes."

Swyne continued attacking England until finally in 1013 Ethelred was driven out after giving a good fight. It is possible that he could have defended and perhaps he found victory for England had he not been so disliked and betrayed by some of his trusted Earls.

"The Danes then came to the Isle of Wight, and pillaged Sussex, Hampshire, and Berkshire. The King Ethelred, having mustered the whole force of England, marched to intercept them as they returned; and then an end would have been put to their savage inroads, had not Edric, the ealdorman, again traitorous, dissuaded the King from fighting, by false reports, fictitious alarms."

Swyne died in 1014, the Danish crowned his son Canute as his successor. The English people sent messengers to Ethelred asking him to come back to England 'If he could promise to be a just King".

This time unlike the child he was when he ascended the throne as a boy ten years old, he was more humble, a Man and a Father. He sent his son Edward to England who assured them that he would govern them more lovingly than he had before and promising to be all that was fitting a King and the people.

Ethelred returned to England and was "received with joy by the whole English Nation."

Meanwhile Canute remained in Gainsborough, with his army until Easter and made a certain agreement with the people of Lindsey. Upon hearing this King Ethelred came with a great army, and taking the country by surprise laid it waste with fire and sword.

Canute, however, who was very crafty, left the people he had deceived to their fate and sailed on board his fleet to Sandwich, and there he put on shore the hostages given to his father, having cut off their hands and noses.

King Ethelred fell ill and died in 1016. His son succeeded him

Edmund II 'Ironside'- (April to November 1016) (son of Ethelred, by an obscure woman, hence a bastard) though he had two half-legitimate brothers, Edward and Alfred, Born of Emma, the whole legitimate line of the Saxon Kings were excluded. One part choosing Ironside, a bastard, the other Canutus a Dane who was a stranger to England.

Edmund was surnamed, 'Ironside' on the account of his prodigious strength and his extraordinary resoluteness in war, was chosen King. After his election he went to Wessex where all the people rendered him their allegiance.

Edmund defeated Canute in several battles and was feared as a warrior. He had given Canute alarm many times and it is said that Canute 'resorted to treachery and aligned with the most treacherous of all, Edric an Ealdorman.'

"Canute and Edric laid their plans for obtaining by treachery the success they could not gain by arms. Edric undertook to betray King Edmund….. The traitorous council of Edric to King Edmund induced him to halt his pursuit of the Danish army in Esesdune. Never had more fatal council ever been given England.

The Murder of King Edmond Ironside:

'Thus is happened one night, this great and powerful King having on occasion to retire to the house for relieving the calls of nature, the son of the ealdorman Edric, by his father's contrivance, concealed himself in the pit, and stabbed the King twice from beneath with a sharp dagger, and leaving the weapon fixed in his bowels, made his escape.

Edric then presented himself to Canute, and saluted him saying, "Hail, thou art sole King of England!" Having explained what had taken place and what he had done. Canute then replied, "For this deed I will exalt you, as merits, higher than all the nobles of England."

He then commanded that Edric should be decapitated and his head placed upon a pole on the highest battlement of the Tower of London."

King Edmund Ironside, after a reign on one year, was buried at Garston buried near King Edgar. It should be noted that Edric was his brother-in-law and that this is the same Edric that had betrayed King Ethelred, preventing any chance of England having victory against the Danes. Edmund left two sons- Edwy and Edward.

Canutus "The Great" (1016-1035) also known as Canute, the Dane became the sole Monarch of the Saxon Monarchy. The beginning of the Danish Dynasty, which did not last long.

Canute married Emma, who had been the wife of King Ethelred. Queen Emma and Ethelred's children Edward and Alfred having been declared excluded from the line of succession by their half-brother Ironside.

Canute had made himself master of a great empire. Even though he was a Dane, it is said he h he treated the Englishmen and Danes as equals. Some say he gave special favor to the Englishmen over his Danish Kinsman.

He restored the laws of England and brought back the 'peace and order as in the days of Edgar'. He then went on a pilgrimage to Rome. From Rome he sent a letter to his subjects and administer just justice to all.

"I have vowed to God," he wrote "to live a life right in all things. To rule justly and piously my realms and subjects, and to administer just judgment to all. If heretofore I have done aught beyond what is just, through headiness or negligence of youth, I am ready, with God's help, to amend it utterly." Canute never wore the crown again, there are poem and tapestry's depicting him choosing God over the Kingdom and Crown.

It makes you wonder that if after the death of Ironside- based on Canute's behavior and his disgust of Edric, his murderer, if he regretted deeply the death of Edmund Ironsides. He seems to have shown a greater compassion for the English and a sincere desire to find forgiveness.

Harold, 'Harefoot' (1035-1039) Son of Canutus and Emma. Was chosen to succeed by the Mercians.

Hardicanute (1039-1042) his half-brother, Hardicanute, the son of a previous wife and concubine of Canute was chosen by the West Saxons to succeed as King. The Empire however was once again breaking up. The Norwegians chose Magnus, a King of their own race.

Hardicanute at this time was in Denmark defending attacks of Magnus. To complicate matters even more, in Normandy, The two sons of King Ethelred and Emma- Alfred and Edward, 'the confessor'- seem to have thought that because of the absence of Hardicanute, they had a chance to return to England. They were in all respect the right and natural order of succession the Kings of England, the Crown of their father that had been stolen by them of the Dane Canute.

Into all this turmoil came Alfred, son of Ethelred II. If he were innocent of any idea of asserting his own rights, he must have been either very young or very unambitious; and why on earth did he come in this particularly dangerous year to give a proof of existence?

Did Alfred come to England to turn the confusion in the land to his own advantage? By attempting to reach his mother Emma, one could conclude that he was trying to enlist his mother onto his side. Emma had been banished by Harold he step-son and sought refuge with Baldwin, the Earl of Flanders

"In this year the innocent Prince Alfred, son of King Ethelred, came hither, and would go to his mother Emma, who sat in Winchester, but the Earl Godwin would not permit it, nor other men also, who could exercise much power; because the public voice was greatly in favor of Harold; though it was unjust. Godwin then impeded him and in durance set him and his companions as they dispersed. And diversely some slew, some they for money sold. Some cruelly killed and some bound, some blinded, scalped and mutilated. No bloodier deed was done in this country since the Danes came. Now is our trust in the beloved God that they possess bliss joyfully with Christ, those who were slain without guilt. The Prince yet lived, every evil they vowed him, until it was resolved that he should be led to Ely, thus bound. As soon as he was near the land, in the ship they blinded him; and him thus blind brought him to the Monks; and there abode the while that he lived, after that, he was buried, as to him was befitting, full honorably, as he was worthy, at the west end, to the steeple, full nigh, in the south porch. His soul is with Christ.

I very seldom see such a significant disagreement or difference in general of such events in historical manuscripts as I do in the death of the Prince Alfred. It is such a horrific and horrible death that he suffered as a young prince that some debate, only came to England to see his mother and others, to try to justify it say to retain his Crown.

It is evident his death provoked many sympathies in England and in actuality caused a new 'Peace' in the Kingdom.

Another account states: 'he came unprovided and practically and undefended. And this emergency Godwin acted with great decision. Before the news of Alfred's arrival could spread through the country. Godwin-the Earl of Wessex and one of the most powerful men in England captured Alfred. He murdered him and all his company.'

Alfred landed in England but was seized by his half-brother Harold. (Other accounts blame Godwin) 'He was blinded with such cruelty that he died'

The Saxon Chronicles convey it was perfectly natural and right of Prince Alfred to attempt to regain his father's throne. Alfred's murder at once gave a solid foundation to national sentiment; popular feeling was so strong that Edward, also son of Ethelred, was able to come to England in 1040. There is some evidence to prove that Hardicanute either recognized Edward as kinship or formally appointed him his successor.

There was no sentimental friendship or love of justice, he was more than likely compelled by the popular opinion of the kingdom. The Danish successors of Canute would more than likely not had possession of England as long as they did had the sons of Ethelred been men of greater statesmanship and skills of war as some of their ancestors.

In 1040 Harold died leaving and Hardicanute came back from Denmark to claim the English crown. Hardicanute was a heartless man, the English people soon wondered why that had chosen him and perhaps regretted not supporting the Children of Ethelred.

Hardicanute brought with him to England his Danish fleet with sailors and housecarls, (household troops in the personal service of the King) ruled and conquered the land.

He raised a 'Danegeld' to satisfy his men- a tax as the principal tool for underwriting continental wars, as well as providing for royal appetites and the costs of conquest, rather than for buying-off menace which had been its primary use in the past.

He sent his houssecarls to force the people to pay the heavy tax. Two of them were killed at Worcester, Hardicanute in retaliation burnt Worcester to the ground.

"Harthacnut caused all of Worcestershire to be ravaged, for the sake of his two housecarls, who announced a heavy impost, when the people slew them within the town, in the monastery."

In 1042 he died 'as he stood at his drink at a bridal'. I do not think that the people of England mourned his death.

The Legend of Queen Emma.

Robert, the Archbishop of Canterbury, persuaded the King that Emma, forty-eight years after her first marriage and fifteen years after the death of her second husband, Canute. Was guilty of too close an intimacy with Aelfwine, Bishop of Winchester.

From her prison, where she was not very strictly confined, Emma writes to those Bishops in whom she trusted, saying, she is far more shocked at the scandal against Aelfwine, than at the scandal against herself. She is even ready to submit to the ordeal of burning iron in order to prove the Bishop's innocence.

The other Bishops advise the King to allow the trial, but the Norman Archbishop uses very strong language. Saying that Emma is "a wild thing, not a woman; her daring went so far that, she called her slimy lover, Christ the Lord, and so forth.

He said "She may make compurgation for the Bishop, but who will make compurgation for herself? Yet, if she will make a double purgation, if she will walk over four burning shares for herself, and five for the Bishop, her innocence shall be allowed."

Preparations for the ordeal are made accordingly, Emma passing the night before in prayer at the shrine of St. Swithun, who, in answer to her supplications, appears to her, announcing himself,

"I am St. Swithun whom you have invoked; fear not, the fire shall do you no hurt."

The next day, the King with his attendant courtiers assemble; the nine ploughshares are made red-hot, and placed upon the pavement in the Church. Emma entered and says- "Oh God, who didst save Susannah from the malice of the wicked elders, save me,"

She then treads with her bare feet upon the glowing metal: but she senses nothing. She has touched it, yet she asks of the Bishops who lead her by the hand, "When shall we come to the ploughshares?"

They then show her that she has already passed over them. Upon examination, her feet are found to be uninjured.

The Bishops exclaimed- "See the Miracle!"

The King is now thoroughly convinced of her innocence, and repenting his cruelty towards his Mother he casts himself at his mother's feet, exclaiming, "Mother, I have sinned before heaven and before you."

He was whipped both from the Bishop and his mother, he restored all their confiscated property, and then banished the Archbishop.

.

Edward III 'The Confessor', (1042-1066)

"In this year came Edward, maternal brother of Hardicanute, son of King Ethelred, from beyond sea, who before had for many years been driven from this country: and yet was sworn King. And then he dwelt so in his brother's family while he lived."

So little had the hereditary succession of the Saxon Kings been regarded, it always seemed to straighten itself out after a small detour here and there. Edward was the son of Ethelred.

After Hardicanute was advanced to Royal Dignity and after the murder of his brother Alfred- Edward had been accepted and lived as a Prince in the Royal household.

He had been brought up in Normandy with his brother from childhood. After the death of his father, his mother Emma had married Canute, it was then that the two Princes were excluded from the royal line and sent to Normandy

Some say that he was crowned while at court. I have not found any account of a coronation or even so must as a feast proving that to be true. Edward married Godwin's daughter, Edith, in 1045.

The marriage of Edith, to the new King did nothing to raise Godwin to any greatness as had perhaps hoped. There seems to be a great struggle between the Earl Godwin and his son-in-law King Edward.

Unlike that of his Father in law, Edward did his best for his Norman favorites. One of them Robert of Jumieges eventually was appointed Archbishop of Canterbury. Between Godwin and the Normans there was no goodwill, and although Godwin was to have been of 'fair repute, and never spited the Normans that was not the case with his son. Godwin's eldest son was Swegen, 'a young man of a brutal nature.'

Swegen angered all of his countrymen by seducing the Abbess of Leominster, and then by murdering his cousin Beorn. The Earl Godwin, in his blind family affection, clung to his wicked son and insisted on his being allowed to retain his Earldom.

"Earl Swegen spoke with his father and with Earl Beorn, and prayed Beorn to go with him to the king at Sandwich, and aid him to the Kings friendship. They then went as if they would go to the King. Then Swegen, while riding begged of him that he would go with his to his ships, saying his shipmen would go from him, unless he the more speedily came.

They then went both to where his ships lay. When they came tither, Earl Swegen prayed him that he would go with him onboard. He refused vehemently, so long until his shipmen seized him, and threw him onto the boat, and bound him, and rowed to the ship, and put him therein.

They then hoisted their sails and sailed west to Exmouth, and then slew him. They took the body and buried it in a church. Then came his friends and sailors from London and took him up, and conveyed him to Winchester, to Old Monastery, and he is there buried by King Canute, his Uncle."

After this the animosity between the Earl and the King broke out openly. Edward's brother-in-law Eustace, Count of Boulogne, visited England. A disturbance broke out in Dover, and a riot ensued, some of the townsmen as well as some of his own men were slain.

Edward called on Godwin, in whose Earldom Dover was, to punish the townsmen. Godwin refused and Edward summoned him to Gloucester to account for his refusal. In the end Godwin was banished and all of his family with him.

Godwin returned to England in 1052 with his sons, except Swegen. They were welcomed back and Godwin was restored his Earldom.

It became necessary to make arrangements for the throne. Edward the Confessor was growing old and had no issue. Godwin growing not only insolent but intolerable to him, he declared Edward the son of Edmund Ironside (his cousin) his heir.

He then sent a message to the King of Hungary to return his

nephew Edward, which he did upon receipt of his request. The King of Hungary had already married Edward to his niece Agatha, daughter to Henry Emperor of Germany.

Upon Edward and his wife's return, the confessor declared that he or his sons should succeed in his Hereditary Kingdom of England.

Unfortunately Edward died almost immediately after his arrival, leaving only one infant son, Edgar. This was a great disappointment to the Confessor. Naturally, the thought arose of looking on Harold as his successor. Even though that was contrary to all customs to give the throne to anyone not of the royal line.

The custom had been necessarily broken in favor of Canute, so Edward thought it might be better to break it in favor of an English Earl rather than place a child on the throne, when danger threatened England from Normandy.

During the remainder of Edwards's life, Harold proved himself a great warrior worthy of the crown. In 1063 he invaded Wales and reduced it to submission. About the same time Elfgar died and his son Edwin succeeded him in the Earldom of the Mercians.

In 1066 England was then ruled by two great families. Edwin Earl of the Mercians and his brother Morkere ruling the North and West.

Harold and his brothers, the sons of Godwin, ruling the South and the East. The two houses had long been rivals, and after Edwards death there would be no one in the country to control the rival feud.

Edward whose life was at an end was filled with gloomy forebodings. Died on January 5, 1066 and was buried in the church he had founded before his death, The Church of Earl's Barton.

Chapter Three

THE NORMANS
1066 - 1154

THE NORMAN INVASION:

King Harold (1066) Harold was at once chosen King and crowned at Westminster January 1066. Although he had no true claim to the throne. His sister Edith had been married to King Edward. The child Edgar was still too young to rule. Harold had proven himself as worthy and had been the choice of successor by King Edward.

"In this year 1066 King Harold came from York to Westminster, at that Easter; and that Easter was then on the day 16th before Kalends of May. Then was, all over England such a token seen in the heavens, as no man ever before saw. Some men said that it was comet star, which some men call the haired star; and it appeared first on the eve of the 8th before the Kalends of May, and shone all the seven nights. And soon after Harold gathered so great a ship force, and also a land force, as no King here in the land had ever before done, because it was made known to him that William the Bastard would come hither and would win this land. All as it afterwards happened."

William the Conqueror (1066-1087) William after hearing of the death of King Edward, and of his rival's coronation William the Conqueror landed in England sometime in September determined to claim the Crown of England.

According to the principals in England, he had no right to it whatever. He contrived however to put together as many good reasons he did which seemed- in the eyes of those that were not Englishmen a good case.

William claimed that Edward had selected him as heir, there is no proof that supported that claim. He also claimed that Harold had at some former time been 'wrecked upon the French coast, and had been delivered up to William, who had refused to let him go until he had sworn solemnly, placing his hand on a chest which contained the relics of the most holy Norman Saints, and swore his allegiance.

All through the summer Harold was watching for his Rival's coming. The greater part of his force however when September arrived need to go home to attend their Harvest. They had hardly gone when Harold received word that his Brother had joined forces against him with Herald the Ruthless, the sea-rover who was King of Norway.

Tostig had refused to accept the orders of the King when he and his Father had been banished in 1051 for their involvement in an uprising that killed innocent Northumbrians and the death of two of the King's men. Tostig was angry that Harold had escaped the punishment of the rest of the family and had actually been elevated 'beyond means' while he had sunk low.

Convinced that Harold had instigated the entire situation. He sought vengeance. He was planning an attack on Harold but met with opposition from the Earl Edwin, another enemy he blamed for his situation in life.

"Tostig, the Kings brother, came into Humber with sixty ships; and Edwin the Earl came with a land force and drove him out. A boatmen forsook him and he went to Scotland with twelve vessels. There he met Harold the King of Norway with three-hundred ships. Tostig submitted to him and became his man."

Tostig and the Norman King reached England and had laid

waste to Yorkshire and then they sailed up the Humber. The two Northern Earls Edwin and Morkere met them but were hard pressed in the battle being greatly outnumbered. Marching swiftly northwards the King learned that the Earls had been defeated, and York had agreed to submit to the Norsemen.

Harold hurried on faster, and came upon the invaders unawares as they lay on both sides of the Derwnet at Stamford Bridge. Those on the western side, unprepared, were soon overpowered. By evening Harold the Ruthless and Tostig himself, with the bulk of the invaders were slain.

"Then came Harold our King unawares of the Northmen, and met them beyond York, at Stanford Bridge, with a great army of English people. There during the day was a very severe fight on both sides. There was slain Harold the Ruthless and Tostig the Earl. And the Northmen who were there with them to fight. The English from behind quietly struck them, some escaped to their ships, some were drowned, some were burned and this in several ways they perished so that few were left; the English had possession of a place of carnage. The King then gave his protection the son of the King of Norwegians and to their Bishop, and to the Earl of Orkney, and to all those who were left in the ships; and they went up to our King and swore oaths that they ever would observe peace and friendship towards this land. The King let them go home with 24 ships. These two battles were fought within five days."

Harold did not have much time to celebrate. As they were toasting the victory in York, Harold received a message of the landing of the Norman at Pevensey. Having just come to the rescue of Edwin and Morkere they gave him no assistance in return.

The King had to defend Sussex without any help from the North or the Midlands. The Earls having no love or goodwill of each other's houses. England was a house divided against itself. Harold had shown what an English King could do, who fought not for this or that part of the country, but for the whole of England. It was the lack of this national spirit in Englishmen which caused his ruin.

"Then came William, Earl of Normandy into Pevensey, on the eve of St. Michaelmas: soon after they were on their way, they constructed a Castle at Hastings-port. This was then made known to King Harold, and he gathered a great force, and went to meet him and William came unawares, before his people were set in order."

The Battle of Senlac: 1066

Harold as soon as he reached the point of danger, drew up his army on the long hill of Senlac on which the Battle Abbey now stands.

The Battle Abbey

On October 14, William marched forth to attack him. The military equipment of the Normans was better than that of the English. Where the weapons on either side are unlike, battles are decided by the momentum. That is to say- by the combined weight and speed of the weapons employed.

The English fought on foot mostly with two handed axes; the Normans not only on horseback with lances but also with infantry, some of them being archers. Harold had in his favor the slope of the hill up which the Normans would have to ride. He took advantage of that and positioned his men with their shields in front of them on the edge of the hill.

The position was a strong one in the means of defense. However it was not a strong one should he need to change his position as the day might need. William, on the other hand, had not only a better armed force but a more flexible one as well.

The English were brave enough but William was a more intelligent leader than Harold. Twice after the battle began the Norman horseman had charged up the hill only to be driven back. William in finding that the hill was not to be stormed by a direct attack, decided to storm the English with a shower of arrows. He then ordered his left wing to 'turn and fly' It was successful. The English rushed down the hill in pursuit, and the Normans faced round and charged their pursuers up the slope. The English was thrown into confusion, they held out stoutly as the Norman Horsemen now occupied one end of the hill.

Slowly and steadily the Normans pressed on as until they reached King Harold who was surrounded by his personal warriors fighting beneath his standard. There all the Norman attacks were in vain until William called out to his bowman ordering them to shoot their arrows into the air. Down came the arrows in showers upon the heads of the English. One of the arrows pierce Harold's eye, stretching him lifeless on the ground.

"The King never the less strenuously fought against William with those who would follow him. There was a great slaughter made on each side. There was slain King Harold, and Leofwin the Earl, his brother and many good men. The Frenchman had possession of the place of carnage, all as God granted them for the people's sins. Archbishop Aldred and the townsmen of London would then have child Edgar for King, all was true and natural right. And Edwin and Morcar vowed to him that they would fight together with him."

William Rufus, The Red, (1087-1100) William was the second son of the Conqueror, succeeded his elder brother Robert- who was still alive at the time. Just before William the Conqueror died he decided that William Rufus, rather than his older brother, Robert Curthose, should be king of England. He was crowned by Lanfranc, the Archbishop of Canterbury, on 26th September, 1087.

The following year some Normans, including Odo of Bayeux, Robert of Mortain, Richard Fitz Gilbert, William Fitz Osbern and Geoffrey of Coutances, led a rebellion against the rule of Rufus in order to place Robert Curthose on the throne. However most Normans in England remained loyal and William and his army successfully attacked the rebel strongholds at Tonbridge, Pevensey and Rochester. The leaders of the revolt were exiled to Normandy.

In 1091 William invaded Normandy. Such was the size of his army that Robert Curthose agreed a peace settlement. This gave William control over large areas of Normandy. The two men also agreed on a joint campaign to take Maine and Cotentin, an area that Curthose had sold to his brother Henry Beauclerk. In the summer of 1091 Henry was forced to surrender Cotentin after a siege of only fifteen days.

William returned to England in August 1091 and soon afterwards marched against King Malcolm III, whose Scots army had invaded the country in his absence. The campaign was a success and Malcolm was forced to submit at the Firth of Forth.

In March 1094 William went on another expedition to Normandy. To pay for the campaign he imposed heavy taxes. Some of this money was used to bribe Philip of France not to support Robert Curthose. After paying his Norman soldiers to continue the war, he returned to England.

In 1095 William decided to bring Robert of Mowbray, the Earl of Northumberland, to justice. He took Newcastle and Tynemouth before besieging Mowbray at Bamborough. William was forced to end this campaign when he heard the Welsh had captured Montgomery. By the time he reached the area the Welsh had abandoned Montgomery and had withdrawn to the mountains.

William was very unpopular with the Church. Unlike his father, William the Conqueror, he was not a committed Christian. His father's policy of spending considerable sums of money on the Church was reversed. When he needed to raise money, he raided monasteries.

On 2nd August 1100, King William went hunting at Brockenhurst in the New Forest. Gilbert de Clare and his younger brother, Roger of Clare, were with the king. Another man in the hunting party was Walter Tyrel, who was married to Richard de Clare's daughter, Adelize. Also present was William Rufus' younger brother Henry. During the hunt, Walter Tyrel fired an arrow at a stag. The arrow missed the animal and hit William in the chest. Within a few minutes the king was dead. Tyrel jumped on his horse and made off at great speed. He escaped to France and never returned again to England. There was little suspension if this was an accident or a plan. There is little evidence to prove either true.

Most people expected Robert Curthose to become king. However, his younger brother Henry Beauclerk decided to take quick action to gain the throne. As soon as he realized William was dead, Henry rushed to Winchester where the government's money was kept. After gaining control of the treasury, Henry declared he was the new king.

Supported by Gilbert de Clare and Roger of Clare, Henry was crowned king on 5th August. Although Robert threatened to invade England, he eventually agreed to do a deal with Henry. In return for an annual payment of 2,000 pounds. Although Robert was furious, he accepted Henry as king of England.

Henry I (1100-1135) In 1106 Henry I invaded Normandy and captured Robert at the battle of Tinchebrai. Robert was brought back to England and spent the rest of his life as a prisoner at Devizes, Bristol and Cardiff.

Henry married Edith, the daughter of King Malcolm III of Scotland. After her death in 1118, he married Adelaide of Louvain. Henry's son, William was drowned in November, 1120.

Although he acknowledged being the father of over twenty

children, almost as many as Charles II, he decided that Matilda, his only legitimate child left alive, should be his heir. Henry I died in December 1135.

However, Stephen, the Son of the Conquerors sister, succeeded Henry. Although Henry willed Matilda as his heir, and was in the direct line of succession. (Matilda is the line that Queen Elizabeth of England claims as an ancestor.)

In 1125- **Stephen (1135-1154)** married Matilda of Boulogne and two years later swore an oath recognizing his cousin, Matilda, the daughter of Henry I, as heir to the English throne. Although Stephen had broken his promise and quickly crowned himself king of England, he did recognize her hereditary rights.

At the time of her father's death, Matilda was with her husband, Geoffrey of Anjou in Normandy. It was not until 1139 that Matilda landed in England with her army. Stephen was eventually captured at the battle of Lincoln in February 1141. Henry of Winchester acknowledged her as Queen, for a short time all of England submitted to her- however her reign was short. Matilda was very harsh where Stephen was soft hearted and good natured. Matilda had seized lands of the Church and ordered Londoners heavy fines as a punishment for supporting Stephen. The people 'rand their bells and the citizens in arms swarmed out of their houses like bees out of a hive." Matilda was forced to flee.

Stephens's army captured Robert of Gloucester and he was taken prisoner. After a while Matilda was forced to set King Stephen free in exchange for her brother. Fighting continued for some time although both sides longed for peace.

Stephen took one castle after another, one victory after another. In 1148 Matilda was forced to surrender the battle.

The Treaty of Winchester was signed in November, 1153. This treaty recognized Matilda's eldest son, Henry, as the next king of England. In return, Matilda agreed that Stephen's son, William, would be allowed to keep his family lands in Normandy.

Stephen was the last of the Norman kings he died in October 1154

*Henry the Second succeeded Stephen, Maud. Henry's Mother was still living. So his succession was not hereditary for Hares non est vi-vinsis.

Richard the First succeeded Henry the Second.

John Succeeded Richard, Arthur the son of Jeffery, Johns elder Brother who was at that time still alive. (John of Gaunt)

Henry the Third succeeded John, Eleanor, and Arthur's Sister then alive who was the heir apparent before him. So of the seven successors after the Conqueror, only one- Richard I, succeeded as heir to his Father the Conqueror.

It is true Edward the First succeeded as heir to Henry III and that Edward II succeeded as heir to Edward I, yet Edward III did not succeed as heir to Edward II, he being alive at the time of Edwards succession.

That Richard II was heir to Edward the Black Prince. The eldest son of Edward III, yet neither Henry the 4th, 5th or Henry 6th were heirs of Edward the 3rd, but were descendants of Philippa who was the daughter of Lionel Duke of Clarence, John of Gaunt elder brother.

So from the succession of 14 Kings after William the Conqueror, there were o,nly Four- Richard I, Edward I, Edward II, and Richard II who succeeded rightfully as heirs to William the Conqueror, or who were his true heirs.

Edward IV succeeded right, as heir to Philippa, who was the daughter of the Duke of Clarence, yet if what Richard III said is true, his brother.

"Edward IV was contracted to Eleanor Boteler, before he married Elizabeth" This being a true statement, then Edward V did not (if it may be called a succession) succeed right, nor could Henry VII claim any right to the Crown of England in Right of his wife Elizabeth, the eldest daughter of Edward IV.

Weather it is true or not, that Edward was contracted to Eleanor Boteler before his marriage, as referred to also in Philippa Gregory's The White Queen, matters little and is of no consequence.

That Richard III succeeded although he was not heir, Edward the Earl of Warwick, the son of George Duke of Clarence and Richards's eldest brother was at that time still alive and the rightful heir to the throne. Therefore Richard did not succeed in the hereditary line. As we learned earlier he did meet an untimely end.

Chapter Four

THE PLANTAGENETS
1154 – 1399

Henry II- 1154-1189- Henry was also known as 'Curtmantle.' The Eldest son of Matilda and Geoffrey Plantagenet. He was the Grandson of Henry I and the Great-Grandson of William I and Matilda of Flanders. Henry was twenty-one years old when he inherited the royal throne of England.

He is described with descriptions like- as strong and thick set, and was as active as he was strong. 'His restlessness was the dismay of his courtiers.' And 'Eager to see everything for himself, he was always on the move; Henry was as busy with his mind as he was with his body.

He had a love for horses as much as books. It is said that Henry was ready to chat to anyone whatever their rank. His ceaseless energy was combined with a strong will, a clear perception of the limits beyond which action would be unwise, a good eye for ability in others. More importantly, he had an ability to utilize those abilities for his own service.

As King Henry was eager to bring the Clergy under his rule. He desired to establish a Kingdom of one law under his command. To ultimately make these clerks punishable by his own courts. This desire followed his predecessors and ultimately caused great turmoil between Kings and Churchman in future generations.

Henry needed to fill the vacancy for the Archbishop of Canterbury. He devised a plan to name his friend and Chancellor-Thomas Becket, who had been active as a reformer in his service.

Thomas did not favor this appointment, he warned Henry, "I warn you, if such a thing should be, our friendship will soon turn to bitter hate."

Henry did not heed this warning and appointed Thomas as Archbishop of Canterbury. Whom soon after this appointment asked to surrender his Chancellorship. He was unable, he said, to serve two masters. Henry should have seen where this was leading too.

The struggle soon insured. The power of a King who wanted to assert his rights of the crown. And between that of an Archbishop who believed he was himself a greater man because he believed that he was fighting the cause of God. Not yet did the people believe in the Divine right of Kings, which was at this time only the desire of King Henry. One he wanted to make a reality.

In 1164 Henry summoned a Great Council to meet at Clarendon. He directed his oldest members to put in writing the customs observed by his Grandfather. Their report was intended to settle all disputes between the King and the Clergy, it was drawn up and is known as the 'Constitutions of Clarendon'. Printed in full on the following pages.

The most important of these articles declared that clergy should not leave the realm without the King's leave; that no tenant-in-chief of the King should be excommunicated without the King's knowledge; that no villain should be ordained without his Lord's consent; that a criminous clerk should be sent to the ecclesiastical court for trial, and that after he had been convicted or plead guilty that the Church should then leave him to the lay court for punishment.

To all of this Sir Thomas was violently and adamantly opposed. After six days of argument and failure to come to any type of agreement with the King, Thomas left the Council- refusing to agree to the Constitutions.

Henry had both his Grandfather and his Great-Grandfather's characters in him. From Henry I he had an orderly spirit, and could not completely and forcefully uphold and force the Constitutions. However, he had also the violence and stubbornness of William II. So when Henry learned that John the Marshal had a suit against Thomas the Archbishop and that Thomas had refused to plead in the lay court, King Henry fined him. He then summoned him to his Castle at Northampton to give an account of all the money that he as Chancellor had received for the King. Which would have amounted to about a $500,000 today.

Thomas was found guilty and King Henry declared him a traitor. Today the charges would have been embezzlement or fraud. Thomas refused to listen or accept the King's ruling, immediately claiming he was under the protection of the Pope. Henry was greatly angered and the two created a public altercation in which Henry banished Thomas from the England.

"This is a fearful day" said an attendant of the King.
"The day of Judgment will be more fearful" Replied Thomas.
Thomas soon fled to France. Henry in his anger banished as many as 400 of the Archbishops family and friends.

Constitutions of Clarendon: 1164

1. If a controversy concerning aversions and presentation of churches arise between laymen, or between laymen and clerks, or between clerks, it shall be treated of and terminated in the court of the lord king.

2. Churches of the fee of the lord king cannot, unto all time, be given without his assent and concession.

3. Clerks charged and accused of anything, being summoned by the Justice of the king, shall come into his court, about to respond there for what it seems to the king's court that he should respond there; and in the ecclesiastical court for what it seems he should respond there; so that the Justice of the king shall send to the court of the holy church to see in what manner the affair will there be carried on. And if the clerk shall be convicted, or shall confess, the church ought not to protect him further.

4. It is not lawful for archbishops, bishops, and persons of the kingdom to go out of the kingdom without the permission of the lord king. And if it please the king and they go out, they shall give assurance that neither in going, nor in making a stay, nor in returning, and will they seek the hurt or harm of king or kingdom.

5. The excommunicated shall not give a pledge as a permanency, nor take an oath, but only a pledge and surety of presenting themselves before the tribunal of the church, that they may be absolved.

6. Laymen ought not to be accused unless through reliable and

legal accusers and witnesses in the presence of the bishop, in such wise that the archaeon do not lose his right, nor any thing which he ought to have from it. And if those who are inculpated are such that no one wishes or dares to accuse them, the sheriff, being requested by the bishop, shall cause twelve lawful men of the neighborhood or town to swear in the presence of the bishop that they will make manifest the truth in this matter, according to their conscience.

7. No one who holds of the king in chief, and no one of his demesne servitors, shall be excommunicated, nor shall the lands of any one of them be placed under an interdict, unless first the lord king, if he be in the land, or his Justice, if he be without the kingdom, be asked to do justice concerning him: and in such way that what shall pertain to the king's court shall there be terminated; and with regard to that which concerns the ecclesiastical court, he shall be sent thither in order that it may there be treated.

8. Concerning appeals, if they shall arise, from the archaeon they shall proceed to the bishop, from the bishop to the archbishop. And if the archbishop shall fail to render justice, they must come finally to the lord king, in order that by his command the controversy may be terminated in the court of the archbishop, so that it shall not proceed further without the consent of the lord king.

9. If a quarrel arise between a clerk and a layman or between a layman and a clerk concerning any tenement which the clerk wishes to attach to the church property but the layman to a lay fee: by the inquest of twelve lawful men, through the judgment of the chief Justice of the king, it shall be determined, in the presence of the Justice himself, whether the tenement belongs to the church property, or to the lay fee. And if it be recognized as belonging to the church property, the case shall be pleaded in the ecclesiastical court; but if to the lay fee, unless both are holders from the same bishop or baron, the case shall be pleaded in the king's court. But if both vouch to warranty for that fee before the same bishop or baron, the case shall be pleaded in his court; in such way that, on account of the inquest made, he who was first in possession shall not lose his possession, until, through the pleading, the case shall have been proven.

10. Whoever shall belong to the city or castle or fortress or demesne manor of the lord king, if he be summoned by the archaeon or bishop for any offense for which he ought to respond to them, and he be unwilling to answer their summonses, it is perfectly right to place him under the interdict; but he ought not to be excommunicated until the chief servitor of the lord king of that town shall be asked to compel him by law to answer the summonses. And if the servitor of the king be negligent in this matter, he himself shall be at the mercy of the lord king, and the bishop may thenceforth visit the man who was accused with ecclesiastical justice.

11. Archbishops, bishops, and all persons of the kingdom who hold of the king in chief have their possessions of the lord king as a barony, and answer for them to the Justices and servitors of the king, and follow and perform all the customs and duties as regards the king; and, like other barons, they ought to be present with the barons at the judgments of the court of the lord king, until it comes to a judgment to loss of life or limb.

12. When an archbishopric is vacant, or a bishopric, or an abbey, or a priory of the demesne of the king, it ought to be in his hand; and he ought to receive all the revenues and incomes from it, as demesne ones. And, when it comes to providing for the church, the lord king should summon the more important persons of the church, and, in the lord king's own chapel, the election ought to take place with the assent of lord king and with the counsel of the persons of the kingdom whom he had called for this purpose. And there, before he is consecrated, the person elected shall do homage and fealty to the lord king as to his liege lord, for his life and his members and his earthly honors, saving his order.

13. If any of the nobles of the kingdom shall have dispossessed an archbishop or bishop or archaeon, the lord king should compel them personally or through their families to do justice. And if by chance any one shall have dispossessed the lord king of his right, the archbishops and bishops and archdeans ought to compel him to render satisfaction to the lord king.

14. A church or cemetery shall not, contrary to the king's justice, detain the chattels of those who are under penalty of forfeiture to the king, for they (the chattels) are the king's, whether they are found within the churches or without them.

15. Pleas concerning debts which are due through the giving of a bond, or without the giving of a bond, shall be in the jurisdiction of the king.

16. The sons of rustics may not be ordained without the consent of the lord on whose land they are known to have been born.

Since the Conquest, no eldest son had succeeded his Father on the throne. Henry wanted to ensure that his son did. He asked the Church- that the Kingdom of England pass upon his death to his eldest son.

'He therefore determined to adopt a plan which had been practiced and successful with the Kings of France. It was to have a young Henry chosen and crowned in his own lifetime, so that when he died his son would be ready to step into his Father's place.'

A Coronation was planned and on June 14, 1170 young Henry was crowned by the Archbishop of York. Unfortunately, it did not go as planned. On the day before the coronation, the Archbishop, Roger, who performed the ceremony, received a notice of excommunication from Thomas that had been ratified by the Pope.

This angered and frustrated Henry, however he also wanted to be assured that the Coronation of his son would be valid. Henry then, saw no other choice but to make peace with Thomas. They soon agreed to let the past be forgotten on both sides. Henry welcomed Thomas back into England but unfortunately Henry's hopes of peace were not to be.

On December 1, 1170 Thomas arrived in England. He refused to release from excommunication all the Bishops who had taken part in young Henry's Coronation- unless they would admit the wrongs done to him. Thomas had forgot nothing.

Henry was again outraged.

"What a parcel of fools and bastards!" Henry cried, impatiently, "Have I nourished in my house none that can be found to avenge me on one upstart clerk!"

Four of Henry's Knights reportedly took him at his word, and left at once for Canterbury.

Thomas had trouble of his own, much more pressing than that of the Bishops. While in his absence Ranulf de Bronc and others had been in the custody of his lands which they presently refused to surrender back to him. On Christmas day, Thomas did what Thomas did best, and excommunicated them and repeated the excommunication of the Bishops.

On December 29, the four Knights sought him out, and it is not believed that they had intended to do him harm. However, the excommunication of the King's servants was a breach of the Constitutions and they asked him- in the King's name, to leave the Kingdom. Thomas seems to have started an altercation and at this point the Knights armed themselves.

The Archbishop was convinced to take refuge in the church by his followers.

The Knights rushed in crying "where is the traitor? Where is the traitor?"

Thomas rushing forward replied, "No traitor here, only a priest of God."

Another altercation ensued, the Knights threw Thomas to the ground and struck him dead."

Henry had four sons:
Henry who had married Margaret of France died young in 1183
Richard 'Lionheart' who married Berengaria of Navarre
Geoffrey who married Constance of Brittany and died in 1185
John- 'Lackland' who married second Isabella of Angouleme

Richard 'Lionheart' (1189-1199)

King Richard has been depicted in many motion pictures, the most famous one being Sean Connery in the Robin Hood- Prince of Thieves movie in 1991

King Richard is known widely for his Crusades. Having determined to embark on his holy crusades, he was eager to raise money to pay for them. Richard sold offices to those who wished to buy them, the right to leave office to those who wished to retire and with the Pope's consent sold the right to remain at home to those who had taken the Cross.

Richard appointed Hugh of Puiset, Bishop of Durham and William of Longchamp's, Bishop of Ely to secure order during his absence.

I think it important to include the 'code of laws' that King Richard set forth to be observed during his expedition. The punishments assigned by this ordinance are worthy of notice, though somewhat barbaric of the age.

1. If a man killed another while on board ship, he was to be bound to the dead body, and cast into the sea. If the murder was committed on land, he was to be buried alive with the dead man.

2. If anyone was convicted of having drawn his knife for the purpose of wounding another, or having struck a crusader to draw blood, he was to lose his hand. If the blow was not followed by blood, he was thrice to be plunged into the sea.

3. If a man used opprobrious language, or unjustly reproached another, he was to be fined an ounce of silver.

4. A convicted robber was to be shaved, tarred and feathered

5. The general order of all persons during a voyage was that they were to obey the commanders appointed by the King as they would the monarch himself.

Richard named his nephew, Arthur, Duke of Brittany -the Son

of his late Brother Geoffrey's son, as his heir. 'In case of his own death without children. This shows both his suspicion and dislike for his brother John.

Richard endeavored to establish the title of the young Duke of Brittany to be considered as his presumptive successor, as to put it beyond all without question. Also, to form for him such connections that would secure his easy accession in the event that throne becoming vacant.

The historians of the time attribute the Bishop of Ely's personal enmity towards John. All of the negotiations that took place at this time focused towards a strict alliance between the King of Scotland and the young Prince Arthur.

The Chronicle of Mailros states distinctly, that Richard not only solemnly declared Arthur to be the heir of all his dominions, in case of his own death without children, but that he caused his bishops, counts and his barons to recognize the young Prince as such and bound them to his cause on an oath. Chronicles of Mailros 1191- This chronicle is exceedingly valuable and seems to have been compiled with great care by the Monks of Melrose.

Richard had great success and great failure in his Holy Crusades. Historians debate and always will do so on King Richard as a good King for England vs King Richard a Holy and passionate man of strong convictions. There is no doubt the Crusades cost England greatly, financially as well as the sorry state the country was left in without the King maintaining order.

However, this is one of the most romanticized and greatest historical tales from Shakespeare to Hollywood.

This is a story from a day of Crusades:

Richard, as ardent in pleasure as in war, enjoyed the amusement of falconry, sometimes forgetting about his own safety and the enemy. On one occasion the royal party would have paid dearly for their lack of attention during this pastime, if a quick thinking gentleman, named William de Pratelles, had not cried aloud, "I am the king!" By this noble lie the attention of the Saracens was drawn upon himself, while the real sovereign escaped. Shortly afterwards, a body of Templars fell into an ambush of the Turks. Richard sent the earl of Leicester to the aid of the brave but exhausted knights, and promised to follow straight. Before he could buckle on his armor, he heard that the enemy had triumphed. Despising all personal solicitude, and generously declaring he "should not deserve the name of king if he abandoned those whom he had vowed to succor", he flew to the place of combat, plunged into the thickest of the fight, and his impetuosity received its usual reward of success. The fortifications of Jaffa were at length restored, a vigorous renewal of the war was determined on, and Plantagenet declared to the Saracens that the only way of averting his wrath would be to surrender to him the kingdom of Jerusalem, as it existed in the reign of Baldwin the leper. Saladin did not reject this proposal with disdain, but made a modification of the terms, in offering to yield Palestine from the Jordan to the sea. The negotiation lasted for some time. Richard was deceived and cajoled by the presents and blandishments of Saphadin, who was the brother of Saladin, and the Christians were ashamed that their leader should be so friendly with an infidel. The barons soon saw, and compelled their royal lord to see, the artifice of the Turks, who resumed their attacks, and the negotiation were broken off.

King Richard died in 1199 and was succeeded by his brother John:

King John 1199-1216: 'Lackland' John was born on Christmas Eve 1167 at Beaumont Palace in Oxfordshire, to the parents, Henry II and Eleanor of Aquitaine. After he was born his father jokingly nick-named him Sans Terre or Lackland, probably because, as the youngest of Henry II's five sons, it was difficult to find a portion of his father's French possessions for him to inherit. It seems ironic then, that John Lackland was eventually to inherit the entire Angevin Empire.

Eleanor of Aquitaine, one of the most fascinating women in medieval history in her own right, adored Richard "The Lionheart" as her favorite son. But soon Eleanor's husband, John's father would betray them.

John's youth was divided between his eldest brother Henry's house, where he learned the art of knighthood, and the house of his father's advisor, Ranulf Glanvil, where he learned the business of government. As the fourth child, inherited lands were not yet available to him and only helped to give rise to his nickname, Lackland.

Lackland was also a born cynic, with a rascally sense of humor, hopeless, deceitful and entirely without scruple, he possessed some of the restless energy of his father and was prone to the same violent rages, but unlike his father, John was unstable and cruel and a very flawed individual. His distrust of others verged on paranoia. After eight hundred years, John remains quite the individualist of the House of Plantagenet

When it became time to marry, John sought the hand of Isabella of Gloucester, but as they were both the great-grandchildren of Henry I, they needed papal dispensation to marry, which was granted. However, after ten years of marriage with no heirs produced, the marriage was annulled in 1199. Isabelle never became Queen. The second wife, Isabella of Angouleme, produced two sons and three daughters. Isabella, was the daughter of Count of Angouleme. He also had several illegitimate children, including an illegitimate daughter, Joan. Joan went on to marry Llywelyn the Great Ruler of All Wales, from which the Tudor line of Monarchs descended.

Reign:

John Lackland was crowned King 27 May 1199 at Westminster Abbey; John was an able administrator interested in law and government but he neither trusted others nor was trusted by them.

John was 32 years of age when he succeeded to the throne. On Richard, The Lionheart's deathbed, in 1199, it was reported that he announced John as his heir to the throne. There were arguably better claims, such as Arthur of Brittany, the son of his deceased elder brother, Geoffrey, but with a dying man's declaration, it was clear of the King's wishes, and John didn't waste any time. Lackland quickly seized the royal treasury at Chinon and his coronation took place soon after on Ascension Day in 1199. This caused Phillip Augustus, in accordance to his policy to weaken the Angevin Empire to rebel and create a division between The Plantagenet's and to support Arthur's claim, by attacking Normandy.

Most of his reign was dominated by war with France. Following the peace treaty of Le Goulet there was a brief peace, but fighting resumed again in 1202. John had lost Normandy and almost all the other English possessions in France to Philip II of France by 1204. He spent the next decade trying to regain these without success and was finally defeated by Philip Augustus at the Battle of Bouvines in 1214.

He was also in conflict with the Church. In 1205 he disputed the pope's choice of Stephen Langton as Archbishop of Canterbury. He issued heavy taxes which were disputed within the Church. This caused John to become excommunicated by the Pope in attempts to recover his French possessions made him unpopular and were unsuccessful. So Pope Innocent III placed England under an interdict, suspending all religious services, including baptisms, marriages, and burials.

Many of his barons rebelled, and in June 1215 they forced King John to sign a peace treaty accepting their reforms. Eventually, John submitted, accepting the papal nominee, and agreed to hold the kingdom as a fief of the papacy; an annual monetary tribute was paid to the popes for the next 150 years by successive English monarchs. This treaty, later known as Magna Carta, limited royal powers, defined feudal obligations between the King and the barons, and guaranteed a number of rights.

The Death of John:

King John Lackland was in a state of deep despair and decided to return home. He avoided East Anglia which was rebel territory at the time and navigated around the Wash. (tidelands) His baggage, however, took a different route through some marshes. The outcome for his personal belongings including the crown jewels and all he had inherited from his grandmother Matilda, the Empress of Germany. Gone in the "Wash!" All of the king's possessions were swept away by an unexpected coming tide.

Now the grieved king was depressed at the loss and was mourning his ill fortune and suffering severely from dysentery to top it all off. He even needed to be carried to Newark Castle and in a messenger sent for a physician. He tried to console himself with a diet consisting mostly of peaches.

On a stormy night of October 18, 1216, John's condition worsened and he soon died at Newark. His death left England in a state of anarchy and civil war. There were even rumors that the king had been poisoned. Despite his obvious flaws and short comings, evidence exists that John was not as bad as his posthumous reputation would seem to suggest.

King John Lackland was 49 years, 9 months and 24 days of age when he died. He was also related to Elizabeth II as her 21st great grandfather.

The Document 'Magna Carta'

The following Article is printed with permission by Nancy Troutman and the National Public Telecomputing Network:

The Magna Carta:

John, by the grace of God, king of England, lord of Ireland, duke of Normandy and Aquitaine, and count of Anjou, to the archbishop, bishops, abbots, earls, barons, justiciaries, foresters, sheriffs, stewards, servants, and to all his bailiffs and liege subjects, greetings. Know that, having regard to God and for the salvation of our soul, and those of all our ancestors and heirs, and unto the honor of God and the advancement of his holy Church and for the rectifying of our realm, we have granted as underwritten by advice of our venerable fathers, Stephen, archbishop of Canterbury, primate of all England and cardinal of the holy Roman Church, Henry, archbishop of Dublin, William of London, Peter of Winchester, Jocelyn of Bath and Glastonbury, Hugh of Lincoln, Walter of Worcester, William of Coventry, Benedict of Rochester, bishops; of Master Pandulf, sub deacon and member of the household of our lord the Pope, of brother Aymeric (master of the Knights of the Temple in England), and of the illustrious men William Marshal, earl of Pembroke, William, earl of Salisbury, William, earl of Warenne, William, earl of Arundel, Alan of Galloway (constable of Scotland), Waren Fitz Gerold, Peter Fitz Herbert, Hubert De Burgh (seneschal of Poitou), Hugh de Neville, Matthew Fitz Herbert, Thomas Basset, Alan Basset, Philip d'Aubigny, Robert of Roppesley, John Marshal, John Fitz Hugh, and others, our liegemen.

1. In the first place we have granted to God, and by this our present charter confirmed for us and our heirs forever that the English Church shall be free, and shall have her rights entire, and her liberties inviolate; and we

will that it be thus observed; which is apparent from this that the freedom of elections, which is reckoned most important and very essential to the English Church, we, of our pure and unconstrained will, did grant, and did by our charter confirm and did obtain the ratification of the same from our lord, Pope Innocent III, before the quarrel arose between us and our barons: and this we will observe, and our will is that it be observed in good faith by our heirs forever. We have also granted to all freemen of our kingdom, for us and our heirs forever, all the underwritten liberties, to be had and held by them and their heirs, of us and our heirs forever.

2. If any of our earls or barons, or others holding of us in chief by military service shall have died, and at the time of his death his heir shall be full of age and owe "relief", he shall have his inheritance by the old relief, to wit, the heir or heirs of an earl, for the whole barony of an earl by £100; the heir or heirs of a baron, £100 for a whole barony; the heir or heirs of a knight, 100s, at most, and whoever owes less let him give less, according to the ancient custom of fees.

3. If, however, the heir of any one of the aforesaid has been under age and in wardship, let him have his inheritance without relief and without fine when he comes of age.

4. The guardian of the land of an heir who is thus under age, shall take from the land of the heir nothing but reasonable produce, reasonable customs, and reasonable services, and that without destruction or waste of men or goods; and if we have committed the wardship of the lands of any such minor to the sheriff, or to any other who is responsible to us for its issues, and he has made destruction or waster of what he holds in wardship, we will take of him amends, and the land shall be committed to two lawful and discreet men of that fee, who shall be responsible for the issues to us or to him to whom we shall assign them; and if we have given or sold the wardship of any such land to anyone and he has therein made destruction or waste, he shall lose that wardship, and it shall be transferred to two lawful and discreet men of that fief, who shall be responsible to us in like manner as aforesaid.

5. The guardian, moreover, so long as he has the wardship of the land, shall keep up the houses, parks, fishponds, stanks, mills, and other things pertaining to the land, out of the issues of the same land; and he shall restore to the heir, when he has come to full age, all his land, stocked with ploughs and wainage, according as the season of husbandry shall require, and the issues of the land can reasonable bear.

6. Heirs shall be married without disparagement, yet so that before the marriage takes place the nearest in blood to that heir shall have notice.

7. A widow, after the death of her husband, shall forthwith and without difficulty have her marriage portion and inheritance; nor shall she give anything for her dower, or for her marriage portion, or for the inheritance which her husband and she held on the day of the death of that husband; and she may remain in the house of her husband for forty days after his death, within which time her dower shall be assigned to her.

8. No widow shall be compelled to marry, so long as she prefers to live without a husband; provided always that she gives security not to marry without our consent, if she holds of us, or without the consent of the lord of whom she holds, if she holds of another.

9. Neither we nor our bailiffs will seize any land or rent for any debt, as long as the chattels of the debtor are sufficient to repay the debt; nor shall the sureties of the debtor be distrained so long as the principal debtor is able to satisfy the debt; and if the principal debtor shall fail to pay the debt, having nothing wherewith to pay it, then the sureties shall answer for the debt; and let them have the lands and rents of the debtor, if they desire them, until they are indemnified for the debt which they have paid for him, unless the principal debtor can show proof that he is discharged thereof as against the said sureties.

10. If one who has borrowed from the Jews any sum, great or small, die before that loan be repaid, the debt shall not bear interest while the heir is under age, of whomsoever he may hold; and if the debt fall into our hands, we will not take anything except the principal sum contained in the bond.

11. And if anyone die indebted to the Jews, his wife shall have her dower and pay nothing of that debt; and if any children of the deceased are left under age, necessaries shall be provided for them in keeping with the holding of the deceased; and out of the residue the debt shall be paid, reserving, however, service due to feudal lords; in like manner let it be done touching debts due to others than Jews.

12. No scutage (tax) of aid shall be imposed on our kingdom, unless by common counsel of our kingdom, except for ransoming our person, for making our eldest son a knight, and for once marrying our eldest daughter; and for these there shall not be levied more than a reasonable aid. In like

manner it shall be done concerning aids from the city of London.

13. And the city of London shall have all it ancient liberties and free customs, as well by land as by water; furthermore, we decree and grant that all other cities, boroughs, towns, and ports shall have all their liberties and free customs.

14. And for obtaining the common counsel of the kingdom anent the assessing of an aid (except in the three cases aforesaid) we will cause to be summoned the archbishops, bishops, abbots, earls, and greater barons, severally by our letters; and we will moreover cause to be summoned generally, through our sheriffs and bailiffs, and others who hold of us in chief, for a fixed date, namely, after the expiry of at least forty days, and at a fixed place; and in all letters of such summons we will specify the reason of the summons. And when the summons has thus been made, the business shall proceed on the day appointed, according to the counsel of such as are present, although not all who were summoned have come.

15. We will not for the future grant to anyone license to take an aid from his own free tenants, except to ransom his person, to make his eldest son a knight, and once to marry his eldest daughter; and on each of these occasions there shall be levied only a reasonable aid.

16. No one shall be distrained for performance of greater service for a knight's fee, or for any other free tenement, than is due therefrom.

17. Common pleas shall not follow our court, but shall be held in some fixed place.

18. Inquests of novel dissension, of mort d'ancestor, and of darrein presentment shall not be held elsewhere than in their own county courts, and that in manner following; We, or, if we should be out of the realm, our chief justice, will send two judiciaries through every county four times a year, who shall alone with four knights of the county chosen by the county, hold the said assizes in the county court, on the day and in the place of meeting of that court.

19. And if any of the said assizes cannot be taken on the day of the county court, let there remain of the knights and freeholders, who were present at the county court on that day, as many as may be required for the efficient making of judgments, according as the business be more or less.

20. A freeman shall not be amerced for a slight offense, except in

accordance with the degree of the offense; and for a grave offense he shall be amerced in accordance with the gravity of the offense, yet saving always his "contentment"; and a merchant in the same way, saving his "merchandise"; and a villain shall be amerced in the same way, saving his "wainage" if they have fallen into our mercy: and none of the aforesaid amencements shall be imposed except by the oath of honest men of the neighborhood.

21. Earls and barons shall not be amerced except through their peers, and only in accordance with the degree of the offense.

22. A clerk shall not be amerced in respect of his lay holding except after the manner of the others aforesaid; further, he shall not be amerced in accordance with the extent of his ecclesiastical benefice.

23. No village or individual shall be compelled to make bridges at river banks, except those who from of old were legally bound to do so.

24. No sheriff, constable, coroners, or others of our bailiffs, shall hold pleas of our Crown.

25. All counties, hundred, and tithing's (except our demesne manors) shall remain at the old rents, and without any additional payment.

26. If anyone holding of us a lay fief shall die, and our sheriff or bailiff shall exhibit our letters patent of summons for a debt which the deceased owed us, it shall be lawful for our sheriff or bailiff to attach and enroll the chattels of the deceased, found upon the lay fief, to the value of that debt, at the sight of law worthy men, provided always that nothing whatever be thence removed until the debt which is evident shall be fully paid to us; and the residue shall be left to the executors to fulfill the will of the deceased; and if there be nothing due from him to us, all the chattels shall go to the deceased, saving to his wife and children their reasonable shares.

27. If any freeman shall die intestate, his chattels shall be distributed by the hands of his nearest kinsfolk and friends, under supervision of the Church, saving to everyone the debts which the deceased owed to him.

28. No constable or other bailiff of ours shall take corn or other provisions from anyone without immediately tendering money therefor, unless he can have postponement thereof by permission of the seller.

29. No constable shall compel any knight to give money in lieu of

castle-guard, when he is willing to perform it in his own person, or (if he himself cannot do it from any reasonable cause) then by another responsible man. Further, if we have led or sent him upon military service, he shall be relieved from guard in proportion to the time during which he has been on service because of us.

30. No sheriff or bailiff of ours, or other person, shall take the horses or carts of any freeman for transport duty, against the will of the said freeman.

31. Neither we nor our bailiffs shall take, for our castles or for any other work of ours, wood which is not ours, against the will of the owner of that wood.

32. We will not retain beyond one year and one day, the lands those who have been convicted of felony, and the lands shall thereafter be handed over to the lords of the fiefs.

33. All kydells for the future shall be removed altogether from Thames and Medway, and throughout all England, except upon the seashore.

34. The writ which is called praecipe shall not for the future be issued to anyone, regarding any tenement whereby a freeman may lose his court.

35. Let there be one measure of wine throughout our whole realm; and one measure of ale; and one measure of corn, to wit, "the London quarter"; and one width of cloth (whether dyed, or russet, or "halberget"), to wit, two ells within the selvedges; of weights also let it be as of measures.

36. Nothing in future shall be given or taken for a writ of inquisition of life or limbs, but freely it shall be granted, and never denied.

37. If anyone holds of us by fee-farm, either by scavage or by borage, or of any other land by knight's service, we will not (by reason of that fee-farm, savage, or borage), have the wardship of the heir, or of such land of his as if of the fief of that other; nor shall we have wardship of that fee-farm, savage, or borage, unless such fee-farm owes knight's service. We will not by reason of any small serjeancy which anyone may hold of us by the service of rendering to us knives, arrows, or the like, have wardship of his heir or of the land which he holds of another lord by knight's service.

38. No bailiff for the future shall, upon his own unsupported complaint, put anyone to his "law", without credible witnesses brought for

this purposes.

39. No freemen shall be taken or imprisoned or disseized or exiled or in any way destroyed, nor will we go upon him nor send upon him, except by the lawful judgment of his peers or by the law of the land.

40. To no one will we sell, to no one will we refuse or delay, right or justice.

41. All merchants shall have safe and secure exit from England, and entry to England, with the right to tarry there and to move about as well by land as by water, for buying and selling by the ancient and right customs, quit from all evil tolls, except (in time of war) such merchants as are of the land at war with us. And if such are found in our land at the beginning of the war, they shall be detained, without injury to their bodies or goods, until information be received by us, or by our chief justice, how the merchants of our land found in the land at war with us are treated; and if our men are safe there, the others shall be safe in our land.

42. It shall be lawful in future for anyone (excepting always those imprisoned or outlawed in accordance with the law of the kingdom, and natives of any country at war with us, and merchants, who shall be treated as if above provided) to leave our kingdom and to return, safe and secure by land and water, except for a short period in time of war, on grounds of public policy- reserving always the allegiance due to us.

43. If anyone holding of some escheat (such as the honor of Wallingford, Nottingham, Boulogne, Lancaster, or of other escheats which are in our hands and are baronies) shall die, his heir shall give no other relief, and perform no other service to us than he would have done to the baron if that barony had been in the baron's hand; and we shall hold it in the same manner in which the baron held it.

44. Men who dwell without the forest need not henceforth come before our justiciaries of the forest upon a general summons, unless they are in plea, or sureties of one or more, who are attached for the forest.

45. We will appoint as justices, constables, sheriffs, or bailiffs only such as know the law of the realm and mean to observe it well.

46. All barons who have founded abbeys, concerning which they hold charters from the kings of England, or of which they have long continued possession, shall have the wardship of them, when vacant, as they ought to

have.

47. All forests that have been made such in our time shall forthwith be disafforsted; and a similar course shall be followed with regard to river banks that have been placed "in defense" by us in our time.

48. All evil customs connected with forests and warrens, foresters and warreners, sheriffs and their officers, river banks and their wardens, shall immediately by inquired into in each county by twelve sworn knights of the same county chosen by the honest men of the same county, and shall, within forty days of the said inquest, be utterly abolished, so as never to be restored, provided always that we previously have intimation thereof, or our justices, if we should not be in England.

49. We will immediately restore all hostages and charters delivered to us by Englishmen, as sureties of the peace of faithful service.

50. We will entirely remove from their bailiwicks, the relations of Gerard of Athee (so that in future they shall have no bailiwick in England); namely, Engelard of Cigogne, Peter, Guy, and Andrew of Chanceaux, Guy of Cigogne, Geoffrey of Martigny with his brothers, Philip Mark with his brothers and his nephew Geoffrey, and the whole brood of the same.

51. As soon as peace is restored, we will banish from the kingdom all foreign born knights, crossbowmen, sergeants, and mercenary soldiers who have come with horses and arms to the kingdom's hurt.

52. If anyone has been dispossessed or removed by us, without the legal judgment of his peers, from his lands, castles, franchises, or from his right, we will immediately restore them to him; and if a dispute arise over this, then let it be decided by the five and twenty barons of whom mention is made below in the clause for securing the peace. Moreover, for all those possessions, from which anyone has, without the lawful judgment of his peers, been disseized or removed, by our father, King Henry, or by our brother, King Richard, and which we retain in our hand (or which as possessed by others, to whom we are bound to warrant them) we shall have respite until the usual term of crusaders; excepting those things about which a plea has been raised, or an inquest made by our order, before our taking of the cross; but as soon as we return from the expedition, we will immediately grant full justice therein.

53. We shall have, moreover, the same respite and in the same manner in rendering justice concerning the disafforestation or retention of those

forests which Henry our father and Richard our brother afforested, and concerning the wardship of lands which are of the fief of another (namely, such ward ships as we have hitherto had by reason of a fief which anyone held of us by knight's service), and concerning abbeys founded on other fiefs than our own, in which the lord of the fee claims to have right; and when we have returned, or if we desist from our expedition, we will immediately grant full justice to all who complain of such things.

54. No one shall be arrested or imprisoned upon the appeal of a woman, for the death of any other than her husband.

55. All fines made with us unjustly and against the law of the land, and all amercements, imposed unjustly and against the law of the land, shall be entirely remitted, or else it shall be done concerning them according to the decision of the five and twenty barons whom mention is made below in the clause for securing the peace, or according to the judgment of the majority of the same, along with the aforesaid Stephen, archbishop of Canterbury, if he can be present, and such others as he may wish to bring with him for this purpose, and if he cannot be present the business shall nevertheless proceed without him, provided always that if any one or more of the aforesaid five and twenty barons are in a similar suit, they shall be removed as far as concerns this particular judgment, others being substituted in their places after having been selected by the rest of the same five and twenty for this purpose only, and after having been sworn.

56. If we have disseized or removed Welshmen from lands or liberties, or other things, without the legal judgment of their peers in England or in Wales, they shall be immediately restored to them; and if a dispute arise over this, then let it be decided in the marches by the judgment of their peers; for the tenements in England according to the law of England, for tenements in Wales according to the law of Wales, and for tenements in the marches according to the law of the marches. Welshmen shall do the same to us and ours.

57. Further, for all those possessions from which any Welshman has, without the lawful judgment of his peers, been disseized or removed by King Henry our father, or King Richard our brother, and which we retain in our hand (or which are possessed by others, and which we ought to warrant), we will have respite until the usual term of crusaders; excepting those things about which a plea has been raised or an inquest made by our order before we took the cross; but as soon as we return (or if perchance we desist from our expedition), we will immediately grant full justice in accordance with the laws of the Welsh and in relation to the foresaid

regions.

58. We will immediately give up the son of Llywelyn and all the hostages of Wales, and the charters delivered to us as security for the peace.

59. We will do towards Alexander, king of Scots, concerning the return of his sisters and his hostages, and concerning his franchises, and his right, in the same manner as we shall do towards our other barons of England, unless it ought to be otherwise according to the charters which we hold from William his father, formerly king of Scots; and this shall be according to the judgment of his peers in our court.

60. Moreover, all these aforesaid customs and liberties, the observances of which we have granted in our kingdom as far as pertains to us towards our men, shall be observed b all of our kingdom, as well clergy as laymen, as far as pertains to them towards their men.

61. Since, moreover, for God and the amendment of our kingdom and for the better allaying of the quarrel that has arisen between us and our barons, we have granted all these concessions, desirous that they should enjoy them in complete and firm endurance forever, we give and grant to them the underwritten security, namely, that the barons choose five and twenty barons of the kingdom, whomsoever they will, who shall be bound with all their might, to observe and hold, and cause to be observed, the peace and liberties we have granted and confirmed to them by this our present Charter, so that if we, or our justifier, or our bailiffs or any one of our officers, shall in anything be at fault towards anyone, or shall have broken any one of the articles of this peace or of this security, and the offense be notified to four barons of the foresaid five and twenty, the said four barons shall repair to us (or our justifier, if we are out of the realm) and, laying the transgression before us, petition to have that transgression redressed without delay. And if we shall not have corrected the transgression (or, in the event of our being out of the realm, if our justifier shall not have corrected it) within forty days, reckoning from the time it has been intimated to us (or to our justifier, if we should be out of the realm), the four barons aforesaid shall refer that matter to the rest of the five and twenty barons, and those five and twenty barons shall, together with the community of the whole realm, distrain and distress us in all possible ways, namely, by seizing our castles, lands, possessions, and in any other way they can, until redress has been obtained as they deem fit, saving harmless our own person, and the persons of our queen and children; and when redress has been obtained, they shall resume their old relations towards us. And let whoever in the country desires it, swear to obey the orders of the said five

and twenty barons for the execution of all the aforesaid matters, and along with them, to molest us to the utmost of his power; and we publicly and freely grant leave to everyone who wishes to swear, and we shall never forbid anyone to swear. All those, moreover, in the land who of themselves and of their own accord are unwilling to swear to the twenty five to help them in constraining and molesting us, we shall by our command compel the same to swear to the effect foresaid. And if any one of the five and twenty barons shall have died or departed from the land, or be incapacitated in any other manner which would prevent the foresaid provisions being carried out, those of the said twenty five barons who are left shall choose another in his place according to their own judgment, and he shall be sworn in the same way as the others. Further, in all matters, the execution of which is entrusted, to these twenty five barons, if perchance these twenty five are present and disagree about anything, or if some of them, after being summoned, are unwilling or unable to be present, that which the majority of those present ordain or command shall be held as fixed and established, exactly as if the whole twenty five had concurred in this; and the said twenty five shall swear that they will faithfully observe all that is aforesaid, and cause it to be observed with all their might. And we shall procure nothing from anyone, directly or indirectly, whereby any part of these concessions and liberties might be revoked or diminished; and if any such things has been procured, let it be void and null, and we shall never use it personally or by another.

62. And all the will, hatreds, and bitterness that have arisen between us and our men, clergy and lay, from the date of the quarrel, we have completely remitted and pardoned to everyone. Moreover, all trespasses occasioned by the said quarrel, from Easter in the sixteenth year of our reign till the restoration of peace, we have fully remitted to all, both clergy and laymen, and completely forgiven, as far as pertains to us. And on this head, we have caused to be made for them letters testimonial patent of the lord Stephen, archbishop of Canterbury, of the lord Henry, archbishop of Dublin, of the bishops aforesaid, and of Master Pandulf as touching this security and the concessions aforesaid.

63. Wherefore we will and firmly order that the English Church be free, and that the men in our kingdom have and hold all the aforesaid liberties, rights, and concessions, well and peaceably, freely and quietly, fully and wholly, for themselves and their heirs, of us and our heirs, in all respects and in all places forever, as is aforesaid. An oath, moreover, has been taken, as well on our part as on the art of the barons, that all these conditions aforesaid shall be kept in good faith and without evil intent.

Given under our hand - the above named and many others being witnesses - in the meadow which is called Runnymede, between Windsor and Staines, on the fifteenth day of June, in the seventeenth year of our reign.

This is but one of three different translations I found of the Magna Carta; it was originally done in Latin, probably by the Archbishop, Stephen Langton. It was in force for only a few months, when it was violated by the king. Just over a year later, with no resolution to the war, the king died, being succeeded by his 9-year old son, Henry III. The Charter (Carta) was reissued again, with some revisions, in 1216, 1217 and 1225. As near as I can tell, the version presented here is the one that preceded all of the others; nearly all of its provisions were soon superseded by other laws, and none of it is effective today.

Henry III (1216-1272)

Henry of Winchester, better known as Henry III, was a pious king overshadowed by his rivalries with his barons and other nobles. He became king at the age of nine when his father, King John, died.

After several years of being too young to rule his kingdom on his own, he finally took full control in 1227. From there he tried multiple times to regain the lands of France that had once belonged to his father. These campaigns we futile and he was further humiliated after he attempted but failed to pay his son's way into being the King of Sicily.

His relationship with his nobles was strained once again when he unsuccessfully attempted to help the Pope against the Holy Roman Emperor. Tensions rose but Henry believed that kings should act accordingly and thus he followed the charters which wouldn't allow him to take unjust action against his barons and nobles. This seemed to have eased tensions.

For as many contentions as he had with those surrounding him, Henry was an incredibly pious king. He contributed greatly to churches and even helped in the rebuilding of Westminster Abbey which began in 1245. He was known for being extravagant in his spending due to his piety but he was redeemed for being incredibly charitable. As much as he was known for being problematic with his barons and nobles he was equally known for his religious standpoints and his contribution to building.

Towards the end of his reign, Henry would seek to annul past transgressions with his enemies and even gave some of them their titles and lands back. He wanted peace in his kingdom after a long reign of tumultuous relationships. He would fall ill and die in 1272 leaving behind his wife, Eleanor of Provence, and his son, Edward I of England. He was entombed in Westminster Abbey. Attempts were made to make him a saint but nothing came of it. Henry died leaving behind a legacy of being neither an innately good nor an innately bad king of England. -

Javaneh Fennell was the contributing Author of Henry III

Edward I (1239-1307) 'Longshanks' While on a crusade in 1272, his father died leaving Edward as the unopposed heir to the throne. He was named Edward Longshanks for his unusually domineering height for the times. He was the son of Henry III and Eleanor of Provence.

In his youth he was highly encouraged to appreciate the arts and education by his parents. He was very well educated in literature, learning both Latin and French. His Father had awarded the fifteen year old Edward the Duchy of Gascony as a gift before his marriage to the nine year old Eleanor of Castile. Edward took his new lands seriously and spent a year in Gascony to be better acquainted with it.

Edward was able to watch his father's political failures first hand and for a time took the side of one of Henry's enemies, Simon de Montfort. Edward reconciled with his father, helping him get rid of de Montfort and fight the civil wars with the barons. With Edward's help the realm came to find relative peace for some time.

While on a crusade in 1272, Henry III died leaving Edward as the unopposed heir to the throne. He was politically savvy, successful in battle and geared towards peace in his kingdom making him a greatly desired King by the Barons who swore an oath to his claim in his absence. He would not make his way to his kingdom until 1274. With his reputation as a fierce warrior alongside his extreme height and pension for a temper, Edward was intimidating enough to receive the support he gained from the barons in England while he was on crusade. In the early portion of his reign, the Welsh princes proved trivial for the king. Thanks to his astute skills in battle, Edward squashed the Northern Welsh attempts to give Wales's independence and brought Wales into England. Coincidentally, Edward and Eleanor had a son in Wales at this same time. They named him Edward and gave him the title of Prince of Wales. He would be the first English Prince of Wales and the tradition of giving the heir this title still exists to this day.

Not only did the Prince of Wales begin a tradition within the reign of Edward, but so did regular meetings with Parliament. His battles and efforts in building up Wales had resulted in severe debt. He summoned the largest assembly of the time to work out and resolve the taxes, which would be increased due to the debt, to meet twice a year. This would continue and Parliament became more and more important to the king over time. His first Parliament would establish and define many rights and laws of England and explore all aspects of the government including extortion, freedom of men and criminal cases. The first Parliament enacted many new laws and legislation which fit in well with Edward's father's ideals of a well working government.

Edward would go on to establish feudal framework in England with Parliament. This would lead to Edward demanding feudal allegiance from the King of Scotland. This conflict would take over the remainder of Edward's reign and the upcoming war would be called the Great Cause. Scotland and England shared relative peace for years due to treaties dating back to 1174. In 1290, Scotland was left without an heir and Edward determined he had the authority to resolve this matter. He gave John Baliol the entirety of Scotland, who swore allegiance to Edward. Baliol was not well received and eventually retracted his allegiance to Edward. Edward in return decided that Scotland was no longer independent. William Wallace would come to lead a rebellion against Edward but Wallace would be captured and taken to London to be executed. Edward's health was failing him when a Scottish representative, Robert the Bruce, rebelled and named himself King of Scotland. Edward would die shortly after in 1307, less than a month after turning 68.

Although his later years were plagued with failures, Edward's reign was considered rather successful. He named his son, who would be Edward II, as his successor to the throne. The Scottish people remember Edward I as a tyrant but for the most part the world regards him as an important figure in shaping the politics and laws of England. Edward followed in his father's footsteps and tried to maintain unity in all of England, hoping to increase the arts and building in his entire kingdom.

- Javaneh Fennell, was the contributing Author for Edward I

EDWARD I.

Edward II (1307-1327) Edward was as different as possible from his Father. He was not wicked as some claimed of William and John, but he detested public business. He thought the only advantage of being King was that he would have the leisure to amuse himself.

During his Father's reign he devoted himself to a man named Piers Gaveston. Gaveston who had encouraged the young Edward in 'his pleasures and taught him to mistrust his father.' His Father banished Gaveston, however, immediately upon his accession Edward II brought him back and named him Regent.

Edward went to France and married Isabella the daughter of Phillip IV. While he was in France, the barons who hated and resented Gaveston, started an uprising under Thomas, Earl of Lancaster.

In 1308 the King yielded to the Barons and sent Gaveston out of the country to Ireland- as his Lieutenant. The Barons were fed up with Edward and in 1310 in Parliament made plans to remove him from any and all Government. 21 barons were appointed Lords Ordained, to draw up ordinances. Gaveston was to be banished for life. The King was to appoint officers with only the barons' consent. He was not to go to war or leave the Kingdom.

The ordinances may have been justified in so far as they restrained the authority of a King as incapable as Edward II. Constitutionally, it was a huge step backward for the right of the King and monarchy in general. It took all the power from the King and placed it in the hands of the barons or better known now as the "Parliament"

In 1313 Sterling was the only fortress of importance in Scotland that was still under English control. It surrendered to the Scots on June 24, 1314. Even Edward who had no concern for matters of State was devastated by this and declared War. He then placed himself at the head of the Army. He was determined to gain Sterling back.

Lancaster however, and all whom he could influence, refused to follow him on the grounds that he had broken the ordinances by declaring war without the Barons permission.

Edward was not going to listen to the Barons and he reached Bannockburn a year later. His Army was described as one of confusion. Bruce however over ran the archers that the English had so prized and Edwards's army turned and fled.

All of Scotland and all of England was now lost to Edward. Both Scotland and England had suffered grievously from the result of the Battle at Bannockburn. However that did not influence the continuous English invasions into southern Scotland. Nor the

Scottish invasions into northern England that spread far and wide.

"No nation can suppress the liberty of another
without endangering its own."

Lancaster took over the power of England and battled Bruce who continued to ravage England. Edward was banished alongside his new favorite Hugh le Despenser. Whose Father had actually raised up an Army in support of the King. In 1322 Edward defeated Lancaster at Boroughbridge and had him tried and beheaded at Pontefract.

Parliament met in 1327 in Westminster, filled with the Kings enemies. The Queen with her lover- Robert Mortimer; were conspiring against her husband as well. Edward was pressured into signing a declaration of his own wrong doing and incompetency, and formally resigned the Crown.

"The deposition of Edward II, for his enforced resignation was practically nothing less than that it was the work of a faithless wife and of unscrupulous partisans, but at least they clothed their vengeance in the forms of Parliamentary action. It was the action of Parliament in losing the feudal ties by which vassals were bound to an unworthy King that it rose to the full position of being the representative of the nation and at the same time virtually proclaimed that the wants of the nation must be satisfied at the expense of the feudal claims of the King"

King Edward lived for eight months after surrendering his Crown. He was brutally murdered, assumed a plot concocted by his Wife or Mortimer- perhaps both, at Berkley Castle. Mortimer took over England as Regent.

Edward III (1327-1377) Edward was only fourteen at the age of his accession. For three years power was in the hands of his mother's lover, Mortimer. Robert Bruce, though old and sick with leprosy, was anxious to wring from England an acknowledgment of Scottish independence, in spite of an existing truce. He sent an army to ravage the Northern counties of England. Edward himself led an English force far superior in numbers and equipment. There was actually no fighting except one night when the Scots broke into the English camp and almost succeeded in carrying off King Edward.

Mortimer was at his wits end and in 1328 agreed to an acknowledged treaty of the complete independence of Scotland. It was a wise thing for Edward to do, yet England felt defeated. Mortimer became quite unpopular with the English people. There was a conspiracy against him and in 1330 he executed Prince Edmund, the Kings brother.

Although the King was still only 15 years old and under Mortimer's control, he was married with a child of his own. He was growing tired of virtually being kept a prisoner under the thumb of his Mother, Queen Isabella and Mortimer. One night through a secret passage in the rock where the castle stood, Edward brought in a small army of Mortimer's enemies. His Mother pled in vain for the life of her lover. "Fair son, have pity on the gentle Mortimer"

Despite her pleas for his life, Mortimer was hung and Edward took over complete control of England as King.

His mother, whose brothers were Louis X, Phillip V, and Charles IV, who had successfully reigned in France. The crown had now passed to Isabella's cousin, after the death of her third brother Charles, who died in 1328. Phillip VI now was King of France although Edward had a very strong claim and was now of age.

In 1331 Edward visited France and a treaty was made between the two Kings in which Edward abdicated all his hereditary rights to the Crown of France.

In 1333 the Scots advanced into England. The English won the Battle of Berwick. Edward began his attacks against David Bruce on Scottish soil. One after another for two years.

Phillip VI had personal motives for not wanting Scotland to be crushed. While Edward was doing everything he could to bring the Scots into submission and trying to keep control of Aquitaine, which was held by England. Phillip welcomed David Bruce into France and gave him protection. This ended any treaty Edward had made with his cousin, and making France a new enemy of England.

In 1336 French sailors attacked the Isle of Wight. Edward was so determined to resist, the long war began. It is known as 'The Hundred Years War"

In reality, Aquitaine, was Phillip's personal motive for siding with the Scot's. To Edward, his priority was to first defend England and secondly Aquitaine against the French and Scottish aggressors. It is somewhat obvious he felt betrayed by Phillip, and more than likely refused to ever negotiate with him.

He won, with large offers of money, the alliance of the Princes of the Empires bordering France and even that of the Emperor Lewis the Bavarian.

Many battles ensued, in the end, Edward's cause seemed to have been lost. All countries seemed to become better skilled in battle. The French at this time took on the terms of 'chivalry' in historical documents. Archers mastered their craft. Trade seems to have been increased, more than likely to support the wars. Edward even brought 'Flemish weavers into England' and he implemented wool manufacturing.

Edwards other great resource of support came as the implementation of taxation from export.

Edward the Black Prince: b. 1330-d.1376

This infamous Prince was never King. He was the son of Edward III and the Father of Richard II, being born during the '100 Years War' it is no surprise that he was a great warrior at a very young age. He was not known as the Black Prince until after the 16th century.

His nickname is supposed to have been derived from his wearing of black armor which seemed to be his 'signature'. In 1333 he was made Earl of Chester and just four years later in 1337 he became the Duke of Cornwall, being the first duke ever created in England and a title held by the Prince of Wales even today.

Edward who introduced the feathers and motto "Ich Dien". The feathers are thought to have been part of his mother's court of arms. A more romantic theory is he took the feathers from the helmet warn by King John of Bohemia whom he defeated at the battle of Crécy. The motto is known to have formed part of the arms of King John. It's worth mentioning that 'Ich Dien' is actually German, 'I serve'.

In 1345 the prince first accompanied his father on a foreign expedition. His real career begins, however, with Edward III's Norman Campaign of 1346. On landing at La Hogue he was knighted by his father, becoming one of the original 'Knights of the Garter' and took a prominent part in the whole of the campaign. After at the Siege of Calais in October 1347 he returned to England with his father.

In September 1355 he was sent to Gascony at the head of an English army. He was warmly welcomed by the Gascons and at once led a foray through Armagnac and Languedoc. By November he had gone as far as Narbonne, before returning to Bordeaux- where he kept his Christmas court. In August 1356 he started another expedition, this time in a southerly direction. He penetrated as far as the Loire, but was compelled to retire before the superior forces of King John of France. On the 19th of September the two armies met in the battle of Poitiers. It was the hardest-fought and most important battle of the 'Hundred Years War' and Edward's victory was due both to the excellence of his tactical disposition of his forces and to the superior fighting capacity of his army. Edward's own tactics and the captivity of King John attested the completeness of his triumph.

Edward the Black Prince

He treated his prisoner with almost ostentatious magnanimity, taking him to Bordeaux, they sailed to England in May 1357. On the 24th of that month he led his prisoner in triumph through the streets of London. In 1359 he took part in his father's invasion of Northern France. In October 1361 Edward married his cousin Joan, the daughter and heiress of the Earl of Kent who was the younger son of Edward I, by his second wife Margaret of France. Apparently the king had no knowledge of the marriage but approved of his sons choice anyway! In July 1362 handed over to him all his dominions in Southern France, with the title of Prince of Aquitaine.

In February 1363 Edward and Joan sailed Gascony, which became his ordinary place of residence for the next eight years. He maintained a brilliant court at Bordeaux and did his best to win the support of the Gascons. He was not however, successful in winning over the greater nobles, who with John, Count of Armagnac at their head was dissatisfied with the separation from France and looked with suspicion on Edward's attempts to reform the administration.

Edward was better able to conciliate the towns, whose franchises he favored and whose trade he fostered, hoping that he would prove a counterpoise to the aristocracy. He kept the chief posts of the administration mainly in English hands, and never really identified himself with local life and traditions of the region.

In 1367 'Pedro the Cruel', the deposed king of Castile visited Edward at Bordeaux and persuaded him to restore him to his throne by force. In February 1367 Edward led an army into and over the pass of Roncesvalles. By the 3rd of April, after a difficult march Edward attacked and defeated Bertrand du Guesclin in the last of his great victories. He then proceeded to Burgos and restored Pedro to the throne of Castile. He remained in Castile for four months, living principally at Valladolid.

His army wasted away during the hot Spanish summer and Edward himself contracted the beginnings of a mortal disease. In August 1367 Edward led a remnant of his troops back through the pass of Roncesvalles and returned to Bordeaux early in September. Having exhausted his resources on the Spanish expedition he was forced to take from the estates of Aquitaine extraordinary sources of supply. A hearth tax, for five years was willingly granted to him. The greater barons however saw this as a pretext for revolt.

The Count of Armagnac, who had already made a secret understanding with Charles V appealed against the hearth tax to the Parliament of Paris. Edward was called to explain himself. In January 1369 he declared that he would answer them in Paris with sixty thousand men behind him.

Needless to say, war broke out again and Edward III resumed the title of 'King of France'. Thereupon Charles V declared that all the English possessions in France were forfeited. Before the end of 1369 Aquitaine was in full revolt. With weak health and impaired resources the Black Prince showed little activity in dealing with his insurgent subjects or in warding off French invasion. Although too ill to ride on horseback he insisted on commanding his troops and on the 19th of September 1370 he captured the city of Limoges, putting the population to the sword. What would now be considered a horrendous war crime was common, even normal in those days.

Early in 1371 be returned England, leaving the impossible task of holding Gascony to John of Gaunt.

John of Gaunt is an important character in early Welsh/English history. The Ancestor of Queen Elizabeth II of whom the present Monarchy in England claims their descent...

In August 1372 he joined his father in an expedition to France but contrary winds prevented their landing. After this he abandoned military life for good. In October he resigned his principality on the ground that he could not afford to retain any longer so expensive a charge. His health in rapidly declined but he still followed politics with interest and did what he could to support the constitutional opposition of the great ecclesiastics to the administration of John of Gaunt and the anti-clerical courtiers. His last public act was to inspire the attack on Lancaster's influence made by the Good Parliament in the spring of 1376. The famous Parliament was still in session when he died at Westminster on the 8th of July. Edward, the Black Prince was never king.

He was buried in the east end of Canterbury Cathedral on the 29th of September, where his magnificent tomb, erected in accordance the instructions in his will, may still be seen. By Joan,' The Fair Maid of Kent', who died on the 7th of August 1385, the Black Prince left an only son, afterwards King Richard II.

Richard II (1377-1399) Richard the II was born on 6 January 1367 to parents, Edward, The Black Prince and Joan, the 4th Countess of Kent. Richard was immediately given the title, Bordeaux, The Duchy of Aquitaine. He was born at the Archbishop's Palace, Bordeaux, in the English principality of Aquitaine. And what's fascinating is according to some contemporary sources, three kings, "the King of Castille, the King of Navarre and the King of Portugal," were all present at his birth. This little anecdote, and also the interesting fact that his birth fell on the feast of Epiphany, was later used as religious imagery of the Wilton Diptych, where Richard is seen as one of three kings paying homage to the Virgin and Child.

Richard of Bordeaux was the youngest son of Edward, and Joan of Kent. His mother Joan was known as, "The Fair Maid of Kent". Edward was the heir to the throne of England and had distinguished himself as a military commander in the early periods of the Hundred Years' War, particularly in the Battle of Poitiers in 1356. But once he contracted dysentery in Spain in 1370 he never fully recovered so he had to return to England the next year.

His elder brother Edward of Angoulême died in 1371, and Richard became his father's heir. The Black Prince finally succumbed to his long illness in 1376.

Richard was only ten years old, a young boy, when he succeeded his grandfather's throne. Immediately people began to fear that ambitions the King's uncles would influence all political decisions, so instead a regency by the King's uncles was avoided. Instead, England was ruled by a council under the leadership of John of Gaunt, and Richard was tutored by Sir Simon Burley.

The king, with the advice of counsel, was supposedly to implementation of supremacy along with the help of a series of "continual councils" from which John of Gaunt was excluded. Although, Gaunt, together with his younger brother Thomas of Woodstock, Earl of Buckingham, still held a very great informal influence over the business of government. The king's counselors and friends, particularly Sir Simon de Burley and Robert de Vere, Duke of Ireland, increasingly made royal affairs more and more difficult. So much that the mistrust between them resulted in the councils being discontinues in 1380.

Also in the early years of Richard's reign, advisors, the privy counselors began to direct domestic and foreign policy. But then the heavy taxation that fell upon the people proved extremely unpopular and met with so much opposition that it lead to the so-called 'Peasants' Revolt' of 1381. Once again, counseling gone bad within the realm.

Oh The Peasants' Revolt got nasty and heads were going to roll. In 1381, Watt Tyler led the Peasants' Revolt, a kind of a modern expose of "who's not really who," if you will, against the oppressive government and the policies of John of Gaunt. Richard II was so obviously ill-advised. But now people needed to be held accountable. So the fate of his favorite advisors, Michael de la Pole, Robert de Vere and others, was headed up by Thomas, Duke of Gloucester and four other magnates to form the Lords Appellant. "The five Lords Appellant," tried and convicted five of Richard's closest advisors for treason.

In 1397, Richard arrested three of the five Lords, coerced Parliament to sentence them to death and banished the other two.

This was probably the hardest thing a king was ever made to do; (well, until we get to the Tudor era; which we will!)

One of the advisors who had been exiled was Henry Bolingbroke, the future Henry IV. Richard travelled to Ireland in 1399 to repress warring chieftains, as a way of hoping that Bolingboke would return to England and be elected king by Parliament. Richard lacked support and was quickly captured by Henry IV. This King was seriously unlucky.

He met his end in 1399.

Deposed in 1399, Richard was murdered while in prison, the first casualty of the Wars of the Roses between the Houses of Lancaster and York.

Chapter Five

THE LANCASTERS
1399 - 1461

The House of Lancaster

Henry V (1413-1422) Upon his Father's death dismissed the Archbishop Arundel from his Chancellorship, who had supported his father against him. He gave the Chancellorship to his half-uncle, Henry Beauford, Bishop of Winchester- one of the legitimized sons of John of Gaunt and Catherine Swynford.

His first thought was to show that he had confidence in his own title to the Crown, not of vengeance. He liberated the Earl of March and transferred the body of Richard II to a splendid tomb at Westminster.

Many accounts show that when Henry V ascended the throne he was very different as a King than he was as a Prince. 'Henry V on his part, was to show that as King he could forget the past, change his ways and command well. It was as if placing the Crown on his head transformed from careless to pious.

Walsingham writes: 'As soon as he was made King he was changed suddenly into another man, zealous for honesty, modesty and gravity, there being no sort of virtue that he was not anxious to display.'

The Caxion Chronicles, written between 1464-1470 states: 'He was a noble prince after he was King and crowned. Howbeit, before in his youth he had been wild and reckless, and spared nothing of his lusts and desires, but accomplished them after his liking; but as soon as he was crowned, anointed and sacred, anon suddenly he was changed into a new man, and set all his intent to live virtuously, in maintain of Holy Church, destroying heretics, keeping justice and defending of his realm and subjects.'

I think that this is extraordinary that so many historians wrote such similar accounts on the transformation of Henry V. It must be believed that whatever character the Prince displayed, they were much different than his character as a King. Henry was much more respected and praised.

Of this there is a wonderful account of his 'reformed' character in the Brut, the Lambeth Manuscripts MS 84, which has been verified to have been written in the late spring of 1479.

"Henry as Prince of Wales, intended greatly to riot, and drew to wild company. Several gentlemen and gentle-women followed his will and his desires, and all his household were well pleased with his governance except four men, who were full heavy and sore and they would have him forsake riot; therefore he hated these four men most of his household. When Henry became King he summoned all his household to come before him. They were fully glad, supposing that he would promote them to great offices. In their familiarity they came winking and smiling, and making nice semblance unto him. But the King kept his countenance sadly, and said unto them:

"Sirs, ye are people that I have cherished and maintained in riot and wild governance; and here I give you all in commandment that from this day forward ye shall forsake all misgovernance and live after the laws of Almighty God, and of our land." Then he rewarded them all richly, bade them void his household and live as good men, and never more come into his presence, because he would never again have an occasion where he would riot again. But the four persons, which were sorry for his governance, he loved afterwards best, and made them great lords.

Then King Henry sent to Dane Swynford,* Countess of Hereford, which was a well-governed woman, and kept a most worshipful household and the best ruled in the land, for men that were of good disposition. And she sent him twelve gentlemen of said governance. And so this gracious King forsook all wildness and kept strictly his laws with righteousness and justice."

This was a strange error. Catherine Swynford, who was step mother of Henry IV and Duchess of Lancaster, died in 1403. Henry's grandmother, Joan Bohun, Countess of Hereford, survived until

1419. The original story more than likely stated 'his grandmother, the Countess of Hereford,' which was interpreted by a compiler to mean Catherine Swynford, as his grandmother by marriage.

He was determined to uphold the policies of Edward the III as well as the old religion. Henry thought to demand the crown of France as the right of the King of England. However, the consideration that if the claim of Edward III had been in anyway legitimate, it would have descended to the Earl of March and not to King Henry. This was either not considered or it was his true intention when he attacked France in 1415. Whatever his true motives were can only be speculated.

"In 1415 Henry openly made his claim and gathered his army in Southampton. He there detected a conspiracy to place the Earl of March on the throne, which had been formed but Lord Scrope and Sir Thomas Grey, in combination with March's brother-in-law, the Earl of Cambridge, a son of Duke of York, son of Henry III. All three were executed.

"The King discovered a great and perilous conspiracy of three men against him, of whom the one was the Earl of Cambridge, brother to the Duke of York, and of the King's blood; second was Sir Thomas Gray, one of the King's great council; and the third was the Lord Henry Scrope, Treasurer of England, before that a chivalrous Knight.

These three persons had received out of France a right great sum of money, so that they should by treason destroy their Sovereign Lord. When they were taken and had confessed their offence, by the King's just justice they were condemned to lose their heads. And for the same conspiracy several others were put to execution by the Kings commandment."

This must have been a severe blow of betrayal to Henry. One can only imagine how heavy his heart must have been as he sailed to France. However, when he landed at the mouth of the Seine, he must have put it from his mind and focused at the task at hand.

Henry quickly besieged Harfluer- which fell after a heroic defense. Over two-thirds of his army however had perished from dysentery and fever.

Not a Frenchman could be found that would take Henry's claim to be the true King of France. He having only 10,000 men when he reached Agincourt he found the bridges broken and an army of 50,000 men blocking the way. Despite the disarray of his army, and being outnumbered, Henry 'joyfully' prepared for battle.

He knew the Armagnac army that stood to oppose him was of the same character that had been defeated at Crecy. "There were no recognized commanders, no subordination, and no notion of superior military power of the English archers."

Battle of Agincourt, October 25, 1415:

In the early morning, mass was said in the English army. Henry's followers prayed earnestly that their king's right, as they believed to be, might be shown on that day.

Henry's own prayers were long and fervid. He was told that it was the hour of prime, the first hour of prayer. "Now," he said," is good time, for all England prayeth for us, and, therefore, be of good cheer." He then went forth to marshal his army. To a knight who wished that every brave Englishman now at home were there, he replied that he would not have one man more. Few as they were, they were in the hands of God, who could give them the victory. Henry's tactics were those of Cregy. He drew up his archers between thick woods which defended their flanks, and with sharp stakes planted in the ground to defend them in front, placed his dismounted Horsemen at intervals between the bodies of archers.

The French, however, showed no signs of attacking, and Henry, knowing that unless he cut his way through his soldiers would starve, threw tactics to the winds and ordered his archers to advance. He had judged wisely. The French horsemen were on ploughed ground soaked with rain, and when at last they charged, the legs of their horses stuck fast in the clinging mud.

The English arrows played thickly on them. Immovable and helpless, they were slaughtered as they stood. In vain their dismounted horsemen pushed forward in three columns towards the English knights. Their charge was vigorously resisted, and the archers, overlapping each column, drew forth the heavy leaden mallets which each man carried, and fell upon the helpless rout with blows which crashed through the iron headpieces of the Frenchmen. Such as could escape fled hastily to the rear, throwing into wild confusion the masses of their country- men who had not as yet been engaged.

The battle was won, but unfortunately the victory was stained by a cruel deed. Some French plunderers had got into the rear to seize upon the baggage, and Henry, believing that a fresh enemy was upon him, gave orders, which were promptly carried out, to slay the prisoners. The loss of the French was enormous, and fell heavily on their nobility. Among the prisoners who were spared was the young Charles, Duke of Orleans.

Henry's Conquest of Normandy:

Henry had not secured the crown of France, he had however secured his Crown in England. In 1416 Henry had sent his brother, the Duke of Bedford to secure Harfluer against a French attack, while he was diplomatically active in an attempt to win over the side of the Duke of Burgundy and Sigismund, King of the Romans who had actually visited him in England.

In 1417 the quarrels in France had reached a head. The Count of Armagnac, Capturing the Dauphin- Charles, a boy of only fourteen, established a reign of terror in Paris, and the Duke of Burgundy, was summoned by the frightened citizens to their help, levied war against the Armagnac's and marched to Paris.

Henry seized the opportunity and landed in Normandy. Caen was taken by storm, and in a few weeks all Normandy except Rouen had submitted to Henry. There had been a terrible butchery when the citizens rose against the Armagnac's and imprisoned all of them on whom they could lay hands. Then the mob burst into the prisons and massacred the prisoners, the Count of Armagnac himself being one of the number.

Henry's army in the meanwhile closed round Rouen. The magistrates, to prolong the defense, thrust out the poorer inhabitants. Henry, who knew not pity when there was a practical object to be gained, thrust them back.

During five months the poor wretches wandered about half starved, dying off day by day. On Christmas Day, in honor of Christ's nativity, Henry sent some food to the few who were left. Famine did its work within as well as without the walls, and on January 19, 1419, Rouen, the old ducal capital of the Norman kings, surrendered to Henry.

Henry somehow seemed to gain more by the 'follies' of others than by his own skill. Terrified of losing all to Henry, the Burundian's and the Armagnac's seemed for a moment to forget their quarrel and to be ready to join together in defense of their common country. However, the hatred in their hearts could not be rooted out.

At a meeting between the Duke of Burgundy and the Dauphin on the bridge of Montereau, angry words sprang easily to the lips of both. The Duke put his hand on the pommel of his sword, the Dauphines attendants, thinking he was in danger, fell on the Duke and slew him.

The new Duke of Burgundy, Phillip the Good, at once joined Henry against the Dauphine, whom he considered an accomplice in his Fathers murderers. Even Queen Isabella, the mother of the Dauphine, shared in the outcry against her own son.

In 1420 the Treaty of Troyes was signed, in which the Dauphine was disinherited in favor of Henry V, who was to be King of France upon the death of Charles VI. Henry then married Charles' daughter Catherine, and ruled France as regent.

In 1421 his brother, the Duke of Clarence was defeated and slain at Bauge by a force of Frenchman and Scottish axillaries. Henry returned to France and drove the French over to Loire. He besieged Meaux which held out for many months- finally falling in 1422.

Henry was suffering from an illness and died by the end of the year- having given his life to the restoration of the Church in England. Establishing his dynasty at home by means of glory in foreign conquest and by becoming himself a successor of France.

On September 1, 1422 King Henry V succumbed to his disease and dies at Vincennes Castle. Leaving the crown of England and the future Crown of France to his son, Henry VI who at the time of his death was nine months old.

"The King's disease daily increased, until the most Christian King yielded his soul to God, departed this life in the castle of that is called Bois de Vencennes not far from Paris; where at that time was present King Charles and the two Queens. But before his death this most prudent King in his testament disposed the care and guard of the young Prince, his son, and the defense of the Realm of England, to his most dear brother, Humphrie, Duke of Gloucester, who faithfully defended that noble Prince Henry, and governed and protected this Realm in all peace and obedience, until he was passed the state of childhood and of ability to see and provide for the governance of his Realm. But the custody of the body of the young Prince the King committed to his uncle the Duke of Exeter, to endocrine him in all good manners. And the revenues of the Dutchie of Normandy the King bequeathed to his brother John, Duke of Bedford, for the governance and defense of the same Dutchie and the Realm of France."

Henry VI (1422-1461) Henry was born December 6, 1421. King Charles VI of France died October 21, 1422 only a month and a half after Henry V. The infant Henry VI was then recognized as King in the North and East of France.

The Dauphine held lands south of the Loire and some to the north of it. He immediately claimed to reign over the whole of France by hereditary right as Charles VII.

John, Duke of Bedford was, regent of France and his younger brother Humphrey, Duke of Gloucester, regent of England. There were no parties in England conspiring for the Crown. The whole of England was focused on securing its supremacy in France. Bedford married the sister of the Duke of Burgundy, hoping to secure the loyalty and fidelity of the Duke.

Bedford helped to secure the release of King James I to Scotland with an understanding that his subjects would not aid the enemies of England. He then defeated the French army that had been gaining ground in Verneuil.

Unlike his brother, the 'follies' of others did not aid his cause. His brother was as much a hazard to his cause as any enemy. He was a lost battle in himself.

In 1424 The Duke of Gloucester, 'who was as unwise and capricious as he was greedy for power. He had married Jacqueline, the heiress of Holland and Hainault; while her husband was still alive. He had claimed that her marriage was invalid based on the 'grounds of nearness in kin'.

Many others did not agree with this theory.

He then overran Hainault, which was under Jacqueline's former husbands control the Duke of Brabant. This gave great offence to the Duke of Burgundy, who was a cousin and ally of the offended Duke of Brabant and had no wish to see the English holding territory so near to his own country of Flanders.

The Duke of Brabant recovered Hainault and captured

Jaqueline- who had been abandoned by Gloucester. The relationship between the Duke of Burgundy and England never recovered.

Back in England, Bedford's brother was once again in battle, this time with his own Uncle, the Chancellor Henry Beufort, Bishop of Winchester. The feud was so bitter and dividing loyalties in England that Bedford had to visit England to try keep peace.

Beaufort was asked to leave England after signing an agreement and to surrender the Chancellorship to Kemp along with the Bishop of Kent- as long as the King was under age the council and not the protector would govern. Beufort left England and did Bedford returned to his battles in France. Beufort returned in 1428, from Rome, bringing with him the title of Cardinal. Again, he created a storm that was threatening peace in England.

Bedford had found victory in almost all of France North of the Loire except for Orleans and gained governance.

'Frenchman were indeed weary of the foreign yoke and of the arrogant insolence of the rough island soldiers.' Yet in France all military and civil organizations had abandoned the King. Charles was easy-tempered and entirely incapable of carrying on a war successfully, and lacked the inspiration and enthusiasm that could bring his subjects to stand with him The most careful skill required of a good leader. Charles needed a miracle to inspire Frenchmen with the belief that it was possible for them to defeat the victors of Agincourt and Verneuil, and yet without such a miracle irretrievable ruin was at hand.

Joan of Arc-'Jeanne Darc'

Joan of Arc was that miracle, a young maiden of seventeen, and the daughter of a peasant of Domremi, in the Dutchie bar. Battles had actually been far from her home, yet tales of horror had reached her little town and Joan of Arc was 'filled with pity for the realm of France and for its young King' whom she idealized into the pattern of every virtue.

The voices of St. Catherine and St Margaret 'bade her, the chosen of God, to go forth and save the King, and conduct him to Reims to be crowned and anointed with the holy oil from a vessel which, as men believed, had been brought down from heaven in days of old.'

She was told by the Saints that she was to go to Vaucouleurs, where she would find a Knight, Robert de Baudricourt, who would conduct her to Charles. It was some time before she could convince this Knight 'months passed before Baudricourt would do aught but scorn her message'

In February 1429 when the news from Orleans was that of urgency, he consented to take her to Charles. She found Charles at Chinon and as the story goes, convinced him of her divine mission by recognizing him in disguise among his courtiers. Some distrusted her, however her native good sense, her simple and earnest faith, and above all her purity of heart and life disarmed all opposition. She was given an army to lead against the relief of Orleans.

"Joan of Arc rode on horseback clothed in men's armor, with a sword she had taken from behind the alter at St. Catherine, who was by her side. "

Joan was victorious. She triumphed over many battles" and in 1429 Charles was victorious and pronounced the King of France during a Coronation ceremony. After his coronation as The newly proclaimed King and Joan of Arc rode through the town of Le Ferte, this is written: "The people thronged the way, full of enthusiasm, acclaiming the King and shouting their joyful exclamations "Noel!" though it does not appear that any part of their devotion was addressed to Joan herself. "Oh the good people," Joan cried with tears in her eyes, 'how joyful they are to see their noble King! How happy should I be to end my days and be buried here among them!"

The Archbishop who was riding with them asked of her, "Joan," he said, "in what place do you expect to die?"

"When it pleases God." She said. "I know neither the place nor the time."

Another account of Joan- 'She had crowned her King; she had recovered for him one of the richest providences and established a strong base for further action on his part. She had taught the Frenchman how not to fly before the English. She had filled those stout-hearted English how to fly in their turn. This was, from the first, what she had appointed to do, and not one of her promises had been broken."

Joan was betrayed by the Burgundians and sold to the English. She was tried and found guilty of heresy and burnt at the stake on May 30, 1431.

Her conviction was later over turned and the Bishop who tried her was excommunicated from the Church.

France was lost to Henry. But was soon after Crowned the King of England in 1429, months after Charles was crowned in France. He then married King Charles' niece, Margaret of Anjou in April of 1445. A peace was made between Henry and Charles.

Henry is said to have possibly had intermittent bout of 'madness' assumed now to have perhaps been schizophrenia. The dukes took great advantage of this. The Queen Margaret was very active in the government of England during these times. Her authority and power was very much resented by the Dukes, not to mention the continued and gradual loss of properties to France.

The only son of and the heir apparent Edward, Prince of Wales returned from Ireland and resumed a role as Regent against the Dukes and specifically the Earl of Warwick.

The King and Queen were both very protective of Edmund Beaufort, 2nd Duke of Somerset. Whom was at odds with The Earl of Warwick who resented his favors and had his own plans to elevate Edward to the throne.

'The said Duke Richard and the Earl of Warwick seeing that they may not prevail nor withstand the malice of the Duke Edmund; they set and planned the final destruction of the King and gathered privately a power of the people in May and kept them covered privately about in the town of St Albans; and when the King was there, they besieged him that he would send out unto them their mortal enemy, Edmund, Duke of Somerset- 'enemy to all the realm.' Yet he would not do so, saying they would have him by strength and violence. They went through the town and broke down violently the houses. Then came the King out of the abbey with his banner displayed into the same street, and Duke Edmond with him, and the Duke of Buckingham, the Earl of Northumberland and the Lord Clifford and Lord Sudley brought the Kings banner, and there was a sore fight, as for the time, and there at last was slain the said Duke Edmond, the Duke of Northumberland and the Lord Clifford. The King that stood under his banner was hurt in the neck with an arrow. And when the said Duke Edmond and the Lords were slain- the battle ceased. And thus was done."

This erupted the Battle of the Roses known also as the cousin's wars. The infamous battle between the Lancaster's and the York's.

King Henry was in and out of lucidness for the remainder of his life. His Queen personally was involved in trying to preserve the Crown for her son, Edward of Lancaster, Prince of Wales who was slain in the battle of Tewkesbury after a long exile in France. The King had been taken prisoner by King Edward who was declared the rightful King of England, he was supposedly murdered, but died in the Tower of London.

Chapter Six

The House of York
1461 – 1485

Edward IV (1461-1483) Edward had a rare power of winning popular opinion and sympathy. He was very well loved by the population. While some will speculate in part, some of that public opinion being his marriage to Elizabeth Woodville, in his times as well as ours was much romanticized and the common people embraced him. Not much different than the way we did Dianna and Katherine today.

He had however grown up in a very cruel and unscrupulous time. Edward was as great at playing war as he was at being a King.

Edward had no hesitation rushing into battle, clearing his way through slaughter. He rivaled Edward IV and Margaret of Anjou in his ruthlessness on the field of battle.

Born in Rouen, France to Richard Plantagenet, Duke of York and Cecily Neville, Duchess of York. He was the older brother to Richard III as well. He would be a key player in the War of the Roses as his father had a major, legitimate claim to the throne. When the Duke of York was killed in battle, that claim then transferred to Edward who went on to battle for his claim. Henry VI was the king during this time but he would be captured at the Battle of Northampton and imprisoned. Edward would be declared king for the first time in 1461. Edward was considered a military champion and was well known for his accomplishments on the battle field.

Edward IV's initial kingship would come to a temporary halt in 1470. Edward would create some tension with his cousin, the Earl of Warwick, by marrying Elizabeth Woodville. Elizabeth was a relative nobody. This elevated the status of the Woodville's but would enrage the Earl who was setting up a marriage between Edward and the daughter of Louis XI of France.

The Earl of Warwick made an agreement with Louis XI to restore Henry VI to the throne. Louis XI sent over a French fleet forcing Edward to flee his position. Henry VI sat on the throne for just six months before Edward gained enough support to make his way towards London where he captured Henry VI. In several violent battles, Edward eliminated most of the Lancastrians, including Henry VI's heir. Warwick died in battle and two of his daughters would marry Edward's brothers. Edward officially took back his crown and Henry would die in prison.

Edward was now all powerful, He had no competitor to fear. No descendants of Henry IV remained alive. Of the Beufords, the descendants of John of Gaunt by Catherine Swynford (The line Queen Elizabeth II is descended of) the male line perished, and the only representative was young Henry, Earl of Richmond, whose mother, Lady Margaret, was the daughter of the first Duke of Somerset, and the cousin of the two dukes who had been executed at the Battles of Hexham and Tewkesbury. His Father Edmund Tudor, Earl of Richmond, died before his birth. He was the son of Welsh gentleman of no great mark and married Catherine of France, in secret.

Although his political life was tumultuous, he was a fierce warrior who was never defeated in battle and was all around fairly popular. He was known for being a great businessman and aimed to restore order to England. The latter half of his rule would be in relative peace thanks to his success defeating the Lancastrians. He would fall ill in 1483 and live long enough to name his brother, Richard, Duke of Gloucester, as protector of his son and heir, Edward V. His successful reign would come to an end two years after his death with the defeat of Richard III by Henry Tudor. Edward's daughter, Elizabeth of York, would go on to marry Henry Tudor and bring together the houses of Lancaster and York, officially ending the War of the Roses.

By Javaneh Fennell- contributing Author of Henry IV

Richard III (1452-1485) and of Edward V (1483)

One of the most infamous kings in English history, Richard III did not come from humble beginnings. His father was Richard Plantagenet, Duke of York and Cecily Neville, Duchess of York. His family would be one half of the War of the Roses, a conflict that would eventually lead to another infamous king, Henry VIII. Never meant to be a king, Richard would happen on the crown as a Yorkist king anyhow. He was a great supporter of his brother which allowed him many opportunities. As the brother of King Edward IV he became a prince and attained the title of Duke of Gloucester. He married Anne Neville and had a son named Edward. He went into battle many times with his brother and made a name for himself on the battlefield.

Richard's true infamy came after his brother's death though. He would award himself lord protector of his nephews, Edward V and his brother Richard. It was at this time that Richard III deemed the marriage between Edward IV and Elizabeth Woodville invalid making the two princes illegitimate. The two princes were then imprisoned (see The Truth of the Princes in the Tower below) in the tower where they would die, giving Richard the crown. His reign was short, lasting only two years, but he would fight hard to maintain the crown.

After the death of the princes, Richard fought against two important rebellions. The first was against Henry Stafford, 2nd Duke of Buckingham. He defeated his former ally and had him executed for treason. The next rebellion would prove to be his end. Henry Tudor and Jasper Tudor rode across the countryside gaining support and troops against Richard. On 22 August 1452 at the Battle of Hastings, Richard rode into battle as the last king of England to do so. He would be killed while on his horse. His death allowed Henry Tudor to take the crown making him Henry VII. The Plantagenet's would win out the Yorkists in the War of the Roses. Richard III's body would be laid to rest in an unknown place as he was the deposed king and would not be found until 2012 under a car park. Villainized throughout history, Richard III would forever be known as the short lived last Yorkist king.

Written By Javaneh Fennell -Contributing Author of Richard III

The Discovery of King Richard III

In February 2013, The Leicester University held a press conference and confirmed-

"Beyond a reasonable doubt, the individual exhumed at Grayfriars in September of 2012, is indeed Richard III, the last Plantagenet King of England" The announcement came from, Richard Buckley, The lead Archeologist that was among the team that discovered the Skeleton under a Parking lot.

Richard III was killed in the Battle of Bosworth in 1485, fighting the forces of Henry Tudor. King Richard was only 32 years at the time of his death. A recent autopsy report and x-rays have discovered that Richard III suffered severe injuries to his skull and jaw as well as post mortem injuries.

On December 2, 2014 the University of Leicester issued startling revelation. There was a break in the genetic line. Headlines hit the papers from England to America. "Does Queen Elizabeth have the right to sit on the throne?" Well of course she does. What is more important, the Monarchy is big news and everyone is asking.... How does this work? Well that is hard to explain, England's King's most certainly haven't followed the rules of succession. Let us explore our recent events first. King Richard and his DNA.

Statement by Professor Kevin Schürer and Dr Turi King
Issued by University of Leicester Press Office
on 2 December 2014:

The genetics and genealogy research led by the University of Leicester, and published in Nature Communications, discovered that the male line of descent is broken at one or more points in the line between Richard III and Henry Somerset, 5th Duke of Beaufort (1744-1803).

This provides scientific evidence for the first time of a possible question mark over medieval lines of succession in the monarchy.

Critically, there is no evidence whatsoever on when the break occurred, however, it is statistically far more likely that the break in the male line occurred lower down the chain – and therefore not affecting any Royal lineage – including that of the present day.

Historically Royal succession has taken a number of twists and turns over the centuries and is not based on straight linear inheritance. However, the research does pose a question mark over where the break might have occurred- and the potential implications for the historical monarchy.

Professor Kevin Schürer said: "There are one or more breaks in the chain from Richard III to Henry 5th Duke of Beaufort. There are 19 links in that chain, so there is an equal probability of any one of those 19 being broken. From a historical view point, where the break occurred has differential consequences.

"There are five links in that chain between Richard, up through Edward, and then to John of Gaunt. And then the remaining majority of the links are down through the Somerset's and the Beaufort line.

"Now if - and it is a very big IF - the break in the chain is one of those five, between John of Gaunt and Richard III, historians could ask questions – theoretically - about the inheritance of a number of the Plantagenet monarchs. And since Henry Tudor's mother was also a Beaufort descended from John of Gaunt, there is a question here too.

"However, statistically speaking, the break is far more likely to have occurred in the larger part of the chain which does not affect any of the different Royal lines of succession at all."

Professor Schürer, who is the Pro-Vice-Chancellor for Research at the University of Leicester, said "there was absolutely no evidence that a link in the Royal chain of succession had actually been broken."

Dr Turi King said: "The fact that we do not find a match between the living male-line relatives and the skeletal remains is not at all surprising to me. We knew from work that I, and others, have carried out in the past that the incidence of false-paternity, where the biological father is not the supposed father, is historically in the region of 1-2% per generation. Even using a conservative rate, we knew there was a ~16% chance of finding there would be a false-paternity in this chain."

The University of Leicester was the principal funder of the research. Dr King's post is part-funded by The Wellcome Trust and the Leverhulme Trust.

The Dig for Richard III was led by the University of Leicester, working with Leicester City Council and in association with the Richard III Society. The originator of the Search project was

Philippa Langley of the Richard III Society

The Truth of the Princes in the Tower:
Written by Sir Thomas More in the year 1511

Edward V (Prince in the Tower)
With his Uncle, Richard III

It is my opinion that there is good reason to believe that this is a true and accurate account of the death of the Princes in the tower.

Weather one of the Princes in the tower being a fraud, is another story. That of Perkin. However, Sir Thomas More in this account names the place of burial, "under the bottom of the Stair, to never see the light of day." The actual place of burial or where the Princes bones were found did not happen for over a hundred years, during the Reign of Charles II.

"King Richard after his coronation, taking his way to Gloucester to visit, in his new honor, the town of which bare the name of his old, devised as he rode to fulfill that thing which he before had intended. And forasmuch s his mind gave him that, his nephews still living, men would not recognize him or believe that he had the right to the realm, he thought therefore without delay to rid them, as though the killing of his kinsmen could amend his cause, and make him a kindly King. Whereupon he sent one John Grene, whom he specially trusted, unto Sir Robert Brakenbery, Constable of the Tower, with Stawforth; letter and credence also, that the same Sir Robert should in any wise put the children to death. This John Grene sis his errand unto Brakenbury kneeling before our Lady in the Tower, who plainly answered that he would never put them to death to dye therefore, with which answered John Grene returning recounted the same to King Richard at Warwick yet in his way.

Wherewith, he took such displeasure and thought, that same night, he said unto a secret page of his; 'ah whom shall a man trust? Those that I have brought up myself, those that I had went would roost surely some roe, even those save me. Sir quod his page, there lyeth one on your paylet without, that I dare well say, to do your grace pleasure, the thing were right hard that would refuse, Sir James meaning this by Sir James Tyrell, which was a low born man of right goodly parsonage, and for natures gift, worthy to have served a much better Prince, if he had well served God, and by grace obtained as much truth and good will as he had strength and wit. The man had a high heart and sure longed upward, not rising yet so fast as he had hoped, being hindered and kept under by the means of Sir Richard Ratcliff and Sir William Catesby, which longing for no more partners loveth not of the Prince's favors, and namely not from him, whose pride they would bear no favor, kept him by secret drifts out of all secret trust which thing this page well had marked and known. Wherefore the occasion offered, of very special friendship he took his time to put him forward, and by such wise do him good, that all the enemies he had except the devil, could never have done him so much hurt. For upon this pages words King Richard arose, (for this communication had he sitting at the draught, a convenient carpet for such a council.) and came out in the pallet chamber on which he found in his bed Sir James and Sir Tyrel's, of person like and brother of blood, but nothing of Kin in conditions. Then said the King merely to them: What sirs, be ye in bed so soon? And calling up Sir James, brake him to secretly his mind in this mischievous matter. Of which he found him nothing strange.

Wherefore on the morrow he sent him to Brakenbury with a letter, by which he was commanded to deliver Sir James all the keys of the tower for one night, to the end he might accomplish the Kings pleasure, in such thing as he had given him commandment. After which letter delivered and the keys received, Sir James appointed the night next ensuing to destroy them, devising before and preparing the means. The Prince, as soon as the protector left that name and took himself as King, had it shown unto him, that he should not reign, but his Uncle should have the crown. At which word the Prince sore abashed, began to sigh and said: Alas I would my Uncle let me have my life yet, though I lose my Kingdom. Then he that told him the tale, advised him with good words, and put him in the best comfort he could. But forthwith was the Prince and his brother both shut up and all other removed from them, only one called Black Will or William Slaughter except, set to them and see them sure. After which time the Prince never tried his points, not thought of himself, but with that young babe his brother, lingered in thought and heaviness till this traitorous death delivered them of that wretchedness. For Sir James Tyrel devised that they should be murdered in their beds. To the execution whereof, he appointed Miles Forest, one of the four that kept them, a fellow fleshed in murder before time. To him he joined one John Dighton, his own horse keeper, a big broad square strong knave.

Then all the other being removed from them, the Miles Forest and John Dighton, about midnight (the silly children lying in their beds) came into the chamber, and suddenly wrapped them and entangled them, keeping down by force the featherbed and pillows hard unto their mouths, that within a while smothered and stifled, their breathing failing, they gave up to God their innocent souls into the joys of heaven, leaving their tormenters their bodies dead the bed. Which after that the wretches perceived, first by the struggling pains of death, and after long lying still, to be thoroughly dead; they laid their bodies naked out upon the bed and fetched Sir James to see them. Which upon the sight of them caused those murderers to bury them at the stair foot, neatly deep in the ground under a great heap of stones.

Then rode Sir James in great haste to King Richard, and showed him 'all the manner of the murder. The King giving him great thanks and as some say, there made him a Knight. But he allowed not as I have heard, the burying in so vile a comer, saddened that he would have them buried in a better place, because they were a King's sons. Though the honorable courage of a King! Whereupon they say that a priest of Sir Robert Brakenbury took up the bodies again and secretly entered them in such place, as by the occasion of his death, which only he knew of, and could never now come to light. Very truth is it and well known, that at such time as Sir James Tyrell was in the tower, for Treason committed against the most famous Prince King Henry 7th, both Dighton and he were examined and confessed the murder in above manner written, but whither the bodies were removed they could nothing tell. And this as I have learned of them that much knew and little cause had to lie, were these two Noble Princes, these innocent tender children, born of most royal blood, brought up in great wealth, likely long to live to reign and rule the realm, by traitorous tyranny taken, deprived of their estate, shortly shut up in prison and cruelly slain and murdered, they're bodies cast to god, where by the cruel ambition of their unnatural uncle and his dis-righteous tormentors. Which things on every part well pondered, God never gave this world a more notable example, neither in what uncertainty standeth in this worldly well, or what mischief work in the proud enterprise of a high heart, or finally what wretched end ensued such dispiteous cruelty.

For first to begin with the Ministers, Miles Forest at St Martin's prison rotted away. Dighton in deed yet walketh on alive in good possibility to be hanged til he die. But Sir James Tyrel died on Tower hill, beheaded for treason. King Richard himself, as he shall hereafter here, slain in the field, hacked and hewed on horseback dead, his body in despite torn and togged like a cursed dog. And the mischief that he took, within less than three years of the mischief he died. And yet all the meantime spent in much pain and trouble outward, much fear anguish and sorrow within.

For I have heard by credible report of such as were secret with his clamberers, that after this abominable deed done, he never had quiet in his mind, he never thought himself sure. Where he went abroad, his eyes whirled about, his body punily sensed, his hand ever inward on his dagger, his countenance and manner like tyrants, always ready to strike again. He took ill rest at nights, lay long waking and musing, sore worried with care and watch, rather slumbered then slept, troubled with fearful dreams, suddenly sometimes straight up and leaping out of bed and run about the chamber. So was his restless heart continually tossed and tumbled with the tedious impression and stormy remembrance of his abominable deed. Now he outward no long time in rest for hereupon soon after began the conspiracy, or rather good confederation between the Duke of Buckingham and many other gentleman against him. The occasion whereupon the King and the Duke fell out is of several folk.

King Richard III never trusted any man. He was assumed guilty of his nephew's deaths. He was betrayed by those whom he thought he had love. Above all of those, he dishonored his beloved brother and his children- The whitest rose of England's King, Edward.

Perhaps King Richard knew he had no right to wear the crown.

Chapter Seven

THE TUDORS
1485 – 1603

This Chapter was authored by Jennifer Denman

Genealogy of the Beuforts and the Tudors:

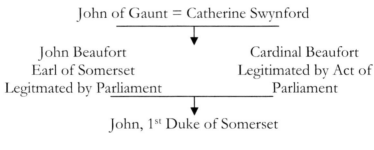

John of Gaunt = Catherine Swynford

John Beaufort
Earl of Somerset
Legitmated by Parliament

Cardinal Beaufort
Legitimated by Act of
Parliament

John, 1st Duke of Somerset

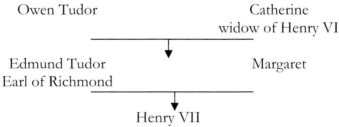

Owen Tudor

Catherine
widow of Henry VI

Edmund Tudor
Earl of Richmond

Margaret

Henry VII

The house of Tudors descended from the male line from the Tudors of Penmynydd, which ruled the Kingdom of England and all of its realms, including their ancestral Wales and the Lordship of Ireland, later the Kingdom of Ireland.

From Henry VII, after the end of The War of The Roses, his much legitimized branch of the English royal House of Lancaster, joined with his marriage to Elizabeth of York, The House of Tudors was born. Through all of his son Henry VIII's notorious fickleness with wives, to his son Edward, Queen Mary, and Queen Elizabeth I, Henry Tudor was able to establish himself as a rightful candidate, not only for the traditional Lancastrian supporters, but also for the discontented supporters. In total, five Tudor monarchs ruled their domains for just over a century. Henry VIII of England was the only in-line male heir of Henry VII to live to the age of maturity.

Many decisions were addressed during The Tudor reign, issues around the Royal succession; including marriage and the succession rights of women, became major political themes, as did the issue known as "The Great Matter," King Henry VIII seeking his divorce from Queen Catherine of Aragon that resulted in the conclusion that Henry, and all monarchs to come, as Supreme Head of the Church of England. Henry VIII's own daughter, Mary tried so hard to overturn that decision and return England back to its Catholic roots during her own reign. I'm sure it was for rather personal reasons, for Henry VIII at the time, but it did, in fact, have very long lasting effects on England, effects that are still in place today.

The House of Stuart came to power in 1603 when the Tudor line failed, as Elizabeth I, The Virgin Queen, died without issue.

Henry VIII of England *Henry VIII* Henry VIII (28 June 1491 – 28 January 1547) was King of England from 21 April 1509 until his death. He was Lord, and later assumed the Kingship, of Ireland, and there were some nominal claims by English monarchs to the Kingdom of France. Henry was the second monarch of the Tudor dynasty, succeeding his father, Henry VII.

Henry VIII was well known for his six marriages, as well his role in the separation of the Church of England from the Roman Catholic Church. He disagreed with the Pope on his "Great Matter," which led him and England, to a forced separation of the Church of England from papal authority. So he made himself, the Supreme Head of the Church of England, and ordered the Dissolution of the Monasteries. His principal dispute was with papal authority, Not with doctrinal matters, he remained a believer in core Catholic theological teachings, despite his excommunication from the Roman Catholic Church. Henry oversaw the legal union of England and Wales with the Laws in Wales Acts 1535 and 1542.

As for his radical changes to the English Constitution and the theory of the divine right of kings to England he began asserting the sovereign's supremacy over the Church of England almost immediately. Many of his chief ministers were used in political gains of fortune and power and then charged with treason. Some were banished or executed and some just fell out of his favor. Political figures such as the Cardinal Thomas Wolsey, Sir Thomas More, Thomas Cromwell, Richard Rich, and Thomas Cranmer were all once very close advisors to The King and after he had gotten what he needed, ironically, they had been charged with crimes and they fell hard from grace.

Despite all of his extravagant splendor, mostly from the stolen proceeds gained by the Dissolution of the Monasteries. Even by withdrawing payments to Rome, Henry was still on the verge of bankruptcy. This is generally blamed on his extravagant personal style, as well as his abundant costly continental wars.

Henry VIII was once described as "one of the most charismatic rulers to sit on the English throne." Another interesting fact about the King was, he was also an author and composer. No one ever really talked about his desire to provide England with a male heir, which more than likely partly was from personal vanity and partly from his own belief that a daughter would never be unable to maintain or strengthen Tudor power and keep the peace that existed following the Wars of the Roses.

Henry Tudor was born at Greenwich Palace, he was the third child and second son of Henry VII and Elizabeth of York. Only three of Henry's siblings survived infancy; Arthur, Prince of Wales; Margaret; and Mary.

In 1493, at the age of two, Henry was appointed Constable of Dover Castle and Lord Warden of the Cinque Ports. He was later appointed Earl Marshal of England and Lord Lieutenant of Ireland at the age three, and was also inducted into the Order of the Bath soon after. The day after the ceremony he was created The Duke of York and a month or so later made Warden of the Scottish Marches. In May 1495, he was appointed to the Order of the Garter. Henry was given a first-rate education from leading tutors, becoming fluent in Latin and French, and learning at least some Italian. Not much else is really known about Henry VIII's early life because he was not expected to become king. In November 1501, Henry also played a considerable part in the ceremonies with the marriage of his brother, Prince Arthur, to Catherine of Aragon. It was Arthur who Charles Brandon was friends with for the most part at this time, but was also friends with Henry, although Brandon was seven years older.

In 1502, Arthur died at the very young age of 15. He had always been somewhat frail, and the causes of his death remain disputed. His death occurred only 20 weeks after the marriage to Catherine. Arthur's death shifted all his duties upon his younger brother, Henry, he was only 10 years old at the time. Henry now became the new Duke of Cornwall in October 1502, the new Prince of Wales, and Earl of Chester in February 1503. Henry VII gave the boy few tasks. Young Henry was strictly supervised and did not appear in public. As a result, the young Henry would later ascend the throne "untrained in the exacting art of kingship."

Henry VII made sure that the marital alliance between England and Spain would still be intact by offering his second son in marriage to Arthur's widow Catherine. Both Isabella and Henry VII were in agreement with the idea so on 23 June 1503, a treaty was signed for their marriage, and they were betrothed two days later. As for the issue of papal dispensation, A papal dispensation was only needed for the "impediment of public honesty" if the marriage had not been consummated as Catherine and her duenna claimed. Henry VII and the Spanish ambassador set out instead to obtain a dispensation for "affinity", which took account of the possibility of consummation. The young Henry's age of only eleven, prevented cohabitation as it were, so this was just an extra step in caution.

Henry VII died on 22 April 1509, and Henry succeeded him as king and adopted the regal name of Henry VIII. After his father's burial on 10 May, Henry precipitously declared that he would undeniably marry Catherine, deciding to leave issues concerning the papal dispensation unresolved. He also added that it had been his father's dying wish that he marry Catherine. Whether or not this was true or not, it was definitely convenient. The Holy Roman Emperor Maximilian I had been trying to marry his granddaughter, Catherine's niece, Eleanor, to Henry; she had now been jilted. The wedding of Henry to Catherine was a low-key event held at the friar's church in Greenwich on 11 June 1509. The coronation, however, was quite the opposite, which was decided to be a double coronation and to be a very grand celebration and a very extravagant one. On 23 June 1509, Henry led Catherine from the Tower of London to Westminster Abbey for their coronation, which took place the following day. It was a huge celebration, with jousting and dancing and all the best tapestries were hung, the tables adorned with the finest of clothes, a true magnificent spectacle, in Westminster Hall. Catherine wrote to her father, "our time is spent in continuous festival".

Afterwards Henry got down to business, he arrested his father's two most disliked ministers, Sir Richard and Edmund Dudley. They were charged with high treason and were executed in 1510. Looking back now, these executions would become Henry's primary tactic for dealing with those who stood in his way; these two executions were just the beginning.

Catherine Parr

Queen Catherine conceived a child quickly, but the child was a girl and was stillborn on 31 January 1510. Then about four months later, she became pregnant again and on New Year's Day 1511, the male child, Henry, was born. After losing their first child, the couple was so relieved to have a boy. There were copious amounts of festivities to celebrate, but, we have to mention the favorite, the jousting tournament. Devastation followed only seven weeks later when the child died. Then Catherine miscarried again in 1514. Finally, Catherine gave birth in February 1516 to a girl, Mary. Marital relations between Henry and Catherine had been on the decline, but they lessened slightly after Mary's birth, and no evidence against to claim that things were not "unusually good" during that time.

Oh but, Henry had mistresses. It was discovered in 1510 that Henry had been having an affair with a daughter of Edward Stafford, 3rd Duke of Buckingham, no one was sure if it was Elizabeth or Anne Hastings, Countess of Huntingdon. Then came Elizabeth Blount, his most significant mistress for about three years, starting in 1516. Blount is one of only two completely undisputed mistresses. There were rumors of numerous other affairs as well, but Catherine did nothing to protest, and in 1518 she herself became pregnant again with another girl, who was also stillborn. Blount, however, gave birth in June 1519 to Henry's illegitimate son, Henry Fitzroy. The young boy was made Duke of Richmond in June 1525, and shocked most into thinking that he was on the path to his eventual legitimization. In 1533, FitzRoy married Mary Howard, but he died childless three years later. At the time of Richmond's death in June 1536, Parliament had enacted the Second Succession Act, which would have allowed him to become king.

Annulment from Catherine

So right around the time of Fitzroy's Dukedom, Henry had begun an affair with Mary Boleyn, another lady-in-waiting to the Queen. Henry's impatience with Catherine's inability to produce the male heir that he so desired was consuming him and driving his animal and biblical instincts to be fruitful and multiply. Anne Boleyn, Mary's sister, soon caught his eye, she was the charismatic young woman in the Queen's entourage. Anne, however, resisted all attempts of the Kings to seduce her, stopped him cold of his offers to become his mistress as her sister Mary Boleyn had. This only made Henry consider all of his three options for finding a dynastic successor and resolving what came to be described in history and also at the time, as the King's "great matter". The options were to legitimize Henry FitzRoy, which would take the pope's intervention and would be open to challenge; marrying off Mary as soon as possible and hoping for a grandson to inherit directly, but Mary was an underdeveloped child and probably unable to conceive before Henry's death. Then there was the issue of rejecting Catherine and marrying someone else of child-bearing age. Who would be able to entice the King and give Henry the male heir needed to ensure that The Tudor Dynasty be secure? Anne Boleyn, the third choice had become the most attractive possibility; actually she had become all that Henry could think about as a way to fix his situation, and the King was absorbed in his desire to annul his marriage to Catherine. It was a decision that would see Henry reject papal authority and initiate the English Reformation.

Henry's motivations and intentions over the coming years were never agreed on. The King, in the early part of his reign, was a devout and well-informed Catholic to the extent that his 1521 publication, Assertio Septem Sacramentorum ("Defense of the Seven Sacraments") earned him the title of "Fidei Defensor," (Defender of the Faith) from Pope Leo X. It was never really made clear why and

Anne Boleyn

when Henry changed his mind on the issue as he grew more intent on a second marriage. By 1527 he had convinced himself that by marrying his brother's wife, he had acted against Leviticus 20:21, an obstruction the Pope had never had the authority to bestow with. It was this argument Henry took to Pope Clement VII in 1527 in the hope of having his marriage to Catherine annulled.

Several other missions ensued, back and forth meetings all were concentrated on arranging an ecclesiastical court to meet in England, with a representative from Clement VII. Clement agreed to the creation of such a court, but he never had any intention of empowering his legate, Cardinal Lorenzo Campeggio, to decide in Henry's favor. Clement called the case back to Rome in July 1529, and then it was clear that the chance for annulment was lost and England's place in Europe had been forfeit. Wolsey bore the blame and was charged in October 1529, his fall from grace was "sudden and total". Woolsey briefly reconciled with Henry in the first half of 1530, but was charged again in November 1530, this time for treason, but died while awaiting trial. Henry appointed Sir Thomas More, to the role of Lord Chancellor and chief minister to Henry. More was intelligent and able, but struggled with the King's appointment because of his religious beliefs as he was a devout Catholic and opponent of the annulment, More initially cooperated with the king's new policy, denouncing Wolsey in Parliament.

After the Archbishop of Canterbury, William Warham, died, Anne's influence, along with the need to find a loyal supporter of the annulment, The King upon recommendation, had Thomas Cranmer appointed to the vacant position. This was approved by the Pope, unaware of the King's hopeful plans for the Church.

Marriage to Anne Boleyn

Henry's choice would be that of the elusive and enchanting Anne Boleyn, she managed to play her political cards exactly right, by showing interest, but keeping the king at an arms' length. So it began with France in the winter of 1532 when Henry met with Francis I at Calais to seek the support of the French king for his new marriage. After returning to Dover in England, Henry and Anne were married in a secret wedding service.

She became pregnant very soon after, and then they decided to have a second wedding service in London on 25 January 1533. On 23 May 1533, to make all things official, Cranmer had convened a special court at Dunstable Priory to rule once again on the validity of the king's marriage to Catherine of Aragon, after which declared the marriage of Henry and Catherine null and void. Five days later, on 28 May 1533, Cranmer declared the marriage of Henry and Anne to be valid. Catherine was formally stripped of her title as queen, becoming instead "princess dowager" as the widow of Arthur. In her place, Anne was crowned queen consort on 1 June 1533.

Queen Anne gave birth to a daughter who was slightly premature on 7 September 1533. The child was christened Elizabeth, in honor of Henry's mother, Elizabeth of York.

The king and queen were not always pleased with married life. The royal couple enjoyed periods of calm and affection, but Anne refused to play by the rules and be a submissive wife and Queen that was expected of her. The King found the qualities that were once so appealing to him, such as high-spiritedness and her opinionated intellect, too independent for the ceremonial role of a royal wife. Henry expected and desired absolute obedience from those who interacted with him in an official capacity at court. This made her many enemies. For his part, Henry disliked Anne's constant irritability and violent temper.

To top it all off, after a false pregnancy or miscarriage in 1534, he saw that failure to give him a son, as a betrayal. As early as Christmas 1534, Henry was discussing with Cranmer and Cromwell the chances of leaving Anne without having to return to Catherine.

Execution of Anne Boleyn

After hearing of Catherine of Aragon's death On 8 January 1536, Henry called for public displays of joy regarding Catherine's death. The queen, although pregnant again, was well aware of the consequences if she failed to give birth to a son. Later that month, the King was unhorsed in a jousting tournament and was badly injured and for a time it appeared that the king's life was in danger. Upon hearing of the king's condition, the queen was sent into shock and suffered miscarriage. The child was a male aged at about 15 weeks old, and on the day of Catherine's funeral, 29 January 1536. The beginning of the end of the royal marriage, given the king's desperate desire for a son and the sequence of Anne's pregnancies has attracted much interest.

The Boleyn family held important positions on the Privy Council, Anne, however, had many enemies, including the Duke of Suffolk. Her own uncle, the Duke of Norfolk, had come to resent her attitude to her power. The Boleyn's preferred France over the Emperor as a potential ally, but the King's favor had already begun to swing towards the latter (partly because of Cromwell), damaging the family's influence. There was also some resentment towards Anne from supporters of reconciliation with Princess Mary, who had now reached maturity. So now a second annulment was now a real possibility, although some believed that Cromwell's anti-Boleyn influence led opponents to look for a way of having her executed, instead.

Anne's downfall was swift after she had recovered from her final miscarriage. There were allegations of conspiracy, adultery and witchcraft all of which remains a matter of debate among historians.

There were even signs of a fall from grace including the King's new mistress, Jane Seymour, being moved into new quarters. Anne's brother, George Boleyn, was refused the Order of the Garter, which was instead given to Nicholas Carew. Between 30 April and 2 May, five men, including Anne's brother, were arrested and charged with treasonable adultery and accused of having sexual relationships with the queen. Anne was also arrested and also accused of treasonous adultery and incest. The evidence against them was unconvincing, the accused were found guilty anyway and condemned to death. George Boleyn and the other accused men were executed on 17 May 1536. At 8 am on 19 May 1536, Anne was executed on Tower Green.

France and the Habsburgs

In 1510, France, along with a still fragile alliance with the Holy Roman Empire in The League of Cambrai, was winning a war against Venice. Henry decided to renew his father's friendship with Louis XII of France, an issue that divided his council. War with the combined force of the two powers would have been extraordinarily difficult. Shortly after, Henry made the decision to also sign a contradictory pact with Ferdinand against France. The problem was now resolved with the creation of the anti-French Holy League with Pope Julius II in October 1511, which brought Louis into conflict with Ferdinand. Henry then brought England into the Holy League afterwards, with an initial joint Anglo-Spanish attack on Aquitaine planned for the spring to recuperate it for England. This glistened in Henry's thoughts and dreams of ruling France, a reality

The next attack, following a formal declaration of war in April, was not led by Henry personally. It was a considerable failure, Ferdinand used it simply to further his own ends. The attack strained the Anglo-Spanish alliance. Nevertheless, the French got booted out of Italy soon after, and the alliance survived. Both parties were intent to win many more victories over the French. After that Henry pulled off a diplomatic coup by convincing the Emperor to join the Holy League. Oddly, Henry had also secured the vowed title of "Most Christian King of France", and possibly coronation by the Pope himself in Paris, if only Louis could be defeated.

On 30 June 1513, Henry invaded France, and his troops defeated a French army at the Battle of the Spurs, a minor result, but one which was snatched by the English for propaganda purposes. Soon after, the English took Thérouanne and handed it over to Maximillian Tournai, a more substantial settlement, followed. Henry led the army personally, complete with large entourage. His absence from the country prompted his brother-in-law, James IV of Scotland, to invade England at the behest of Louis.

The English army, overseen by Queen Catherine, definitively defeated the Scots at the Battle of Flodden on 9 September 1513.

Among the dead was the Scottish king, ending Scotland's brief involvement in the war. These campaigns had given Henry a taste of the military success he so desired. However, despite initial indications that he would pursue a 1514 campaign, Henry decided against that move. He had been supporting Ferdinand and Maximilian financially during the campaign but had got back little and because of it, England's own coffers were now empty.

Pope Leo X replaced Pope Julius, who was then inclined to negotiate for peace with France, which then inspired Henry to sign his own treaty with Louis: It was decided that his sister Mary would become Louis' wife, having previously been pledged to the younger Charles, and peace secured for eight years, which was remarkably long time.

Upon the deaths of his grandfathers, Ferdinand and Maximilian, in 1516 and 1519 individually, Charles of Austria ascended the thrones of Spain and Holy Roman Empire, and Francis I became king of France on Louis' death. Cardinal Thomas Wolsey's careful diplomacy had resulted in the Treaty of London in 1518, pointed at uniting the kingdoms of Western Europe in the rouse of a new Ottoman threat, and it almost seemed that peace might be secured. Henry met Francis I on 7 June 1520 at the Field of the Cloth of Gold near Calais for a "fortnight," (Olde English, meaning fourteen nights,) of lavish entertainment. The goal was for friendly relations and peace in place of the wars of the previous decade. Then there was a strong air of competition that laid to rest any hopes of a renewal of the Treaty of London, and conflict was inevitable.

Marriage to Jane Seymour

Henry was very swift to become engaged to Seymour, in fact it happened day after Anne's execution in 1536. Jane had been one of the Queen's ladies-in-waiting and had caught the eye of the king. They were married just ten days later.

On 12 October 1537, Jane gave birth to a son, Prince Edward, the future Edward VI. The birth was difficult, and the queen died on 24 October 1537 from an infection, known as child bed fever, and she was buried in Windsor. The euphoria that had accompanied Edward's birth turned to sorrow, but it was only over time that Henry came to think about and mourn his wife. Believe it or not, at the time, Henry recovered rather quickly from the shock. Measures were immediately put in place to find another wife for Henry, which, at the determination of Cromwell and the court, and the main focus fell on the European continent.

Charles V was distracted by the internal politics of his many kingdoms and external threats, and Henry and Francis were mostly on good terms, domestic and not foreign policy issues had been Henry's priority in the first half of the 1530s.

In 1536, for Henry granted his sanction to the Laws in Wales Act 1535, which legally annexed Wales, uniting England and Wales into a single nation. Then after he followed with the Second Succession Act (the Act of Succession 1536), which declared Henry's children by Jane to be next in the line of succession and declared both Mary and Elizabeth illegitimate, thus excluding them from the throne. The king was also granted the power to further determine the line of succession in his will, should he have no further issue. However, when Charles and Francis made peace in January 1539, Henry became increasingly uneasy and suspicious of Cromwell. He seemed as spymaster who supplied Henry with a constant list of threats to the kingdom (real or imaginary, minor or serious), and Henry became increasingly paranoid. Expanded by the dissolution of the monasteries, Henry used some of his financial reserves to build a series of coastal defenses and set some aside for use in the event of a Franco-German invasion.

Marriage to Anne of Cleves

It was time for Henry to marry once again to ensure the succession. Cromwell, now Earl of Essex, suggested Anne, the sister of the Duke of Cleves, who was seen as an important ally in case of a Roman Catholic attack on England, for the reason that The Duke's religious beliefs fell between Lutheranism and Catholicism. Hans Holbein the Younger was sent to Cleves to paint a portrait of Anne for the king. It was speculated that Holbein painted her in an overly flattering light, however, it is more likely that the portrait was accurate. Holbein remained in favor at court. After concerning Holbein's portrayal, and advised by the complimentary description of Anne given by his courtiers, the king agreed to wed Anne. Once the king actually saw Anne, he did not share the same opinion at all about Anne's appearance and made it well known that he did not favor her at all. He married her, however, it was not long before

Henry wished to annul the marriage so he could marry another. Anne did not argue, and confirmed that the marriage had never been consummated. The subject of Anne's previous marriage arrangements with the Duke of Lorraine's son eventually provided for the answer, one complicated enough that the remaining impediments to an annulment were removed. The marriage was subsequently dissolved, and Anne received the title of "The King's Sister", two houses and a generous allowance.

It was already clear that Henry had fallen for Catherine Howard, the Duke of Norfolk's niece, the politics of which worried Cromwell, for Norfolk was a political opponent.

Maybe it was the urging by Cromwell to marry Anne of Cleves, or maybe it was shortly after, the religious reformers (and protégés of Cromwell) Robert Barnes, William Jerome and Thomas Garret were burned as heretics, but Cromwell, fell out of favor of the king, and it is unclear exactly why. Cromwell was now in the midst of enemies at court, with Norfolk also able to draw on his niece's position. Cromwell was soon charged with treason, selling export licenses, granting passports, and drawing up commissions without permission, and may also have been blamed for the Cleves failure and the failure of the foreign policy it accompanied. He was subsequently attainted and beheaded

Marriage to Catherine Howard

On 28 July 1540 (the same day Cromwell was executed), Henry married the young Catherine Howard, a first cousin and lady-in-waiting of Anne Boleyn. He was thrilled and very taken by his new queen, she was very beautiful and very young and exciting and entertained the king's appetite for all kinds of enjoyment. He awarded her the lands of Cromwell and a massive array of jewelry. Soon after her marriage, however, Queen Catherine began an affair with the courtier Thomas Culpeper. She employed Francis Dereham, who was previously informally engaged to her and had an affair with her prior to her marriage, as her secretary. The court was informed of her affair with Dereham whilst Henry was away; they dispatched Thomas Cranmer to investigate, who found evidence of Queen Catherine's previous affair with Dereham, and brought it to the king's attention. Henry originally refused to believe the allegations, but Dereham confessed, but it still took another meeting of the council, before

Henry believed and went into a rage, blaming the council before consoling himself in hunting. When questioned, the queen could have just admitted a prior contract to marry Dereham, which would have made her subsequent marriage to Henry invalid, but she insisted that Dereham had forced her to enter into an adulterous relationship. Dereham, meanwhile, exposed Queen Catherine's relationship with Thomas Culpeper. Culpeper and Dereham were executed, and Catherine too was beheaded on 13 February 1542.

Marriage to Catherine Parr

Henry married his last wife, the wealthy widow Catherine Parr, in July 1543. She was reformer at heart, and she argued with Henry over religion. Ultimately, Henry remained committed to a peculiar mixture of Catholicism and Protestantism

The best thing that Parr helped do in her marriage was to reconcile Henry with his daughters Mary and Elizabeth. In 1543, an Act of Parliament put his daughters back in the line of succession after Edward, Prince of Wales. The same act allowed Henry to determine further succession to the throne in his will.

In his late life, Henry became obese, with a waist measurement of 54 inches (140 cm), and needed the help of mechanical device to be moved about. He was covered with extremely painful, pus-filled boils and more than likely suffered from gout. His obesity and other medical problems can be traced from the jousting accident in 1536, in which he suffered a leg wound. The accident re-opened and aggravated a previous leg wound he had sustained years earlier, his doctors found it very difficult to treat. The wound festered for the remainder of his life and became ulcerated, preventing him from maintaining a healthy level of physical activity he had previously enjoyed. The jousting accident is believed to have caused Henry's mood swings, which may have had a dramatic effect on his personality and temperament.

Henry did not suffer from syphilis, that theory has been dismissed by most historians. A more recent theory suggests that Henry's medical symptoms are characteristic of untreated Type II diabetes. Alternatively, his wives' pattern of pregnancies and his mental deterioration have led some to suggest that the king may have been Kell positive and suffered from McLeod syndrome. According to another study, Henry VIII's history and body morphology was probably the result of traumatic brain injury after his 1536 jousting accident, which in turn led to a neuroendocrine cause of his obesity. This analysis identifies growth hormone deficiency (GHD) as the source for his increased adiposity but also significant behavioral changes noted in his later years, including his multiple marriages.

If Henry VIII hadn't become obsessed with food, he may have lived a bit longer, however, his state of obesity hastened his death at the age of 55. Henry died on 28 January 1547 at the Palace of Whitehall, on what would have been his father's 90th birthday.

The last words he spoke, were only rumored to have been, "Monks, monks, monks!" And only maybe he was referencing the monks he had evicted during the Dissolution of the Monasteries. On 14 February 1547, Henry's coffin lay overnight at Syon Monastery, to be en-route for burial in St. George's Chapel. Henry VIII was interred in St George's Chapel in Windsor Castle, next to Jane Seymour. Over a hundred years later, King Charles I (1625–1649) was buried in the same vault.

A little funny to think of it now, for those are the two things for which Henry is most remembered: his six marriages and his break with the Pope (who would not allow an annulment of Henry's first marriage) and the Roman Catholic Church, leading to the English Reformation. Henry became severely obese and his health suffered, contributing to his death in 1547. He is frequently characterized in his later life as a lustful, egotistical, harsh, and insecure king.

Henry VIII was succeeded by his son Edward VI.

EDWARD VI (1537-1553)

EDWARD VI, succeeded as King of England and Ireland upon the death of his father. He was born at Greenwich on the 12th of October 1537. He was the only child and the only male heir that his father longed for so desperately, of Henry VIII and his third wife, Jane Seymour, who died of child bed fever twelve days later. There was once a rumor that the mother's life was deliberately sacrificed by the performance of caesarean, but that rumor had been deemed proved false unsubstantiated. Jane's death, sadly, was little noticed due to all of the rejoicings and celebrating. Everyone at court and in the kingdom was happy to hear of the birth of a male heir to the throne.

In spite of Holbein's spirited portrait of Edward at the age of two, now at Hanover, he was a fragile child, and a short life was predicted for him from his early years. He still was raised with all of the strenuous education one would expect of a royal offspring, until around the age of six, when he was left in the charge of women. When he was only seven his tutor, Dr Coxe, next bishop of Ely, wrote that he could "decline any Latin noun and conjugate any regular verb." Sir John Cheke, Sir Anthony Cooke and Roger Ascham all helped to teach him Latin, Greek and French; and by the age of thirteen he had read Aristotle's Ethics in the original and was himself translating Cicero's De Philosophe into Greek.

Edward was Duke of Cornwall from his birth, but he was never Prince of Wales. He was only nine when he succeeded his father as king of England and Ireland and supreme head of the English church on 28 January 1546. His succession and regency threw power into the hands of Somerset and then of Northumberland, and enabled Gardiner and Bonner to maintain that the royal supremacy over the church was, in abeyance. There were mentions made towards marriage for the king, but none that were hardly even considered, but an excuse, for Somerset's war on Scotland and Northumberland's ensuing alliance with France.

All parties tried to control Edward, not because of his age or health but because of his position, he considered the Great Seal, only a more indispensable secretary to the wielder of authority. The Protector's brother, Edward's own uncle, Thomas Seymour, tried to bribe him with money. Northumberland was more subtle with his attempts and was able to establish a complete domain over his mind, and he went ahead and put him forward at the age of fourteen as entitled to all the power of Henry VIII.

This was all just a mask of Northumberland's making. There is hardly a trace of all of his influence over Edward in the course of history during his reign. One single posthumous effort was made to give him the credit of one humane desire to save Joan Bocher from the flames; but it was recorded with such an apparently cold-blooded indifference for the execution of both his uncles. He also made no attempt to lessen even the harassing treatment which the council paid his sister Mary. This passed for piety with the extremists, and the persecutions of Mary's reign reflected a halo on that of the Protestant Josiah. So strong was the regret that rumors of his survival persisted, and foolish youths resonated about him throughout Mary's and even far into Elizabeth's reign

However it was, he bequeathed a legacy of woe; his health began to fail in 1552, and in May 1553 it was well known that he was dying. But his will and the various drafts of it only deceive the disconcerted and irrational efforts of Northumberland to contrive some means whereby he might continue to control the government and prevent the administration of justice. Northumberland was far too high handed but not unstoppable.

So how did Northumberland plot to control? His plan was devious, he tried to make it seem that Edward wished that Jane Grey was to inherit the throne and his sisters' Mary and Elizabeth were to be excluded from the throne, as not sufficiently pliant instruments. His plan also had Mary Stuart ignored as being under Scottish, Catholic and French influence.

The Duchess of Suffolk, Lady Jane Grey's mother, was also excluded because she was married, and that meant that the Duke, her own husband, might claim the crown under matrimonial laws. So this means that all females were excluded, except Jane, which is laughable, because by his own admittance, on the ground that no woman could reign. Confusingly she was excluded in the first draft, and the crown was left to "the Lady Jane's heirs male." This draft was then manipulated to read "the Lady Jane and her heir's male." Supposedly his last words were vehement injunctions to Cranmer to sign the will, so he did, causing Jane Grey to become Queen for only nine days.

Edward VI died at Greenwich on the 6 July 1553, and was buried in Henry VII's chapel by Cranmer with Protestant rites on the 8th of August, while Mary had Mass said for his soul in the Tower.

Mary I
Queen of England
In Nomine Patris et Filii et Spiritus Sancti

Born: 18 February 1516 Greenwich Palace; Proclaimed Queen: 19 July 1553 St. Paul's Cathedral, London; Coronation: 1 October 1553 Westminster Abbey; Died: 17 November 1558 St. James's Palace; Buried: 14 December 1558 Westminster Abbey

The Last Catholic Queen of England

Mary Tudor was born on 18 February 1516, the only child born to Henry VIII and Catherine of Aragon and was the only child of Catherine's to survive childhood. Now just think, if she had been born a boy, English history would have been different, but certainly not as interesting!

Mary was the center of court attention in her earliest years. But, as the years went by, the strain that her father had put on Catherine, and his constant desire for a male heir started to show and affect his relationship with Mary. After Mary's father looked into his alternatives and sought an annulment from Catherine, their relationship became non-existent. When her father married his second Queen, Anne Boleyn, Mary was declared illegitimate and was to no longer be called "Princess", but rather "The Lady Mary".

The next act of betrayal by her father, stung worse. That happened after Anne Boleyn gave birth to another girl, Elizabeth, Mary was sent to attend the every need of the new baby Princess in her household. All it took was time, and soon the young Elizabeth would also be declared a bastard as well, since her mother also failed to produce a male heir, and lost her head.

True to form, quickly after the death of Anne Boleyn, Henry wed Jane Seymour, who was in favor of reconciliation with the King with his two daughters. Henry and Jane visited Mary and she became encouraged to write letters to the Holy Roman Emperor Charles V, her cousin, and the Pope stated that her parent's marriage had not been valid. Mary was even able to get a secret message to them stating that she wrote the letters under duress. She then returned to court, even though her title of Princess had yet to be restored.

In October 1537, Queen Jane gave birth to Edward, Henry's longed for son and Mary stood as the young Prince's godmother at the christening. The court was soon lurched into mourning when Jane died from child bed fever just two weeks after Edward's birth.

In January 1540, Mary, another stepmother, did Mary once again have. This time, Anne of Cleves was the new bride of her father's but not for long. And, although they shared different religions, Mary Catholic, and Anne a Lutheran, the two women quickly became friends and would remain so until Anne's death in 1557. Unfortunately Anne's marriage to Henry wasn't so long-lived and she was divorced in July of the same year.

Shortly after the annulment of his marriage to Anne of Cleves, Henry took another wife, yes, up to five now, this one was Kathryn Howard. Kathryn was younger than Mary by six years. Kathryn was 18 years old and Mary was outwardly disgusted by her father's actions. There were squabbles between Mary and Kathryn during the young Queen's reign. That reign didn't turn out very well either, as she was arrested, tried and executed for adultery in 1542.

This became a time of emotional turmoil for Mary and she became seriously ill and some say she may have been in danger of losing her life. Her father became very concerned for his daughter's life, enough so that he sent for his own doctors to look after her.

Henry's last Queen was Katherine Parr, who was about four years older than Mary. They were married in 1543, and she survived Henry in his death in 1547. All three of Henry's children attended the wedding at Hampton Court. Mary was friends with her last stepmother, although they did have their religious differences, as Katherine was a strong supporter of the Reformed Church. They got along wonderfully.

When Henry VIII began to fall ill, he drafted his will declaring that Edward would be his heir and Mary was to follow him if the young Prince were to die childless. Elizabeth was also included, and she would take the throne if Mary were to die without an heir. As we know in hindsight, this is exactly what was to happen.

Henry VIII died January 28, 1547, leaving his 9 year-old son as King. The young Edward was a supporter of the Protestant faith, although Mary seems to have hoped at one point he would see the error of his ways and return England to the Church of Rome.

She acted against Edward's Act of Uniformity and openly celebrated Mass, which had been abolished. Edward and Mary constantly struggled with this issue through the rest of the King's short reign.

Around 1552, Edward began to show signs of the illness that would eventually claim his life. He was reported to have a hacking cough that eventually resulted in him spitting up blood and tissue.

Medical historians generally agree that he had tuberculosis.

Fearing Mary would return the country to the Catholic faith, powerful men in the realm, such as John Dudley, Duke of Northumberland and Henry Grey, Duke of Suffolk began to make their plans. Although they made moves to court Mary's favor, they worked secretly with their own agenda. Northumberland married his son Guildford to Suffolk's daughter Jane Grey, who would be in line for the throne after Mary and Elizabeth. By placing Jane on the throne in Edward's wake, they hoped they would have a puppet they could control.

Mary was courted by Duke Philip of Bavaria in late 1539, but Philip was Lutheran and pursuit for her hand was unsuccessful. Over the year 1539, the king's chief minister, Thomas Cromwell, tried to negotiate a potential alliance with the Duchy of Cleves. Suggestions were made that Mary could marry the Duke of Cleves, who was the same age, but nothing was to become of it, instead, a match between Henry and the Duke's sister Anne was agreed upon. After the king saw Anne for the first time, he quickly regretted the deal that was made, but for diplomacy's sake, he went through with the marriage.

Cromwell fell from favor quickly after and was arrested for treason in June 1540; one of the unlikely charges against him was that he had plotted to marry Mary himself. Anne then consented to the annulment of the marriage, which had not been consummated, and Cromwell was beheaded.

On 10 July 1553, Lady Jane was proclaimed Queen by Dudley and his supporters, and on the same day Mary's letter to the council arrived in London. By 12 July, Mary and her supporters had assembled a military force at Framingham Castle, Suffolk. Dudley's support buckled, and Mary's grew. Jane was unseated on 19 July. She and Dudley were imprisoned in the Tower of London. Mary rode into London triumphantly on 3 August 1553 on a wave of popular support. She was escorted proudly by her half-sister Elizabeth, and a procession of over 800 nobles and gentlemen.

One of Mary's first actions as queen was to order the release of the Roman Catholic Duke of Norfolk and Stephen Gardiner from imprisonment in the Tower of London, as well as her kinsman Edward Courtenay. Mary understood that the young Lady Jane was just a pawn in Dudley's scheme, and Dudley was the only conspirator of rank executed for high treason in the immediate aftermath of the coup. Lady Jane and her husband, Lord Guildford Dudley, though found guilty, were kept under guard in the Tower rather than immediately executed, while Lady Jane's father, Henry Grey, 1st Duke of Suffolk, was released. Mary was left in an unusually difficult position, as almost all the Privy Counsellors had been implicated in the plot to put Lady Jane on the throne. So the next order of business was to appoint Gardiner to the council and made him both Bishop of Winchester and Lord Chancellor, he held these offices until his death in November 1555. Susan Clarencieux became Mistress of the Robes. On 1 October 1553, Gardiner crowned Mary at Westminster Abbey.

Spanish marriage

At the late age of 37, Mary turned her attention to finding a husband and producing an heir, trying to prevent her Protestant half-sister Elizabeth, and still successor under the terms of Henry VIII's will and the Act of Succession of 1544, from succeeding to the throne. Edward Courtenay and Reginald Pole were both mentioned as potential suitors, but her cousin Charles V recommended she marry his only son, Prince Philip of Spain. Philip had a son from a previous marriage, and was heir apparent to vast territories in Continental Europe and the New World. As part of the marriage negotiations, a portrait of Philip by Titian was sent to her in September 1553.

Mary was, excluding the brief, disputed reigns of the Empress Matilda and Lady Jane Grey, England's first queen regnant. That meant, under the English common law doctrine of pure luxuries, the property and titles belonging to a woman became her husband's upon marriage. It was feared that any man she married would thereby become King of England in fact and in name. While Mary's grandparents, Ferdinand and Isabella, had retained sovereignty of their own realms during their marriage, there was no precedent to follow in England. Mary acted alone, meaning, she had an act passed by Parliament as follows: Under the terms of Queen Mary's Marriage Act, Philip was to be styled "King of England", all official documents, including Acts of Parliament, were to be dated with both their names, and Parliament was to be called under the joint authority of the couple, for Mary's lifetime only. England would not be obliged to provide military support to Philip's father in any war, and Philip could not act without his wife's consent or appoint foreigners to office in England. Philip was unhappy at the conditions imposed, but he was ready to agree for the sake of securing the marriage. He had no amorous feelings toward Mary and sought the marriage for its political and strategic gains. Philip's aide Ruy Gómez de Silva wrote to a correspondent in Brussels, "The marriage was concluded for no fleshly consideration, but in order to remedy the disorders of this kingdom and to preserve the Low Countries."

After Philip's visit in 1557, Mary thought herself pregnant again with a baby due in March 1558. She decreed in her will that her husband be the regent during the minority of her child. However, no child was born, and Mary was forced to accept that Elizabeth was her lawful successor.

Mary was weak and ill from May 1558, and died aged 42 at St. James's Palace during an influenza epidemic that also claimed the life of Reginald Pole later the same day, 17 November 1558. She was in pain, possibly from ovarian cysts or uterine cancer. She was succeeded by her half-sister. Philip, who was in Brussels, wrote to his sister Joan: "I felt a reasonable regret for her death."

Although her will stated that she wished to be buried next to her mother, Mary was interred in Westminster Abbey on 14 December in a tomb she would eventually share with Elizabeth. The Latin inscription on their tomb, Regno consortes et urna, hic obdormimus Elizabetha et Maria sorores, in spe resurrectionis (affixed there by James VI of Scotland when he succeeded Elizabeth as King James I of England) translates to "Consorts in realm and tomb, here we sleep, Elizabeth and Mary, sisters, in hope of resurrection".

There was never another Catholic King or Queen of England.

Elizabeth I (1558-1603)-

Queen Elizabeth I was not well liked by Jane Austin. While she may have been made famous in movies and well liked in this century, her reputation was smeared by Jane Austin's pen.....

Jane Austin's hatred for Queen Elizabeth:

It was the peculiar misfortune of this woman to have bad Ministers- Since wicked as she herself was, she could not have committed such extensive mischief, had not these vile and abandoned men connived at, and encouraged her in her crimes. I know that it has by many people been asserted and believed that Lord Burleigh, Sir Francis Walsingham and the rest of those who filled the chief offices of State were deserving, experienced, and able Ministers.

But Oh! how blinded such writers and such readers must be to true merit, to merit despised, neglected and defamed; if they can persist in such opinions when they reflect that these men, these boasted men were such scandals to their country and their sex to allow and assist their Queen in confining for the space of nineteen years, A woman who if the claims of relationship and merit were of no avail, yet as a Queen and as one who condescended to place confidence in her, had every reason to expect assistance and protection; and at length in allowing Elizabeth to bring this amiable Woman to an untimely, unmerited and Scandalous Death. ~ Jane Austin

Jane Austin wrote often of Mary Queen of Scots. She truly believed her execution to be a horrible act, unjust and murder. Her dislike of Queen Elizabeth and her advisers was always full of hatred, she believed them to be guilty and was un-forgiving of their acts by her pen.

When writing of Queen Mary, she did not hold back her hatred of Elizabeth at all. Here is another piece written by Jane Austin:

Mary Queen of Scots

~ This woman had the good luck if being advanced to the throne of England, in spite of the superior pretensions, Merit and Beauty of her Cousins Mary Queen of Scotland and Jane Grey. Nor can I pity the Kingdom for the misfortunes they experienced during her reign, since they fully deserved them, for having allowed her to succeed her Brother- which was a double piece of folly, since they might have foreseen that she died without children, she would be succeeded by that disgrace to humanity, that pest of society, Elizabeth. Many were the people who fell martyrs to the protestant Religion during her reign; I suppose not fewer than a dozen. She married Phillip King of Spain who in her sister's reign was famous for building Armadas. She died without issue, and then the dreadful moment came in which the destroyer of all comfort, the deceitful Betrayer of trust reposed in her, and the Murderess of her Cousin succeeded to the Throne. ~ Jane Austin

I think that it is safe to say, Jane Austin, whom we all love~ had no love for the Virgin Queen.

Queen Elizabeth I – The Golden Age

"Take this beauty into your heart, learn it. Someday you will only be able to see this with the eyes of your heart. Then it will be important for you to have the beauty inside you. Memorize the land." -Maria Jose Hobday, Ute Indian and Fransiscan sister, quoting her mother

The reign of Queen Elizabeth I is often referred to as The Golden Age of English history. Elizabeth was an immensely popular Queen, and her popularity has diminished little with the passing of four hundred years. She is still one of the best loved monarchs, and one of the most admired rulers of all time. She became a legend in her own lifetime, renowned for her remarkable abilities and achievements. Yet, about Elizabeth the woman, we know very little. She is a mystery, and was a mystery to her own people.

Elizabeth was the daughter of King Henry VIII and his second wife, Anne Boleyn. She was born on 7 September 1533 at Greenwich Palace. Her birth was yet another huge disappointment for her father. It was a common fact that he wanted a son and heir to succeed him as he already had a daughter, Mary, by his first wife, Catherine of Aragon. He had not divorced Catherine, and uprooted the entire kingdom and changed the religion of the country in the process, only to have another daughter. Elizabeth's early life was filled with turmoil. Her mother failed to provide the King with a son and to top it all off, her mother was executed on false charges of incest and adultery on 19 May 1536. Anne's marriage to the King was declared null and void, and Elizabeth, like her half-sister, Mary, was declared illegitimate and deprived of her place in the line of succession.

The next eight years of Elizabeth's life saw a quick succession of stepmothers. There was Jane Seymour who died giving birth to the King's longed for son, Edward; Anne of Cleves who was divorced; Catherine Howard who was beheaded; and finally Catherine Parr. For generations, historians have debated whether the constant bride changing of her father was responsible for Elizabeth's apparent refusal to marry. It is surely a probability that the tragic fates of Anne Boleyn and Catherine Howard impacted her ultimate decision to fear of marriage, however, there may have been unknown reasons that even history never wrote about, that influenced the Queen's single state, but she was the Queen, and although urged by council, that was her choice.

As a child, Elizabeth was given an immaculate education. It was highly popular amongst the nobility to educate daughters just as well as sons and Elizabeth surpassed everyone at her studies. The Tudor was tutored by famous scholars such as William Grindal and Roger Ascham, and from a very early age it was clear that Elizabeth was remarkably gifted. She had a particular flare for languages, and by adulthood, she could supposedly speak five languages fluently. While the King lived, she was well guarded from political opportunists, but after he died in the January of 1547, and his young son became King Edward VI, she fell prey to those who saw her as a political chess piece. Henry had reinstated his daughters in the line of succession before his death so Mary was to follow Edward, and Elizabeth was to follow Mary. This meant that Elizabeth was now second in line to the throne.

Elizabeth found herself wedged up in treason accounts after the Wyatt rebellion of 1554. Edward had died in the summer of 1553 from prolonged ill health, and Elizabeth's half-sister, Mary, had become Queen Mary I of England, after a brief battle over the throne against the evil schemes of John Dudley, Duke of Northumberland, to make his daughter in law, Jane Grey, queen.

Mary was a very popular monarch, and was constantly suspicious of her Protestant half-sister. It was for this reason that it was not difficult to persuade her that Elizabeth may have been conspiring with Thomas Wyatt and his men to seize the throne. Whether or not the rebellion was to make Elizabeth queen or not is uncertain, and it is also unknown whether Elizabeth had any knowledge of the conspirators' plans. Even if she did have knowledge of them, no one was ever able to prove such allegations that she knew of the actions of Wyatt and his followers. Elizabeth always maintained her innocence of the accusations made against her. She still endured the arrest and being sent to the Tower of London as a prisoner.

There were many supporters to the Queen who would have

liked to see Elizabeth executed, but there was no evidence against her and she was very popular among the people. Elizabeth was kept prisoner at the Tower for two months, instead and then removed to Woodstock Manor in Oxfordshire, where she was kept a prisoner for a year. That house itself was dilapidated so she had to be boarded in the gatehouse with her servants. It was the Queen's husband, Philip of Spain, who had to intervene and request that she be allowed to return to her childhood home of Hatfield in Hertfordshire. Philip was mindful of the Queen's poor health and wanted to advance the friendship of Elizabeth to secure peaceful relations between England and Spain should his wife die and Elizabeth succeed to the throne.

Elizabeth finally succeeded to the throne on 17th November 1558. It was a glorious moment of supreme triumph for the cast about daughter who had spent her life in the shadows. The years following the death of her father had called for soberness and restraint, but now that she was Queen, Elizabeth was determined to enjoy her new found freedom and live life to the full.

She loved all kinds of sports, especially horse riding, and in the early years of her reign spent many hours riding. She loved hunting, hawking, bear baiting, and watching the male courtiers. She had a keen eye for watching them excel at jousts or other sporting contests. Elizabeth also enjoyed music and dancing, pageantry and masques, and could even play the virginals and the lute herself with skill. She enjoyed every part of life at court and at play to its fullest. She had no time for the Puritan theologians who deemed such things irreverent. She also loved watching plays and created the atmosphere responsible for the flourishing of the literary masterpieces of the period against the Puritan demands for the closure of all theatres and playhouses.

Following her formal crowning as Queen on Sunday 15th January 1559 and in the months that followed, the new Queen re-established the Protestant Church in England and restored the sullied coinage. She had also decided to mollify Catholics or to pacify those who did not believe a woman could become the head of the church, Elizabeth became, instead, Supreme Governor of the Church of England, rather than Supreme Head as her father had been. It is next to impossible to know what exactly the Queen's personal religious beliefs were, the church she established is an indication of them. She was a committed Protestant, and reputedly spent time in prayer every day, but she was probably a conservative Protestant.

Elizabeth knew that by not marrying and having a child of her own meant that the succession was unsettled. Elizabeth also did not like to talk about the succession and tried to have mention of it suppressed, but people were extremely anxious about what would happen to the country when she died. However, having a child of her own may not have been an end to all problems as one may have believed.

Many believed that Elizabeth was illegitimate and had no right to the throne anyways, and remaining unmarried and childless provoked some to set things right. Technically because Mary I reigned as the legitimate daughter of Henry VIII, Elizabeth could not and should not have succeeded by hereditary rights. Mary's mother was alive during Anne Boyne's marriage and the birth of Elizabeth. It was believed especially by the Catholics that this marriage was invalid and Elizabeth was illegitimate. Mary, Queen of Scots was the rightful Queen of England and had a the strongest claim to the throne.

Plots were made to make Mary Queen, these would have been formed regardless of whether Elizabeth had a child or not. This threatened Elizabeth and forced her to imprison Mary. Although Elizabeth wanted to feel close ties and have an ally with her cousin Queen, she was advised by several of her trusted advisers, weather true or not, that Mary was an enemy to her crown.

Mary, Queen of Scots was forced to flee her own country, after abdicating her throne in favor of her son, and after the murder of her husband which she was implicated in. Mary sought Elizabeth's help in restoring her to her kingdom. 'As a dear sister and Queen" That proved to be a big mistake, as she was immediately imprisoned. This was meant to protect her just as much to minimize the danger she posed to Elizabeth. Mary was kept a prisoner for almost twenty years. In that time, Elizabeth refused to hear about executing her cousin, but Mary's involvement in the Babington plot of 1586 made the execution, in the eyes of many, unavoidable. It proved to be a traumatic time for Elizabeth, and for a while it seemed that she may not have the strength to order the execution, but she did, and Mary was executed at Fotheringay Castle on 8 February 1587.

Elizabeth was dedicated to her country in a way few monarchs had been or have been since. Elizabeth had the mind of a political genius and nurtured her country through careful leadership and by choosing capable men to assist her, such as Sir William Cecil and Sir Francis Walsingham. Elizabeth was a determined woman, but she was not obstinate. She listened to the advice of those around her, and would change a policy if it was unpopular. In appearance she was extravagant, in behavior sometimes flippant and frivolous, but her approach to politics was serious, conservative, and cautious. When she ascended the throne in 1558, England was an impoverished country torn apart by religious quarrels. When she died at Richmond Palace on the 24th March 1603, England was one of the most powerful and prosperous countries in the world. She had disproven her own father's theory that a woman would not have the power to be powerful.

Elizabeth Tudor is considered by many to be the greatest monarch in English history. She was committed above all else to preserving English peace and stability; her genuine love for her subjects was legendary. Only a few years after her death in 1603, they lamented her passing. In her greatest speech to Parliament, she told them, 'I count the glory of my crown that I have reigned with your love.' And five centuries later, the worldwide love affair with Elizabeth Tudor continues.

More Facts of Interest on Elizabeth I

"Proud and haughty, as although she knows she was born of such a mother, she nevertheless does not consider herself of inferior degree to the Queen, whom she equals in self-esteem; nor does she believe herself less legitimate than her Majesty, alleging in her own favor that her mother would never cohabit with the King unless by way of marriage, with the authority of the Church.... She prides herself on her father and glories in him; everybody saying that she also resembles him more than the Queen does and he therefore always liked her and had her brought up in the same way as the Queen." the Venetian ambassador Giovanni Michiel describes Elizabeth; spring 1557

Did you know? In 1596 Sir John Harington introduced Queen Elizabeth to her first flushing toilet? Sure, flushing toilets have been around since the time of the ancient Minoans, but for the English, they were a new marvel.

Harington, who was known as Elizabeth's "saucy godson," constantly fell in and out of favor with the Queen. However, his flushing toilet remained forever in her favor.

Sir John Harington, or Harrington, August 4, 1561 – November 20, 1612) was a courtier, author, and scientist. He became a prominent member of Queen Elizabeth I's court, and was known as her 'saucy Godson'. But because of his poetry and other writings, he fell in and ultimately out of favor with the Queen, as well as with her successor, King James I of England. Prior to contrary belief, Thomas Crapper did not invent the flush toilet; John Harrington did. The flush toilet is described in his famous work The Metamorphosis of Ajax which had enjoyed considerable popularity on its publication in 1596.

Chapter Eight

THE STUARTS
1603 - 1714

James I (1603-1625) James was named the Successor of Queen Elizabeth. Many Noble Lords supported his succession although there were some that were Leary of the 'barbarous Scots's. Among one of the most noble families in England was the Howards, who fully supported King James.

James had been the King of Scotland since he was an infant. His Mother, Mary- Queen of Scots had made it so before fleeing Scotland. She was executed in February 1587 after being the prisoner of Elizabeth in England for 17 years.

James ruled by the belief of Divine Rights: That he was appointed by God at birth and was a divine ruler of the people. He answered to no one but God himself, not even the Church of England or Rome. This belief was one than was never accepted in England and would end up leading his son to the executioner's block in 1649.

However, this led to many disagreements with his Parliament and led to long periods of King James relying on advice from his favorites.

He is also credited with the revision of the Bible, known as the

King James Version. Despite James' lifestyle he was a devout Christian.

During Elizabeth's time tobacco was introduced into England. James had a hatred of tobacco, he laid a very heavy tax on it, in hopes to hinder its consumption. He also wrote what is called 'Counterblaste to Tobacco', a well-argued attack on smoking that was distributed throughout England.

Among some of his arguments King James states in the document is how unreasonable the pleas in its defense are. How by using tobacco men are guilty of sinful and shameful lust; that is a branch of the sin of drunkenness. And that 'some gentlemen bestow three, sometimes four hundred pounds a year upon this precious stink"

James described it as a "Childish novelty' that was found out by some barbarous indians. It was used against the pox, a filthy disease whereunto these barbarous people are, as all men know, very much subject to the uncleanly and adust (this meaning the color of their skin) constitution of their bodies.'

He then says, "Now good countrymen let us, I pray you, consider what honor or policy can move us to intimidate the barbarous and beastly manners of the wild; godless; and slavish Indians, especially in so vile and stinking a custom?"

James had an absolute aversion to war. He stated, "The greatest gift that our savior gave his apostles, immediately before his assertion was one of peace with them, I know not what fortune was added to my title, at my coming to England."

From what James writes I believe he would have wished that Elizabeth had left him the kingdom in peace. She did not though, she left England bitter enemies with Spain. Within months of ascending the throne, James was in negotiations and peace was starting to be made.

There are many accounts of the gun-powder plot written in contemporary writing from memoirs of earlier times. I am going to relate some of them now. The plot had always been suspicious and the actual guilt of those involved questioned. "The horrid powder-plot suspected to be politically contrived by Cecil, but known to be acted by a few desperados of a religion that detests such treasons" Sir Thomas Birch.

"It was long for I could persuade them here to believe the truth of the said conspiracy; but now lastly, when they see they can no longer dispute the doubtfulness and uncertainty thereof, they report to this consideration, that it is the work of the devil's expressly to banish and extirpate the catholic religion out of England." Sir Thomas Edmonds, dated December 27, 1605

"For it was not he (King James) that guessed from the expression in the letter to lord Monteagle, 'that they should receive a terrible blow this Parliament, and yet they should not see who hurts them," It was not he who guessed that it should be some sudden danger by blowing up of powder, but the Earl of Suffolk, Lord Chaimberlain, and the Earl of Salisbury, as the latter himself relates in a letter to Sir Charles Cornwallis.

The writers themselves on this subject are excusable, having authority to rely on. For such was the flattery of James's courtiers, that they got it inserted into the preamble of the act for a public thanksgiving to almighty God every year on the fifth of November. That the conspiracy would have turned to the utter ruin of this whole Kingdom, had it not pleased almighty God, by inspiring the Kings most excellent majesty with divine spirit to interpret some dark phrases of a letter showed to his majesty, above and beyond all ordinary construction, miraculously discovering this hidden treason.

Tis amazing how any man, who knew it to be such, could publicly receive it, much more that the most great learned and religious King the ever reigned this Kingdom. King James was stilled, But the drawers of this doubted it. Everybody knows that in consequence of the discovery, several of the falsehoods for truths in statutes- for these being enforced by the highest authority, the facts in them declared should be strictly true; otherwise whatever disobedience may be yielded. The enactors will have little esteem or regard for the people, to whom the dealers in untruths seldom appear in amiable light.

"Tis well known, that many of the papists then and now have denied the fact, and imputed the whole of the affair to Salisbury; and we are told, that the opposite principles have confidently asserted, 'that there never was any such thing as the powder-plot, but that it was a plot contriving to endear King James unto the people.'"

Dr. Tilotson, Archbishop of Canterbury

It has been written over and over again, the Gunpowder Plot and Guy Fawkes. It is celebrated in England. We learn in from History lessons to Wikipedia, it was a 'Jesuit' plot to put the Princess Elizabeth on the throne by Catholics. There is always two sides to every story, and with history that rule of thumb is the same.

The 'Popist Plot' of King James:

No this is not a mistake. The only popist plot you have heard, has probably been that of Titus Oates and King Charles II, a "fictitious" plot. This Popish plot was quite real and in the Reign of King James.

"The papists by reason of some extraordinary grown mighty in number, courage and influence. In great hopes of a tolerance, when they saw King James set against the puritans that it became so much the general expectation among them, that in order to clear himself of having intentions of granting it to them, his majesty though proper to declare that 'he never intended it, would spend the last drop of his blood before he would do it, and suppressed that impression on his prosperity, if they should maintain any other religion, than what the truly professed and maintained' - of which I have before taken notice. Not content herewith he ordered the laws against them that he put into execution, and they underwent many hardships.

Upon the discovery of the Popish Plot, there was a general prosecution of all the papists set on foot, as might be expected; but King James was very uneasy at it', says Burnet, 'which was much increased by what Sir Dudley Carleton told him upon his return from Spain, where he had been ambassador; which he said to me from Spain, where he had been ambassador; which he said to me, that sir Dudley Carlton told it to himself, and was much troubled when he saw it had an effect contrary to what he had intended.

When he came home, he found the King at Theobald's hunting in a very careless and unguarded manner: and upon that, in order to the putting him on a more careful looking to himself, he told the king he must either give over that way of hunting, or stop another hunting that he was engaged in, which was priest hunting: for he had intelligence in Spain that the priests were comforting themselves with this, that if he went on against them, they would soon get rid of him.

The king sent for him in private to inquire more particularly into this and what he saw made a great impression on him: but wrought otherwise than as he intended. For the king, resolved to gratify his humor in hunting, and in a careless and irregular way of life, did immediately order all that prosecutions to let fall.

I have the minutes of the council books of the year 1606, which are full of orders to discharge and transport priests, sometimes ten in a day.'

I was inclined at first to call this whole story of Burnet's into question, by reason that Carleton was never as far as I know an ambassador to Spain. On further search I find it probable. In 1605, Carleton, accompanied by Lord Norris into Spain, and it might be here that it was said, what was spoken supposedly to King James. So there is only a small mistake by Burnet and what he said was very probable. The laws were enacted against the Catholics, and the Judges commanded on occasion to 'put them to execution'.

James did however have a great affection for them, he made many of them his favorites. The entire Howard family for example that has been said was the 'Most Catholic family in all of England' and I believe to this day the Howards are still of the Catholic faith.

There is one indisputable writer on this matter that is King James himself:

"Not only the papists grew to that bright of pride, in confidence of my mildness, as they did directly expect, and assuredly promise to themselves liberty on conscience and equality with other of my subjects in all things; but when a number of the best and most faithful of my said subjects, were cast in great fear and amazement of my course and proceedings, ever prognosticating and justly inspecting that sour fruit to come of it, which showed itself early in the powder-treason. How mad did I favor with Knighthood, of known and open recusants? How indifferently did I give audience, and accept both sides, bestowing equally all favors and honors on both professions? How free and continued was my acceptance in ranks and degrees of papists in my court and company? And above all how frankly and freely did I free recusants of their original payments? Besides it is evident what straight order was given out of my own mouth to the Judges, to spare the execution of all Jesuits, notwithstanding their conviction, joining thereunto a gracious proclamation, whereby all priests that were at liberty, and not taken, might go out of the country by such a day: my general pardon having been extended to all convicted priests in prison: whereupon they were set at liberty as good subjects. Time and paper will fail me, to enumeration of all the benefits and favors I bestowed in general, and particular upon papists."

These religious wars continue for several years and again in 1610, where the tug of wars of affect King James from every side, including Spain and France.

'From thence to his dying day he continued always writing and talking against popery, but acting for it. He married his only daughter to a protestant prince, one of the most zealous and sincere of them all, the elector palatine; upon which a great revolution happened in the affairs of Germany. "

Sir Walter Raleigh had been sentenced to the Tower. It was here actually that he became very good friends with Prince Henry, The heir apparent he was called. There was an entire nation waiting for him to succeed his father. The reason being the dislike many had for the way he ran his court and the power that James allowed his favorites. Those being first Sir Robert Carr, who was elevated to Earl Somerset and then the infamous Duke of Buckingham.

"For this young Prince, whose qualities promised Noble destiny for himself and for England, and whose high spirit despised the foolishness and sumptuous squalor of his Fathers Court, Raleigh had a great affection, and for hours the old man and the young Prince discussed many great memories of history and principals which should guide princes in their work of government." It was to Prince Henry the Raleigh dedicated his "History of the World"

The Friendship between the Prince and Raleigh was actually one of mutual respect. Also, I must add, one more thing that separated the bonds between Father and Son. Henry once saying about his Father having Raleigh in prisoned.

"No man but my Father would keep such a bird in a cage"

Here is another interesting memoir that actually surprised me, I had actually never heard any account of the Japanese in England.

In the year 1619, a treaty was concluded between James and the Dutch, with regard to the trade of the East-Indies 'This made them envied by the Dutch, who were determined if possible, to deprive them of the advantages they reaped. A plot therefore was pretended, in which the English, with the assistance of a few Japanese (was spelled Japonese) soldiers, were to siege the fortress, and put the Dutch to the sword. Where upon they were seized and examined, but stiffly denying the fact, they were tortured most barbarously. This produced, what the rack almost always does produce, a confession; hereupon Ten Englishmen, seven of whom were agents, factors and assistants were ordered to be executed, Feb 1623. Six Japanese, and three natives, who all uniformly denied their knowledge of the plot to the last moment."- The Dutch account transmitted to the East-India Company

Charles I (1625-1649)

Charles was not raised to be King, his older brother Henry was supposed to have inherited the crown and there is no doubt that history would have been very different. Henry was everything that Charles was not. Henry was beloved by all of England. He was a great scholar, sure of himself and his position, and raised to Rule. Henry also had the great ability of fairness and righteousness, as well as a way to persuade the people to want to please him.

Charles was weak, easy influenced and unfortunately he was stubborn. He believed in the divine rights of Kings and although he would try to please, he also had a quick temper and when Charles believed that he was right and others were wrong he was unbending.

Charles was very loyal in his faith, although some say that he converted to the Catholic faith shortly before his execution, Charles was very loyal and strict. King Charles II and Henry of Gloucester are reliable resources of his faith and despite accounts of his conversion and the fear of Parliament and people that he could be swayed by his catholic Queen Henrietta Marie.

Prince Henry and Charles both refused to attend mass with her or to even consider the Catholic religion. Henry stating that it was his Father's last request that he should never take up the Catholic faith nor that he wear a crown while his brothers live. This request before his Fathers execution was adhered to throughout Henry's life and the reason that the relationship with his mother did not exist. Queen Henrietta Maria failing in every attempt to convert the young Henry she told him, "She would no more own him as her son." And she "commanded him out of her presence, and forbade him anymore to set foot into her lodgings." Henry then knelt and asked for her blessing in which she refused him. This was the last time the Queen ever saw her son.

The beginnings of the English Civil Wars

It is my opinion- and I believe many will agree that King Charles' fate was sealed when he signed the death warrant of his friend Lord Strafford. Charles having given into the demands of Parliament against his own conscience. 'He unknowingly at that moment, signed his own death warrant.'

There are many accounts of this written in history. Some of them agree with one another and some have completely different perspectives. In exploring these accounts one might find the truth. Or rather I should say, the truth that they believe. I know that everyone has their own opinion of 'truth' -this is only mine. I want to lay out some of the key players- those I call the sacrificial lambs of King Charles' reign. The victims of Parliaments thirst for blood in their much fought for war of power.

I honestly do not believe that any man intended this war without an enemy to go as far as it did. Ending with a headless King. Ending up with the tyrannical leader Oliver Cromwell.

In 1641 and travel through King Charles' monarchy. The first key player was probably the Archbishop Laud. Was he truly guilty of treason or just in the way? Was Lord Strafford a pawn played by Parliament to break the King? So many key events in a ten year span that turned England upside down. So much so it has never been the same.

At this time in England, there was a power struggle between the Parliament and King Charles. There is no dispute in history that King Charles was taken by the reins from day one by Parliament. He was not afforded the normal monies or power that every King before him had had. He had to fight and struggle from the first day to the last.

His favorite- Duke of Buckingham whom everyone despised to their great displeasure had Charles' undivided ear. His was the first bloodshed. Buckingham was murdered. That is another story that I am dying to write so I am not going to get into too much detail here. It will take a considerable amount of pages to give accounts of his character and roles from his numerous enemies. Not many people besides King Charles himself thought Buckingham's death a loss. Most probably were relieved to hear of it- some may have actually celebrated.

Why did Charles have to fight for everything much harder than any other King with Parliament? Why did Parliament believe they could actually control this King? It's not as if Charles was a child. Personally- I believe this change relates back to the types of people that his father King James had 'sold' titles too. James 1 in 1611 created a new title- Baronet (Lessor Baron) which he sold for what be an equivalent today of $150,000. These titles were sold to 'gentleman of quality, commoners some being land owners' These titles did not give them peerage however they were considered gentleman and addressed as Sir. By elevating their status many were admitted into colleges and some even ran for office. By selling titles he inadvertently admitted into the houses a group of non-aristocrat blood.

By 1640 the land owning class was now represented in the House of Lords. They were being elected to Commons in large numbers, defeating candidates the King supported and vice versa. Unlike Buckingham, Warwick and several others who for centuries fought and stood for King and Country, these people wanted rights. They now had reason to believe you can improve your station in life. They did not necessarily believe that the King "inherited" his Kingdom as Charles Stated in 1649 before he was murdered. They did not agree with the Kings ideas, and those of and many high born families, the truth of Divine Rights.

With divine rights, nothing was open to change, they were not of the religious beliefs that many had throughout the years that it was 'a mortal sin to disobey a sovereigns command'. They wanted more. They were strict in their spiritual beliefs and even broke from the Church of England.

From 1628 to 1640 Charles reigned free of Parliament, He would not be told by any man what to do.

Charles I said "Howsoever princes are not bound to give an account of their actions but to God alone........"

Edward Hyde, Lord Clarendon wrote at that time: "No man can shew me a source from whence these waters of bitterness we now taste have more probably flowed, than from this unseasonable, unskillful, and precipitate dissolution of Parliament...."

The battle lines have been drawn. Times had most definitely changed. People were not afraid to disobey or even disagree and argue with their King. These people in the houses were not raised to believe in the sovereigns divine rights. They wanted equality. Equality in the 17th Century? Yes it was there.

I honestly believe the domino effect leading to the Commonwealth started with James. A lavish lifestyle that was in need of support and the selling of aristocratic titles that brought in a different quality people with beliefs different than any in hundreds of years.

Archbishop Laud I can only say was a devout and fair man in my opinion. His ultimate downfall was his beliefs being so strong and unbending. He believed that no man was above the law, rich or poor. As a matter of fact some historians might say he held the gentry and those powerful more accountable than others. Of course this did not sit well with many members of Parliament. In 1637 he tried to introduce the 'Book of Common Prayer' into Scotland. This did not go well with the Scots. The rebellion from the Scots was astronomical in his ultimate downfall.

The Scottish leaders signed the National Covenant. All of Scotland was in an uproar and vowed to protect their Puritan faith even by force. Scotland then excommunicated and rid itself of every bishop. Soon after this uproar spread into England. Laud was arrested by the House of Commons and sent to the Tower in 1640 where he would sit for four years and was ultimately executed despite all of King Charles' efforts to save him.

The charges brought against Archbishop Laud are as follows:

ON the 25th of February 1641 Mr. Pym carry'd up to the Lords the Articles against Archbishop Laud, which is as follows:

1. 'That he traitorously endeavored to subject the fundamental laws and government against the Kingdom, to introduce arbitrary and tyrannical power; and to that end he wickedly and traitorously advised his Majesty that he might raise money at his own will and pleasure without consent of Parliament, which he affirmed was "warrantable by the Law of God"

2. That for the better accomplishment of his traitorous designs, he had procured sermons to "be preached, printed and published against the authority of Parliament and the laws of the land'.

3. He hath by letters, messages, threats and promises to the judges, prevented the course of justice, whereby several of his majesty's subjects have been deprived of their lawful rights and subjected to his tyrannical will, to their ruin and destruction

4. He hath traitorously and corruptly sold justice in the High Commission Court, hath taken unlawful gifts and bribes, and endeavored to corrupt other courts of justice by advising the King to sell places of judicature contrary to law.

5. He hath traitorously caused a Book of Canons to be composed and published contrary to the Kings prerogative, to the fundamental laws and statues, to the right of Parliament, to the 'property and liberty of the subject sending to publication and to the establishment of vast" unlawfully, presumptuous power in himself and his successors. To which is added a wicked and ungodly oath to be taken by all the clergy men and some laymen.

6. That he traitorously assumes a tyrannical power in ecclesiastical matters, and denied ecclesiastical power to be decided by the crown; which he has exercised to the destruction of Kings liege people.

7. That he traitorously endeavored to alter and subvert Gods true Religion by Law, and instead set up popery, superstition and Idolatry, hath maintained popish doctrines and opinions, established superstitious ceremonies without any warrant by law. Hath cruelly persecuted those who have opposed the same by corporal punishments and imprisonments and unjustly vexed others who refused to conform thereunto by suspension, deprivation, degradation contrary to the law.

8. That to advance his traitorous purpose he intruded on the places of diverse great offices and upon the right of his majesty's subjects, and preferred to great promotions in the church such as

have been popishly affected or otherwise unfound and corrupt in doctrine and manners.

9. For the same traitorous and wicked intention he hath employed such men to be his domestic chaplains, whom he knew to be notoriously dis-attached to the reformed religion and hath them committed the Book by which diverse false and superstitious books have been published.

10. He hath traitorously and wickedly endeavored to reconcile the Church of England with the Church of Rome, and consorted and desired papist priests and Jesuits, has kept secret intelligence with "the Pope of Rome" and permitted the a popish hierarchy to be established in this Kingdom.

11. That he in his own person and other officers by his command, have caused, pious, and orthodox ministers to be silenced, suspended, deprived, degraded, excommunicated, without just cause; hath hindered the preaching of god's word, caused his majesty's loyal subjects to forsake the Kingdom and increased Christian ignorance among the people. That he might affect his own traitorous design of corrupting the true religion here established

12. He hath traitorously endeavored to cause division and discord between the Church of England and other reformed churches, and to that end hath suppressed the Dutch and French Churches in this Kingdom.

13. That he hath maliciously and traitorously plotted and endeavored to stir up War and Enmity between his Majesty's two Kingdoms of England and Scotland; and to that purpose hath labored to introduce into the Kingdom of Scotland False innovations in religion and government, tending all popery and superstition, to great discontent of that nation; and for refusing to submit to such innovations, he did traitorously advise his majesty to reduce them by force of arms. And when pacification was made, he so incensed his majesty against his subjects in Scotland that he then by the advice of his Archbishop enter into an offensive war against them.

14. That to preserve himself from being questioned for these and other traitorous courses he hath labored to subvert the ancient course of Parliamentary Proceedings and falsely and maliciously incensed his Majesty against Parliaments.

In both Clarendon and Echard's histories of England they both declare that Archbishop Laud "had meekness of a dove, the Virtue of a philosopher, the piety of a Saint, the constancy of a martyr, the Charity of a primitive Christian, and the perfection of an Angel.

Parliament saw his as traitorous, having a spell over the King and a singular agenda of causing the Kingdoms ruin: Keep in mind this is the same Parliament that had been picking at King Charles' advisers and friends, even wife, one by one for years. Who had refused monies for an army even they stated, "Was just". They could not control the King as they had hoped. They resorted to picking at him by accusations such as these to his most loyal advisers. Denying him what was due to him by birth. It became a game of power. It became a game of manipulation. It ultimately became a game of life and death.

I think that this event was the undoing of any future negotiations between Parliament and King Charles in the future. Even more so than the devastating loss of Buckingham, King Charles never quite recovered or found peace in the act of Strafford's execution.

Historians and I included can only speculate at how King Charles felt. So I thought it appropriate to include in his own words-how he felt. This is an excerpt from the Kings Book that he composed. Although there has been speculation to the authenticity of the authorship, I believe, and have given a brief description in the biographies section, this is the work of King Charles.

It is believed that he started these manuscripts in 1645 or 1646 and continued them more thoroughly during his imprisonment at Carisbrooke Castle in the Isle of Wight.

The Kings Book: Upon raising Armies against the King

I find that I am at the same point and posture I was, when they forced me to leave Whitehall. What tumults could not do, an Army must; which is but Tumults listed, and enrolled to a better order, but as bad an end: My recess hath given them confidence that I may be conquered.

And so I easily may as to any outward strength, which, God knows, is little or none at all. But I have a soul invincible through God's grace enabling me, here I am sure to be conqueror, if God will give me such a measure of constancy, as to fear him more than man, and to love the inward peace of my conscience, before any outward tranquility.

And must I be opposed with force, because they have not reason wherewith to convince me? O my Soule, be of good courage, they confess their known weakness, as to truth, and Justice, who chose rather to contend by armies, than by arguments.

Is this the reward and thanks that I am to receive for those many Acts of Grace I have lately passed, and for those many indignities I have endured? Is there no way left to make me a glorious King but by my sufferings?

It is a hard and disputable choice for a King that loves his People, and desires their love, either to kill his own subjects, or to be killed by them.

Are the hazards and miseries of Civil War in the bowels of my most flourishing Kingdom, the fruits I must now reap after 17 years living and reigning among them, with such a measure of Justice, peace, plenty, and religion, as all nations about either admired, or envied? notwithstanding some miscarriages in Government, which might escape- rather through ill counsel of some men driving on their private ends, or the peevishness of others envying the public should be managed without them, or the hidden and insuperable necessities of State, then any propensity, I hope, of myself either to injuriousness or oppression. Whose innocent blood during my reign have I shed, to satisfy my lust, anger, or covetousness? What widows or orphans tears can witness against me; the just cry of which must now be avenged with my own blood? For the hazards of war are equal, nor doth the Cannon know any respect of persons.

In vain is my person accepted by a parenthesis of words, when so many hands are armed against me with swords? God knows how much I have studied to see what ground of justice is alleged for this war against me that so I might (by giving just satisfaction) either prevent, or soon end so unnatural a motion; which (to many men) seems rather the productions

Of a surfeit of peace, and wantonness of minds, or of private discontents, Ambition and Faction (which easily find, or make causes of quarrel) than any real obstructions of public Justice, or Parliamentary Privilege.

But this is pretended, and this I must be able to avoid and answer before God in my own conscience, however some men are not willing to believe me, lest they should condemn themselves. When I first withdrew from Whitehall, to see if I could allay the insolence of the Tumults, (the not suppressing of which, no account in Reason can be given, (where an orderly guard was granted) but only to oppressed both mine and the two houses freedom of declaring and voting according to every man's conscience) what obstructions of Justice were there further than this, that what seemed just to one man, might not seem so to another?

Whom did I by power protect against the Justice of Parliament?

That some men withdrew, who feared the partiality of their trial, (warned by My Lord of Strafford's death) while the vulgar threatened to be their Oppressors, and Judgers of their Judges, was from that instinct, which is in all creatures to preserve themselves. If any others refused to appear, where they evidently saw the current of Justice and freedom so stopped and troubled by the rabble, that their lawful Judges either durst not come to the Houses, or not declare their sense with liberty and safety; it cannot seem strange to any reasonable man when the sole exposing them to public odium was enough to ruin them, before their cause could be heard or tried. Had not factious tumults overborne the freedom and honor of the two Houses; had they asserted their justice against them, and made the way open for all the members quietly to come and declare their consciences: I know no man so dear to me, whom I had the least inclination to advise either to withdraw himself, or deny appearing upon their summons, to whose sentence according to law (I think) every subject bound to stand.

Distempers (indeed) were risen to so great a height, for want of timely repressing the vulgar insolences; that the greatest guilt of those which were voted and demanded as delinquents was this, that they would not suffer themselves to be over-awed with the tumults, and their patrons; nor compelled to abet by their suffrages, or presence; the designs of those men who agitated innovations, and ruin, both in Church and State.

In this point I could not but approve their generous constancy and cautiousness ; further then this I did never allow any man's refractoriness against the Privileges and Orders of the Houses ; to whom I wished nothing more, then Safety, Fullness, and Freedom. But the truth is, some men, and those not many, despairing in faire and Parliamentary ways by free deliberations, and votes to gain the concurrence of the major part of Lords and Commons, betook themselves (by the desperate activity of factious tumults) to sift and terrific away all those members whom they saw to be of contrary minds to their purposes. How oft was the business of the Bishops enjoying their Ancient places, and undoubted Privileges in the House of Peers, carried for them by fare the major part of Lords? Yet after five repulses, contrary to all Order and Custom, it was by tumultuary, instigations obtruded again, and by a few carried, when most of the Peers were forced to absent themselves.

In like manner, as the Bill against Root and Branch, brought on by tumultuary clamors, and schismatically terrors, which could never pass, till both Houses were sufficiently thinned and over-awed. To which partiality, while in all reason, justice and religion, My conscience forbids me by consenting to make up their votes to acts of Parliament; I must now be urged with an Army, and constrained either to hazard my own, and my Kingdoms ruin by my defense ; or prostrate my conscience to the blind obedience of those men, whose zealous superstition thinks, or pretends, they cannot do God and the Church a greater service, than utterly to destroy that primitive, Apostolically, and anciently Universal Government of the Church by Bishops.

Which if other men's judgments bind them to maintain, or forbids them to consent to the abolishing of it ; mine much more ; who, besides the grounds I have in my judgment, have also a most strict and indispensable Oath upon My Conscience, to preserve that Order, and the Rights of the Church; to which, most Sacrilegious and abhorred Perjury, most unbecoming a Christian King, should I ever by giving my Consent be betrayed, I should account it infinitely greater misery, then any hath, or can befall me; in as much as the least sin hath more evil in it then the greatest affliction. Had I gratified their Anti-episcopal Faction at first in this point, with my consent, and sacrificed the Ecclesiastical Government, and Revenues, to the fury of their covetousness, ambition, and revenge, I believe they would then have found no tolerable necessity of raising an Army to fetch in, and punish delinquents.

That I consented to the Bill of putting the Bishops out of the House of Peers, was done with a firm persuasion of their contentedness to suffer a present diminution in their rights, and honor for my sake, and the Commonwealth which I was confident they would readily yield unto, rather than occasion (by the least obstruction on their part) any dangers to Me, or to My Kingdome. That I cannot add my consent for the total extirpation of that Government (which I have often offered to all fit regulations) hath so much further tie upon my conscience, as what I think Religious and Apostolically; and so very sacred and divine, is not to be dispensed with, or destroyed, when what is only of civil Favor, and privilege of honor granted to men of that Order, may with their consent, who are concerned in it be annulled.

This is the true state of those obstructions pretended to be in point of Justice and Authority of Parliament; when I call God to witness, I knew none of such consequence as was worth speaking of a War, being only such as Justice, Reason, and Religion had made in my own and other men's Consciences.

Afterwards indeed a great shew of delinquents was made; which were but consequences necessarily following upon mine, or others withdrawing from, or defense against violence: but those could not be the first occasion of raising an Army against me. Wherein I was so far from preventing them, (as they have declared often, that they might seem to have the advantage and Justice of the defensive part, and load me with all the envy and injuries of first assaulting them) that God knows, I had not so much as any hopes of an Army in My thoughts. Had the Tumults been honorably and effectually repressed by exemplary Justice, and the liberty of the Houses so vindicated, that all Members of either House might with Honor and Freedom, becoming such a Senate, have come and discharged their Consciences, I had obtained all that I designed by my withdrawing, and had much more willingly, and speedily returned then I retired; this being My necessity driving, the other my choice desiring.

But some men know, I was like to bring the same judgment and constancy, which I carried with me, which would never fit their designs: and so while they invited me to come, and grievously complained of my absence, yet they could not but be pleased with it:

especially when they had found out that plausible and popular pretext of raising an Army to fetch in delinquents: when all that while they never punished the greatest and most intolerable delinquencies of the Tumults, and their exciters, which drove myself and so many of both Houses from their places, by most barbarous indignities, which yet in all reason and honor, they were as loath to have deserted, as those others were willing they should, that so they might have occasion to persecute them with the injuries of an Army, for not suffering more tamely the Injuries of the Tumults.

That this is the true state, and first drift and design in raising an Army against me, is by the sequel so evident, that all other pretenses vanish. For when they declared by Propositions, or Treaties, what they would have to appease them; there was nothing of consequence offered to me, or demanded of me, as any original difference in any point of law, or order of justice. But among other lesser innovations, this chiefly was urged, The Abolition of Episcopal, and the establishment of Presbyterian Government.

All other things at any time propounded were either impertinent as to any ground of a war, or easily granted by me, and only to make up a number, or else they were merely consequential! And accessary, after the war was by them unjustly began.

I cannot hinder other men's thoughts, whom the noise and shew of piety, and heat for reformation and religion, might easily so fill with prejudice, that all equality and clearness of judgment might be obstructed. But this was, and is, as to my best observation, the true state of affairs between us, when they first raised an Army, with this design, either to stop my mouth, or to force my consent: and in this truth, as to my conscience, (who was (God knows) as far from meditating a war, as I was in the eye of the world from having any preparation for one) I find that comfort, that in the midst of all the unfortunate successes of this war, on me side, I do not think my innocence any whit prejudiced or darkened.

Nor am I without that integrity, and peace before God, as with humble confidence to address my prayer to him.

For Thou, O Lord, sees clearly through all the clouding's of humane affaires; Thou judges without prejudice: Thy omniscience eternally guides thy inerrable judgment.

O my God, the proud are risen against me, and the assemblies of violent men have sought after my soul, and have not set Thee before their eyes. Consider my enemies, O Lord, for they are many, and they hate me with a deadly hatred without a cause. For Thou knows, I had no passion, design or preparation to embroil My Kingdoms in a Civil War; whereto I had least temptation; as knowing I must adventure more than any, and could gain least of any by it. Thou, O Lord, art my witness how oft I have deplored, and studied to divert the necessity thereof, wherein I cannot well be thought so prodigally thirsty of my Subjects blood, as to venture my own life, which I have been oft compelled to do in this unhappy war; and which were better spent to save then to destroy my people. O Lord, I need much of thy grace, with patience to bear the many afflictions thou hast suffered some men to bring upon me; but much more to bear the unjust reproaches of those, who not content that I suffer most by the war, will needs persuade the world that I have raised first, or given just cause to raise it.

The confidence of some men's false tongues is such, that they would make me almost suspect my own innocence: Yea, I could be content (at least by my silence) to take upon me so great a guilt before men, If by that I might allay the malice of my enemies, and redeem my People from this miserable war; since thou O Lord knows my Innocence in this thing.

Thou wilt find out bloody and deceitful men; many of whom have not lived out half their days, in which they promised themselves the enjoyment of the fruits of their violent and wicked counsel. Save, O Lord, thy servant, as hitherto thou hast, and in thy due time scatter the people that delight in war.

Arise O Lord, lift up thy self, because of the rage of mine Enemies, which increased more and more. Behold them that have conceived mischief, travelled with iniquity, and brought forth falsehood. Thou knows the chief design of this war is, either to destroy my Person, or force my Judgment, and to make me renege my conscience and thy truth.

I am driven to cross David's choice and desire, rather to fall into the hands of men, by denying them, (thought their mercies be cruel) then into thy hands by sinning against my Conscience, and in that against thee, who art a consuming fire; better they destroy me, then thou should damn me. Be thou ever the defense of my soul, who will save the upright in heart.

If nothing but my blood will satisfy my enemies, or quench the flames of my Kingdoms, or thy temporal Justice, I am content, if it be thy will, that it be shed by mine own subjects hands. But o let the blood of me, though their King, yet a sinner, be washed with the blood of my innocent and peace-making redeemer, for in that thy Justice will find not only a temporary expiation, but an eternal plenary satisfaction; both for my sins, and the sins of my people; whom I beseech thee still own for thine, and when thy wrath is appeased by my death, O remember thy great mercies toward them, and forgive them! O my Father, for they know not what they do.

The Kings Book: Upon the Seizure of the Kings property:

> How untruly I am charged with the first raising
> of an Army, and beginning this Civil War,
> the eyes that only pity me, and the loyal hearts
> that durst only pray for me, at first, might witness,
> which yet appear not so many on my side, as there
> were men in Arms listed against me;
> My unpreparedness for a War may well dishearten those
> that would help me; while it argues (truly) my
> unwillingness to fight; yet it testifies for me, that I am
> set on the defensive part; having so little hopes or power
> to offend others, that I have none to defend myself, or
> to preserve what is mine own from their proration.

Thomas Wentworth, Lord Strafford, 1st Earl of Strafford – A dear and trusted friend to Charles I whose loyalty is unquestionable. Lord Strafford had been for 8 years the 'Lord Deputy of Ireland'. He was summoned back to England in 1640 to be Charles' leading adviser. He was ultimately the sacrificial lamb for a blood thirsty House of Commons. The House of Commons and Parliament had already gone after 12 bishops, imprisoned Archbishop Laud, tried to impeach the Queen and now their eyes are turning towards Strafford. My second part of this series is going to focus on Lord Strafford. His career in Ireland and in England. His relationship with both Parliament and King Charles. His beliefs and his execution.

War and Ship money was at the center of the controversy-

Religion, the houses were very afraid of the Kings Catholic wife Queen Henrietta, thinking she could sway either Charles of a future King. All of this was a growing concern in England. Although Charles himself never confessed to be Catholic, many wondered where his true beliefs lie. King Charles was at odds with both the Scots and the Irish. King Charles needed to wage a war against the Scots and also against Ireland. Much needed was funds for ships and his armies, but without the permission of the House of Commons and that of the Parliament he was hopeless. He had no choice but to go to them for assistance. At the same time the house had already charged and issued warrants for some of his most trusted supporters. King Charles had little trust and faith in his Parliament or so called trusted advisers at the time. The few he trusted becoming victims of the houses themselves such as Lord Digby, Lord Wallis, and as mentioned above-Archbishop Laud. This effectively removed them as advisers from King Charles- Parliaments main grievance against these men. Most of these were trumped charges. For example, they could not charge Laud with 'treason"- that was a crime against a monarch. So for the first time in history, a charge that had not existed before, they charged him as 'treasonous'- an act of treason against country.

The Parliament was called once again. In both Lawrence Echard's History of England and also Edward Hyde, 1st Earl of Clarendon their historical accounts are as follows. These are verified through documents and records of the House of Lords, Commons

There was no breaking up of the Parliament while the Scots Army was in England, which at that time occupied some of the Northern parts of England. The Scots were in no great hurry to return to Scotland either. The court was advised according to Echert "to swim with the stream, and for once to try the effect of popular councils," which Echert says "was an infirm Piece of Policy; for politics is as to think the love of the people a weakening of the Prince; There was no surer way to make him beloved, than to employ those whom the people loved." Parliament truly believed if they could make King Charles feel they were on his side while at the same time encouraging and admitting 'beloved' gentry into the council they would have the upper hand of both the King and the people.

The Earl of Bedford, the Earl of Essex, The Earl of Warwick and Lord Say, were then sworn into the Privy Council to advise King Charles. According to Echert History of England: "They soon showed how unfit they were to have seats at that Board, by telling the King," They ought not to give him any advice- which was disagreeable to the sense of Parliament his great council." They were considered weak. Parliaments plan to admit loyal advisers, although fearful ones, into the Kings council backfired. They would not give King Charles ANY advice. They would not advise against their conscience.

The historian Echert writes "Counseling the King to be only advised by two houses." Which he thought was ridiculous but then goes onto write "If the King had any interest separate from that of the people, he is in the right to unseat those Lords of the Privy Council for giving him such advice. But if the Kings interest and his peoples are inseparable, as common sense teaches one, then the Advice of his Parliament could be the only sure foundation for his majesty to build upon."

Here is my opinion on this: The Parliament takes a few advisers whose families have been loyal and trustworthy to the Kings of England for hundreds of years- making the King feel like he has a trustworthy council for a change. These were loyal men. Parliament put them in a position to advise them hoping they would be more favorable for Parliaments side than his former advisers.

Those former advisers having proved to be unbending and responsible for dissolving Parliament and having no use for them. This being done at a time when those same advisers to King Charles are being attacked and charged with treason or some other charges that landed them in the tower. These men were obviously aware of that fact. So what do these loyal men do? They advise the King to not listen to them. This of course upsetting Parliament.

Our wonderful historians, whom none are completely impartial- write that King Charles has his own agenda, and that his interests must then be "separate of the people." Yet even people in Parliament were in agreement with King Charles. Was this truly about ship monies and armies? Of course not!

In Clarendon's history he writes: "many believed the real necessity of ship-money" and "thought the burden reasonable" One would think if what the King was asking for was necessary and reasonable, why was there such a power war? The Reason: Parliament thought that if they gave the King his much needed army, he would have more power over them.

The King's Book: Upon the Earl of Strafford's Death-

I looked upon my Lord of Strafford as a gentleman whose great abilities might make a prince rather afraid than ashamed to employ him in the affairs of State.

For those were prone to create in him great confidence of undertakings, and this was like enough to betray him to great errors and many enemies; whereof he could not but contract good store, while moving in so high a sphere and with so vigorous a lust, he must needs, as the sun, raise many envious exhalations, which condensed by a popular odium, were capable to cast a cloud upon the brightest merit and integrity.

Though I cannot in my judgment approve all he did, driven, it may be, by the necessities of times and the temper of that people, more than led by his own disposition to any height and rigor of actions; yet I could never be convinced of any such criminousness in him as willingly to expose his life to the stroke of justice, and malice of his enemies.

I never met with a more unhappy conjuncture of affairs than in the business of that unfortunate Earl; when between my own unsatisfaction in conscience, and a necessity, as some told it, of satisfying the importunities of some people, I was persuaded by those that I think wished me well to choose rather what was safe than what seemed just, preferring outward peace of my kingdoms with men before that inward exactness of conscience before God.

And, indeed, I am so far from excusing or denying that compliance on my part (for plenary consent it was not) to his destruction, whom in judgment I thought not by any clear law, guilty of death. That I never bare any touch of conscience with greater regret; which, as a sign of my repentance, I have often with sorrow confessed both to God and men as an act of so sinful frailty, that it discovered more a fear of man than of God, whose name and place on earth no man is worthy to bear, who will avail inconveniences of State by acts of so high injustice as no public convenience can expiate or compensate.

I see it a bad exchange to wound a man's own conscience, thereby to solve State sores; to calm the storms of popular discontents by stirring up a tempest in a man's own bosom.

Nor hath God's justice failed in the event and sad consequences to shew the world the fallacy of that maxim. Better one man perish, though unjustly, than the people be displeased or destroyed. For, in all likelihood, I could never have suffered, with my people, greater calamities, yet with greater comfort, had I vindicated Strafford's innocence, at least by denying to sign that destructive Bill, according to that justice which my conscience suggested me to, than I have done since I gratified some men's unthankful importunities with so cruel a favor. And I have observed, that those who counselled me to sign that Bill have been so far from receiving the rewards of such ingratiating's with the people, that no men have been harassed and crushed more than they. He only hath been least vexed by them who counselled me not to consent against the vote of my own conscience. I hope God hath forgiven me and them the sinful rashness of that business.

To which being in my soul so fully conscious, those judgments God hath pleased to send upon me are so much the more welcome, as a means, I hope which his mercy hath sanctified so to me as to make me repent of that unjust act, (for so it was to me,) and for the future to teach me that the best rule policy is to prefer the doing of justice before all enjoyments, and the peace of my conscience before the preservation of my kingdoms.

Nor hath anything more fortified my resolutions against those violent importunities which since have sought to gain a like consent from me to acts wherein my conscience is unsatisfied, than the sharp touches I have had for what passed me in my Lord of Strafford's business.

Not that I resolved to have employed him in my affairs, against the advice of my Parliament; but I would not have had any hand in his death, of whose guiltlessness I was better assured than any man living could be.

Nor were the crimes objected against him so clear, as after a long and fair hearing to give convincing

The Short Parliament of 1640-

One of Thomas Wentworth, Lord Strafford's main enemies was Sir Henry Vane. It was suggested by Lord Clarendon in his History of the Rebellion- Vane and Hamilton's dislike for Strafford at times, and specifically, The Short Parliament session unintentionally betrayed the King.

Sir Henry Vane was a member of the Privy Council and a great favorite of the Queen Henrietta Marie. It is no secret that King Charles gave into her wishes often and as a result Vane was elevated to Secretary of State in Feb. 1640. Strafford opposed this which added to this personal feud. To add fuel to the fire Strafford continued to make enemies in England. He had made a comment to the King about Holland, "That the King would do well to cut off his head". The Marquis of Hamilton "regarded him with distrust, if not with dislike" Says Clarendon. Lastly Clarendon states "He had an enemy more terrible than all the others, and like to be more fatal- the whole Scottish Nation, provoked by the declaration he had procured of Ireland"

Weather King Charles realized it or not his Privy Council was at odds with each other. Two of Strafford's enemies seated beside him. Other notable members of the Privy Council were Laud, Cottington and the Earl of Northumberland. I am not certain your opinion of this but I personally believe that did not run like a well-oiled machine. Weather it had anything 'Significant' to do with the Kings downfall can be debated.

One significant incident comes to mind and that was the dismissing of the "short" Parliament. I discussed this briefly in part one. There was a large majority of Parliament members that were in favor and more than likely would have voted in favor of the King.

What happened in the short Parliament is a mystery and will probably always remain that way. There are many accounts of what happened. We do know two things that has been documented and I believe everyone agrees upon.

1. Charles sincerely desired coming to terms with his Parliament.
2. There is significant evidence a majority of that Parliament also wanted to come to terms with King Charles.

So if both sides were both desirous of reaching an agreement what went terribly wrong that king Charles walked into Parliament the morning of May 5, 1640 and dissolved it.

The day before King Charles dissolved the Short Parliament Hyde (Clarendon) rose and spoke in favor of the king's proposal, knowing some did not want to completely give into the kings demands but would be favorable towards a compromise. Clarendon said: "those who desired to give the king a supply, though in not such a proportion, nor it may be that matter" The form of his question was disputed, So he proposed: "to the end that every man might frankly give his yes or his no, that the question might be put only upon the giving the king a supply; which if carried in the affirmation, another question might be put upon the proportion and the manner." THIS was acceptable! This would have granted the King his supply! Clarendon later writes had this been voted- "for its immediate purpose of securing the assent of a majority of the House to a course witch at any rate would have left the door open to an amicable settlement." It was generally believed that had the question been put and carried in the affirmative, and had not sir Henry Vade stood up and not said these words. There is no doubt in my mind at that our historical testimonies of the 17th century would be in a positive light that day. Instead, these events brought the commons to a standstill and ultimately it was dissolved and a civil war was brewing.

Sir Henry Vane ~ "It has always been my custom to deal plainly and clearly with this house in all things. I can now but assure you that the putting and carrying that question could be of no use; I am most sure and have the authority to tell you so. If you pass a vote for giving the king a supply, if it is not in the proportion and manner proposed in his majesties message it cannot be accepted by him and therefore desire that question might be laid aside"

Ok, yes this was recorded by Edward Hyde, Lord Clarendon in his famous history. Yes- Mr. Hyde was the speaker of the question that Sir Vane laid aside. So it could very easily be argued there is a personal conflict in Clarendons writing on this particular event. I would agree; if several others had not stated the same account. Strafford for one, accused Vane of "misleading the commons and misleading his majesty of the commons" Vane was eventually dismissed from the Kings Privy Council and relieved of his title of Secretary of State.

It has been said that evening Vane went to King Charles and told him that the house was against him and they were not going to vote favorably towards him. Strafford could not counter his claims because he was unfortunately laid up in bed and had little to do with these meetings. What if he had been there?

What truly happened in this 3 week short Parliament we will never completely know. What we do know is the King was not granted these funds at this time and shortly after was force to recall them in what was called The Long Parliament.

The Battle of Edgehill: October 23, 1642-

England's war against the King and his belief of Divine Rights. A war of Parliament and Crown. The first battle of many in what is now known as the English Civil Wars. A battle that has divided historians today the same as it had 372 years ago divided the many participants who took arms. Who took arms and sides in a divided cause against their own kin. A War of Father against Son, Brother against Brother and Friends opposing Friend.

It would be wonderful to be able to go back in time and do a few interviews and ask the question "Why did you chose to fight for this side?" We today can only speculate as to each individuals reasoning for being on whatever side they chose. Some who fought for the Royalists (The Cavaliers) fought out of loyalty for their King, as many generations before them had. Loyalty was honor. Some took arms for the Parliamentary side for religious reasons. Fearing that King Charles had Catholic sympathies. Many will say some fought for the side they thought would win. King Charles himself believed if he could grow a strong enough army he would be able to sway soldiers onto his side. Whatever the reasons, there are so many factors, many were confused as to the actual reasons these wars began.

It has been said of the Civil Wars, it was a war "few men welcomed and fewer understood." To try to sum it up, I would have to say it was a private battle between Parliament and King. A King who whole-heartedly believed in Divine Rights. Who believed no one could tell the King his limits, he ruled by God's Grace alone. A Parliament who he had made concessions too that never seemed satisfied. A group of Puritans who ruled Parliament that King Charles thought was, in today's terms, a radical and unruly group whom he would never be able please- so he sought control them by force.

On the evening of October 22, 1642- by accidental mistake it was discovered the Parliamentary Army was at the Kings door. King Charles' army stood ready for battle the next morning. King Charles rode before his troops wearing an ermine robe over his battle armor shortly before 2pm and addressed his soldiers.

"Friends and soldiers! You are called Cavaliers and Royalists in a disgraceful sense... Now show yourselves no malignants, but declare what courage and fidelity is within you. Fight for the peace of the Kingdom and the Protestant religion. The value of the Cavaliers hath honored that name both in France and other countries, and now let it be known in England, as well as horseman and trooper. The name of Cavalier, which our enemies have striven to make odious, signifies no more than a gentleman serving his King on horseback. Show yourselves, therefore, now courageous Cavaliers, and beat back all opprobrious aspersions cast upon you." King Charles, Edgehill

A small exchange of artillery started off the battle shortly after 2pm. Round one was given to the Parliament army. However, Dragoons were then soon embedded in a skirmish from both sides, which was bested by the royalist's army. Prince Rupert leading his men on, riding from one to the other giving his men orders to " March as close as possible keeping their ranks with sword in hand, to receive the enemy's shot without firing either carbine or pistol, till we break in amongst the enemy and then make use of our firearms as need should require" The Prince then took his place at the head of the right hand army, with approximately 1,400 troops he deployed into two lines. The second line to remain in reserve. Rupert led the front line in advance. Starting with a walk that progressed to a jog and then a full charge run. Swords drawn and firearms raised Rupert shouted a battle cry " THE KING AND THE CAUSE" The Parliamentarian Army with the Cavaliers charging towards them in what was a 'demonic force' was a remembrance of what had happened only days earlier at Powic Bridge, where the cavaliers slaughtered the rebels. The Parliamentary Army pulled back in what could be considered a panic. The retreating soldiers some say and it has been recorded "retreated all the way to St Albans some 40 miles away"

Wilmot's front line of the Royalist Army also devastated and out power ranked their opponents with catastrophic results. The Parliamentary Army was in flight. The battle given to the Cavaliers, the Royalist and of course the King found Victory.

What happens later is of little effect, little actual evidence and perhaps even a bit exaggerated. The truth of the matter we will never really know. I am only including it for what I call an "ah ha" moment. A little unknown fact of history that we didn't know until now.

It was said that against Rupert's clear instructions the Cavaliers charged forward, the Royalist commanders- sir John Byron and Lord Digby eager to be in at the kill. Some say Rupert was at the head of these blood crazed men urging them on. The Plunderer-in-chief. NOTE: There is no actual evidence Rupert himself participated in this 'Plundering' there are accounts that Rupert urged his men to return with him to the battlefield.

The Ah ha moment? It was here, with Rupert's alleged conduct, the word Plunder was introduced to England. "Many towns and villages he plundered, wrote May, which is to say robbed for at that time was the word first used in England, being born in Germany when that stately country was so miserably wasted and pillaged y foreign armies, and committed to outrages upon those who stood affected to the Parliament, executing some and hanging servants at their masters doors for not discovering of their masters. (May, History of the Long Parliament)

As with all historians my version of events will vary with others. Some call it a draw, that there was no actual victor. I on the other hand will hands down give this battle to the King and his army of Cavaliers. The amount of casualties has also been debated over the last 372 years. It is estimated somewhere between 1,500-3,000 men. I believe the number to be on the higher side given that the actual combat was given over to flight and therefore the retreaters were essentially 'slaughtered'.) I might also note that Prince Charles ll was also present at Edgehill, although there is little written of it and doubtful he participated in anyway.

In 1647 the King was betrayed and taken into custody of Oliver Cromwell, or the commonwealth, by Cornet Joyce. At this time the Parliament and all those fighting for Parliament against the King never imagined where it would lead. I think it is safe to say, that no one at this time wanted to murder the King.

On June 3, Joyce appeared at Holby. It seems there he received news 'which led him to think that a Presbyterian body of troops was approaching to take custody of the Kings person." Late in the evening him "foreseeing that the dangers and instructions from Cromwell have arrived" There is some dispute as to whether Cromwell actually ordered the King to be taken into custody, however, he seemed delighted he had been afterwards.

Charles the next morning "stepping out on the lawn, asked Joyce for a sight of commission which authorized him to give such orders. Joyce replied, "This is my answer" Pointing towards his soldiers.

King Charles was betrayed again when he had escaped to Carisbrooke Castle seeking the assistance of Colonel Hammond. The King and Cromwell not coming to any truce, Charles had started to hear officers talking about 'Bringing the King to Justice for his crimes," The King fled to the Isle of Wight. It is assumed and more than likely true that his escape was instigated by Cromwell himself to put the King in bad light, not able to be trusted, so that it would sway the mind of Parliament they will never control the King.

King Charles was at this time secretly conspiring with the Scots, Rupert and in close communications with many people. All the while Parliament was in negotiations with him. Ireton drew up an agreement call 'The heads of Proposals' it provided for a constant succession of biennial Parliament. Giving complete religious liberty to all but Catholics. And another article drawn up "The Agreement of the People."

Charles grew more and more hostile towards Cromwell every day and on Dec. 26, 1647 entered into 'The Engagement' with the Scottish commissioners. The King agreed to Presbyterism in all of England for three years and suppress all heresy. The Scottish army was to advance into England and secure the King's restoration to power with the wishes of a free Parliament chosen after the destruction of the existing one.

The English Parliament had no knowledge of this agreement, however, because Charles refused to accept their term they replied with a vote on January 17, 1648 of No Address. They were done negotiating with the King.

Although the majority of England was willing to take accept the King at his word, many were still worried by the Army he still controlled. There was an insurrection in Wales and in Colchester. The Kings army, led by Hamilton, was defeated by Fairfax on August 28th.

On January 4, 1649 the House of Commons declared, 'The people were, under God, the source of all just power, and that the House of Commons, being chosen by the people formed the Supreme power in England. Having no need of either the King or the House of Lords."

On January 19, a special High Court of Justice was created for the trial of the King. Charles was brought to Westminster. Many lords refusing to sit in the trial. Of the 135 members named only 67 were present when the trial began.

Fairfax was among then appointed but he refused. When his name was called his wife, Anne, called out "He is not here! And will never be; you do wrong to name him." Fairfax did remove himself from Cromwell's service. I think his actions alone prove that he was against Cromwell's decision to put the King on trial. I also personally believe he had deep regret's for his part in it. He was pardoned years later by Charles II for his involvement against the King. Fairfax also refused to sign the death warrant.

The Trial of Charles I
Saturday Jan. 20, 1649

The court being thus seated and silence made, the great gate of the said hall was set open to the end that all persons (without exception) desirous to see or hear might come into it, upon which the hall was presently filled and silence again ordered.

This done, Colonel Thomlinson, who had the charge of the Prisoner, was commanded to bring him to the court, who within a quarter of an hour's space brought him, attended with about twenty officers with partisans marching before him, there being other gentlemen to whose care and custody he was likewise committed marching in his rear.

Being thus brought up within the face of the court, the Sergeant at Arms with his Mace receives and conducts him straight to the Bar, having a crimson velvet chair set before him. After a stern looking upon the court and the people in the galleries on each side of him, he places himself, not at all moving his hat or otherwise showing the least respect to the court, but presently rises up again and turns about, looking downwards upon the guards placed on the left side and on the multitude of spectators on the right side of the said Great Hall.

After silence made among the people, the act of Parliament for the trying of Charles Stuart, King of England, was read over by the Clerk of the Court, who sat on one side of a table covered with a rich Turkey carpet and placed at the feet of the said Lord President, upon which table was also laid the Sword and Mace. After reading the said act, the several names of the commissioners were called over, everyone who was present rising up and answering his call.

Charles, having again placed himself in his chair with his face towards the court, silence being again ordered, the Lord President stood up and said: "Charles Stuart, King of England, the Commons of England being deeply sensible of the calamities that have been brought upon this nation (which is fixed upon you as the principal author of it) have resolved to make inquisition for blood, and according to that debt and duty they owe to justice, to God, the kingdom, and themselves, and according to the fundamental power that rests in themselves, they have resolved to bring you to trial and judgment, and for that purpose have constituted this High Court of Justice before which you are brought."

This said, Mr. Cook, Attorney for the Commonwealth, standing within the Bar on the right hand of the Prisoner, offered to speak, but the King, having a staff in his hand, held it up and laid it upon the said Mr. Cook's shoulder two or three times, bidding him hold. Nevertheless, the Lord President ordering him to go on, Mr. Cook said: "My Lord, I am commanded to charge Charles Stuart, King of England, in the name of the Commons of England, with treason and high misdemeanors. I desire the said charge may be read."

The said charge being delivered to the Clerk of the Court, the Lord President ordered it should be read, but the King bid him hold. Nevertheless, being commanded by the Lord President to read it, the Clerk began:

The Charge of the Commons of England against Charles Stuart, King of England, of High Treason and other high crimes, exhibited to the High Court of Justice.

That the said Charles Stuart, being admitted King of England and therein trusted with a limited power to govern by and according to the laws of the land and not otherwise, and by his trust, oath, and office being obliged to use the power committed to him for the good and benefit of the people and for the preservation of their rights and liberties, yet nevertheless out of a wicked design to erect and uphold in himself an unlimited and tyrannical power to rule according to his will, and to overthrow the rights and liberties of the people, yea to take away and make void the foundations thereof and of all redress and remedy of misgovernment, which by the fundamental constitutions of this kingdom were reserved on the people's behalf in the right and power of frequent and successive Parliaments or National Meetings in Council, he (the said Charles Stuart) for accomplishment of such his designs and for the protecting of himself and his adherents in his and their wicked practices to the same ends, hath traitorously and maliciously levied war against the present Parliament and the people therein represented.

The charge being read, the Lord President replied: "Sir, you have now heard your charge read, containing such matter as appears in it. You find that in the close of it, it is prayed to the court in the behalf of the Commons of England that you answer to your charge. The court expects your answer."

The King: I would know by what power I am called hither. And when I know what lawful authority, I shall answer. Remember, I am your King your lawful King and what sins you bring upon your heads and the judgment of God upon this land, think well upon it. I say think well upon it before you go further from one sin to a greater. Therefore let me know by what lawful authority I am seated here and I shall not be unwilling to answer. In the meantime, I shall not betray my trust. I have a trust committed to me by God, by old and lawful descent. I will not betray it to answer to a new unlawful authority. Therefore, resolve me that, and you shall hear more of me.

Lord President: If you had been pleased to have observed what was hinted to you by the court at your first coming hither, you would have known by what authority. Which authority requires you in the name of the people of England, of which you are the elected King to answer them?

The King: No, sir, I deny that.

Lord President: If you acknowledge not the authority of the court, they must proceed.

The King: I do tell them so England was never an elective kingdom but an hereditary kingdom for near these thousand years. Therefore, let me know by what authority I am called hither. I do stand more for the liberty of my people than any here that come to be my pretended judges. And therefore let me know by what lawful authority I am seated here, and I will answer it. Otherwise, I will not answer it.

Lord President: Sir, how really you have managed your trust is known. Your way of answer is to interrogate the court, which beseems not you in this condition. You have been told of it twice or thrice.

January 22,
Lord President: Sir, you may remember, at the last court you were told the occasion of your being brought hither and you heard a charge against you containing a charge of High Treason and other high crimes against this realm of England. You heard likewise that it was prayed in behalf of the people that you should give an answer to that charge, that thereupon such proceedings might be had as should be agreeable to justice. You were then pleased to make some scruples concerning the authority of the court, and knew not by what authority you were brought hither. You did divers times propound your question and were as often answered that it was by the authority of the Commons of England assembled in Parliament that did think fit to call you to account for those high and capital misdemeanors wherewith you were then charged. Since that, the court hath taken

into consideration what you then said. They are fully satisfied with their own authority and they hold it fit you should stand satisfied with it too, and they do require it that you do give a positive and particular answer to this charge that is exhibited against you. Their authority they do avow to the whole world that the whole kingdom are to rest satisfied with it. And thereunto you are to lose no more time, but give a positive answer thereunto.

The King: When I was here last, 'tis very true I made that question. And truly, if it were only my own particular case, I would have satisfied myself with the protestation I made the last time I was here against the legality of this court and that a King cannot be tried by any superior jurisdiction on earth. But it is not my case alone it is the freedom and the liberty of the people of England. And do you pretend what you will, I stand more for their liberties for if the power without law may make laws, may alter the fundamental laws of the kingdom, I do not know what subject he is in England that can be sure of his life or anything that he calls his own. Therefore, when that I came here I did expect particular reasons to know by what law, what authority, you did proceed against me here. I am your King by what authority to you try me?

Lord President: Sir, you have offered something to the court. I shall speak something unto you that the sense of the court. Sir, neither you nor any man are permitted to dispute that point. You are concluded. You may not demur to the jurisdiction of the court that if you do, I must let you know that they overrule your demurrer. not They sit here by the authority of the Commons of England, and all your predecessors and you are responsible to them.

The King: I deny that. Show me one precedent.

Lord President: Sir, you ought not to interrupt while the court is speaking to you. This point is not to be debated by you, neither will the court permit you to do it. If you offer it by way of demurrer to the jurisdiction of the court, they have considered of their jurisdiction. They do affirm their own jurisdiction.

January 23,

This court took into consideration the managing of the business of the court this day in the hall and the King's refusal to answer (notwithstanding he had been three several times demanded and required thereunto) and have thereupon fully approved of what on the court's part had then passed, and resolved that notwithstanding the said contumacy of the King and refusal to plead (which in law amounts to a standing mute and tacit confession of the charge) and notwithstanding the notoriety of the fact charged, the court would nevertheless, however, examine witnesses for the further and clearer satisfaction of their own judgments and consciences, the manner of whose examination was referred to further consideration [at] the next sitting, and warrants were accordingly issued forth for summoning of witnesses.

January 24th and 25th,

The Prisoner is brought to the Bar, and proclamation is again (as formerly) made for silence, and the Captain of the Guard ordered to take into his custody all such as should disturb the court.

Some discourse was used by the President for vindicating the Parliament's justice, explaining the nature of the crimes of which the Prisoner stood charged, and for which he was to be condemned, and by way of exhortation of the Prisoner for serious repentance of his high transgressions against God and the people and to prepare for his eternal condition.

Lord President: The court then, sir, hath something else to say unto you, which, although I know it will be very unacceptable, yet notwithstanding they are willing and are resolved to discharge their duty.

Sir, the difference has been: who shall be the expositors of this law, sir? Whether you and your party, out of courts of justice, shall take upon them to expound the law, or the courts of justice who are the expounders, nay, the sovereign and highest court of justice, the Parliament of England, that is not only the highest expounder but the sole maker of the law. Sir, for you to set yourself with your single judgment, and those that adhere unto you to set themselves against the resolution of the highest court of justice that is not law. Sir, as the law is your superior, so truly, sir, there is something that is superior to the law and that is indeed the parent or author of the law and that is the people of England. For, sir, as they are those that at the first (as other countries have done) did choose to themselves this form of government, even for justice's sake, that justice might be administered, that peace might be preserved, so, sir, they gave laws to their governors, according to which they should govern. And if those laws should have proved inconvenient or prejudicial to the public, they had a power in them, a power reserved and innate to alter them as they should see cause.

Sir, the term traitor cannot be spared. We shall easily agree it must denote and suppose a breach of trust, and it must suppose it to be done by a superior. And therefore, sir, as the people of England might have incurred that respecting you, if they had been truly guilty of it as to the definition of law, so on the other side when you did break your trust to the kingdom, you did break your trust to your superior. For the kingdom is that for which you were trusted. And therefore, sir, for this breach of trust when you are called to account, you are called to account by your superiors "when a king is summoned to judgment by the people, the lesser is summoned by the greater." And, sir, the people of England cannot be so far wanting to themselves, God having dealt so miraculously and gloriously for them, they having power in their hands and their great enemy, they must proceed to do justice to themselves and to you. For, sir, the court could heartily desire that you would lay your hand upon your heart and consider what you have done amiss, that you would endeavor to make your peace with God.

Truly, sir, these are your high crimes tyranny and treason. And there is a third thing too, if those had not been, and that is murder, which is laid to your charge. All the bloody murders that have been committed since the time that the division was betwixt you and your people must be laid to your charge that have been acted or committed in these late wars. Sir, all I shall say before the reading of your sentence it is but this the court does heartily desire that you will seriously think of those evils that you stand guilty of. Sir, you said well to us the other day, you wished us to have God before our eyes. Truly, sir, I hope all of us have so. That God that we know is a King of Kings and Lord of Lords, that God with whom there is no respect of persons, that God that is the avenger of innocent blood, we have that God before us, that God that does bestow a curse upon them that withhold their hands from shedding of blood, which is in the case of guilty malefactors and those that do deserve death.

The sentence formerly agreed upon and put down in parchment writing was by the court's command solemnly pronounced and given, the tenor whereof followed:

Now, therefore, upon serious and mature deliberation of the premises and consideration had of the notoriety of the matters of fact charged upon him as aforesaid, this court is in judgment and conscience satisfied that he (the said Charles Stuart) is guilty of levying war against the said Parliament and people, and of maintaining and continuing the same, for which in the said charge he stands accused. And by the general course of his government, counsels, and practices, before and since this Parliament began (which have been and are notorious and public, and the effects whereof remain abundantly upon record), this court is fully satisfied in their judgments and consciences that he hath been and is guilty of the wicked designs and endeavors in the said charge set forth; and that the said war hath been levied, maintained, and continued by him as aforesaid, in the prosecution and for the accomplishment of the said designs; and that he hath been and is the occasioned, author, and continuer of the said unnatural, cruel, and bloody wars, and therein guilty of High Treason and of the murders, rapines, burnings, spoils, desolations, damage, and mischief to this nation acted and committed in the said war and occasioned thereby.

For all which treasons and crimes this court doth adjudge that he, the said Charles Stuart, as a tyrant, traitor, murderer, and public enemy to the good people of this nation, shall be put to death by the severing of his head from his body.

Monday, 29 January 1649.
At the High Court of Justice for the trying and judging of Charles Stuart, King of England, and January 29, 1649.

Whereas Charles Stuart, King of England, is and standeth convicted, attainted, and condemned of High Treason and other high crimes, and sentence upon Saturday last was pronounced against him by this court to be put to death by the severing of his head from his body, of which sentence execution yet remained to be done, these are therefore to will and require you to see the said sentence executed in the open street before Whitehall, upon the morrow, being the thirtieth day of this instant month of January, between the hours of ten in the morning and five in the afternoon of the same day, with full effect. And for so doing, this shall be your sufficient warrant. And these are to require all officers, soldiers, and others, the good people of this nation of England, to be assisting unto you in this service.

Given under our hands and seals. (Signed by John Bradshaw, Oliver Cromwell, and 57 other commissioners.)

The death-warrant of King Charles I. The signature of Cromwell is seen on the left, third from the top.

Charles' visit with his Children before his execution a true account of that meeting. This is the visit, an excerpt from my Novel: Secrets of a Princess:

Elizabeth was so overcome with sadness. She had such a terrible tightness from her chest to her belly. It was most painful. She did not want to succumb to tears, not that she wanted to hide the pain that the man of the devil was causing her. To her family and her Father. It was for her Father, she did not want to cause him more pain with her grief. As hard as she tried, she could not help it. Her tears fell freely;

her hands and lips shook uncontrollably.

Her father came to her and picked her up, she clung to him as he sat her upon his knee. Elizabeth touched her Father's face, caressed his cheeks. She wanted to never forget him. He too was clinging to Elizabeth soaking in his daughter with his eyes.

"Darling child, I am so glad that you have come. Please do not grieve and torment thyself darling Elizabeth. "He wiped the tears from her eyes gently and held her more closely to him.

"There is so much to say to you and not time. I fear my child that you will forget"

Elizabeth shook her head as she looked into his eyes. "I will write down all that you say to me, thou I will never forget."-

Her father smiled as he stroked her chestnut hair.

"I have feared the cruelty of our injustice is too great to permit writing. There is much I want to say to you child which I cannot to another."

He wiped the tears from his daughters red teary and swollen face.

"My darling Elizabeth, do not grieve, this is a glorious death. I shall die for the laws and the religion of the land."

Elizabeth wanted to die with him, she held him closer. "Elizabeth, I have forgiven my enemies and pray God will forgive them also. I command that thy children all forgive them."

He lowered his voice so that the other people in the room could not hear. "Do not grieve fair child, Stand strong. And trust in Amice Andros, of Guernsey. He whilst help you child. I desire you to leave this land, for thy are unjust and not with God. Leave Elizabeth go far and not look towards the throne, they meant to have thy family at war within and only our blood to cover thy land."

Elizabeth understood the message he had given her, and he continued in a soft voice as their keepers came closer to hear.

"Tell your mother 'that thy thoughts had never strayed from her, and that thy love for her would be the same to the last;' I command you both to love her and be obedient to her." Elizabeth confirmed that she would.

He pressed into her hand an object, "Do not look now darling, it is a gift, the last gift I shall ever give to you made from thy own hands. Hold dear to your heart darling forever and do not forget, never forget that always shall I be with you. Stand strong Elizabeth and draw courage from me, never falter in thy beliefs that you have been taught, never falter. Trust in God Elizabeth,"

Tears were coming from his face and the spectators around them noticed.

Elizabeth could hear one of the guards say, "throughout, has not shed a tear, and now...."

"Do not grieve for me child, I beg of you darling, I should die a Martyr. Withal I doubt not but God would restore the throne to your brother Charles, and that then you should be all happier than we could possibly have been if I had lived. Pray child, for thy brother Charles."

He kissed her cheeks and her forehead and lifted Elizabeth off his lap as her little brother Gloucester ran forward to take his turn. Her father handed her his Bible, she took it and slipped it along with the object her father had given her into her pocket.

Elizabeth's grief was burning, she did not want to leave, and she wanted to sit on his lap for all eternity and not to leave him. For she knew that this was the last time that she would have happiness at all with him. She was so sad; this was not a happy time and began to cry more.

Elizabeth heard her father speaking "Dear boy, now will they cut off thy father's head.' His tone and manner was much different than with Elizabeth. Elizabeth had always wanted to have that expectation from her father as well.

'Heed, my child, what I say; they will cut off my head, and perhaps make thee a king; but, mark what I say! You must not be a king as long as your brothers Charles and James live; therefore, I charge you, do not be made a king by them. For they will cut off your brothers' heads when they catch them, and cut off thy head too at the last. And therefore I charge you, do not be made a king by them! '

Her brother sighed deeply and replied, 'I will be torn in pieces first.'

Elizabeth was overcome with grief. One of the guards came to her as she began to collapse. The darkness surrounded her she cried, "No! I want to stay, I don't want to leave him!"

CHARLES II: The Merry Monarch

I honestly do not and will never understand why Charles is and was called the merry monarch. There were very few years in his entire life Charles had any reason to be 'Merry"

"The Characcter of the young man, who was emerging from battle his scars – the cynic, the sceptic, the opportunist, who distrusted high sounding as much as he sought to make the most of one night's pleasure- should surprise nobody, unless the surprise is that his spirit was not broken altogether"

Portrait of King Charles I saying farewell to his children, Princess Elizabeth and Prince Henry, Duke of Gloucester before his execution 1649

The Kings Speech at his Execution:

Believe it you will never do right, nor God will never prosper you, until you five God his due, the King his due (that is, my successors) and the People their due, I am as much for them as any of you. You must give God his due by regulating rightly His Church (according to the Scripture) which now out of order. For to set you in a way particularly now I cannot, but only this. A national synod freely called, freely debating among themselves, must settle this, when that every opinion is freely heard.

For the King, indeed I will not, then turning to a gentlemen that touched the Ax, said, hurt not the ax, that may hurt me (meaning if he did blunt the edge) For the King, the laws of the land will clearly instruct you for that. Therefore because it concerns my own particular, I only give you a touch of it.

For the people. And truly I desire their liberty and freedom as much as anybody whomsoever. But I must tell you that their liberty and freedom consists in having of government; those laws by which their life and their goods may be most their own. It is not for having share in government, Sir that is nothing pertaining to them. A subject and a sovereign are clean different things, and therefore until they do that, I mean, that you do put the people in that liberty as I say, certainly they will never enjoy themselves. It was for this that now I am come here. If I would have given way to an arbitrary way, for to have all laws changed according to the power of the sword I needed not to have come here. And, therefore, I tell you, and I pray God it be not laid to your charge, that I am the martyr of the people.

After the Execution of his Father, Charles knew of his father's death when he was addressed as 'Your Highness' and Charles knew his Father had been executed. No one had to tell him, some say he cried and there are others that say he was unaffected- I would like to believe the accounts that he was very upset and swore revenge. What parent wouldn't want a child to say that after the murder of a parent. Unfortunately I doubt that it really the case.

I believe that there is enough correspondence between King Charles I and his Son Charles II to believe they did have a love for each other. I also think it fair to say there is a probability that the letter that Charles was to have sent Oliver Cromwell, "a blank sheet with only a signature so that as Cromwell could name his terms of the Kings life" may have actually been true.

There is an account of writer James Heath in those times, who was a companion and spent time with Prince Rupert that the letter was actually from the Prince Rupert and not Prince Charles.

I do think that could very well be, Prince Rupert was much closer to Charles that his son. This more than likely because Prince

Charles really had not known his Father. The Civil wars and the King being exiled created a relationship gap that was not the fault of either of them.

Charles writes very often of his love for his children and that of his wife as well. There are also many accounts of King Charles speaking of his Children. And Even visiting, princess Elizabeth and Prince Henry at Penhurst Palace, 'every week'. While they were all prisoners of Cromwell.

It seems that King Charles II did make a very good effort to regain his throne. Cromwell was busy in Ireland dealing with a rebellion. Ormond who was a protestant had left Ireland, and handed over Dublin to the Parliamentary forces in 1647. The Irish tried to resist the English Commonwealth.

Records show that both Prince Rupert and Prince Maurice had visited Ireland in 1650. Shortly after that Rupert was trapped in Lisbon by Cromwell's Admiral Blake. Who had sat at the mouth of the river and then entered under the orders that Prince Rupert was under the King of Portugal's protection.

Oliver Cromwell had declared England 'The Commonwealth of England in an act of Parliament making England a Republic. He was soon named the 'Lord Protector.' Thomas Fairfax had resigned his commission and Cromwell placed himself at the Head of the Army as well, going on to defeat Charles II. He took victories in both the Battle of Dunbar and Worchester.

The Act of Parliament Passed May 19, 1649

Be it Declared and Enacted by this present Parliament and by the Authority of the same, That the People of England, and of all the Dominions and Territories thereunto belonging, are and shall be, and are hereby Constituted, Made, Established, and Confirmed to be a Commonwealth and Free-State: And shall from henceforth be Governed as a Commonwealth and Free-State, by the Supreme Authority of this Nation, The Representatives of the People in Parliament, and by such as they shall appoint and constitute as Officers and Ministers under them for the good of the People, and that without any King or House of Lords.

Charles II could not find any other means of support to fight the Commonwealth. Against the protests of his friends Charles decided to go along with the demands of the Scots if he could gain their support in waging a battle in England against the now called "Lord Protector." Oliver Cromwell. -

The History of the Rebellion, Lord Clarendon

The Commonweath of England

Charles went to Scotland in 1650, after James Graham, the Marquis of Montrose had already left to make negotiations with the Scot's. Unknowing to either Montrose or Charles the Scot's had their own plans. Knowing that the young King was at their Mercy for his Crown. The Scot's seized Montrose, who had waged a battle on behalf Of Charles II. Unknowing that the King had made his own negotiations with the Scot's. It is said that Charles had sent a letter to Montrose to desist. Other historians say that Charles allowed Montrose to be a pawn in negotiations. Personally, I believe that the Scots knew the King was at their mercy and used Montrose as a way to show him that. A month after Montrose' death, the Scots had Charles staying in Edinburgh, where his friends head was displayed on a pike.

Execution of James Graham, Montrose
In the two days after his being captured, he was brought before the Parliament, and bitterly reviled by the earl of Loudon the chancellor. Who upbraided him with having broken the covenants, rebelling against God, the king, and the kingdom, and committed many horrible murders, treasons, and impieties. He told them, that as the king had condescended to treat with them, he would behave

towards them with more reverence than he should otherwise have expressed for such an assembly.

He said he had taken and kept the first covenant, while they prosecuted the purposes for which it was ordained; that he had never subscribed the second, which was productive of the most monstrous rebellion; that he had raised forces by virtue of his majesty's commission, and acted like a faithful subject, without perpetrating those cruelties that were laid to his charge, or suffering any blood to be shed but in battle; on the contrary, he had always put a stop to the carnage as soon as he possibly could take such a step with any regard to his own safety, and had saved the lives of many persons. Then present, to whose evidence he appealed. He observed, that he had laid down his arms, and quitted the kingdom at his late master's command, that he had now he was returning to Scotland.   He advised them to consider the consequence of proceeding against him in this manner, and demanded a fair trial by the laws of the land, or by the law of nations. He was condemned to be hanged next day on a gallows thirty feet high; and the sentence implied, that he should be afterwards quartered, and his members exposed in different parts of the kingdom. During this short interval, he was persecuted by their ministers, who told him, his sufferings in this. Life would be but an easy prologue to those which he would undergo hereafter and, without scruple, pronounced his eternal damnation.

He heard them with scorn, observing, that they were a miserable, deluding and deluded people, and would mostly bring that poor nation to the most insupportable servitude, He declared, he was as well pleased to hear that his head should be placed on the Tolbooth, as he should be to know that his picture hung in the king's bed-chamber and wished he had flesh enough to be distributed among all the cities of Christendom, as a testimony of the cause for which he suffered.

At the place of execution, the hangman tied about his neck, with a cord, an elegant Latin book, containing the history of his exploits, written by Dr. Wishart, who had been his chaplain. He smiled at this mark of impotent malice, saying, he was prouder of that collar than ever he had been of the garter. He demeaned himself with undaunted courage, and the most pious resignation. He expatiated on the virtues of his murdered master; spoken praise of the justice and goodness of the present king, and fervently prayed that they might not betray him as they had betrayed his father. After some devout ejaculations, he cheerfully submitted to the sentence, which was executed with every circumstance of barbarous exultation.

Such was the ignominious death of James Graham, marquis of Montrose, a nobleman of illustrious birth, unspotted faith, amazing courage, and incredible courage. He possessed the romantic virtues of heroism "above all his contemporaries. He thirsted after glory with the greediest appetite: he seemed insensible of danger; and thinking himself equal to the most arduous enterprise, achieved a series of the most surprising adventures. Thirty of the officers taken with Montrose, were executed in different parts of the kingdom; and, among these, colonel Urrey, who had shifted sides so often, as some men do, since the beginning of the troubles. Colonel Whiteford saved his own life by saying, when he was brought to the place of execution, that he was to suffer for no other reason, but because he had slain Doriflaus, who was concerned in the murder of the late king.

The magistrate then present suspended the execution, in order to report this expression to the council, who thought proper to avoid reproach, by sparing the colonel's life.

Charles II in Scotland and the Battle of Dunbar

After the death of Montrose, the king finding himself absolutely without other resource, subscribed the terms which the Scottish commissioners had presented, embarked at Scheveling, (the port of the Hague) with the earl of Lanark, now duke of Hamilton, and his kinsman the earl of Lauderdale, who were obnoxious to the rigid Presbyterians, that when they arrived in Scotland, they found it necessary to retire to their respective houses for their personal safety. The king was obliged to sign the covenant, before the Scots would allow him to set his foot on shore.

Then the marquis of Argyle received him with demonstrations of the most profound respect: but all his English domestics of any quality, were removed from his person, except the duke of Buckingham. Daniel O Neal was apprehended, as an Irishman who had been in arms for the late king, and banished from Scotland by order of the council : and they dismissed Mr. Robert Long, principal secretary of state, Sir Edward Walker clerk of the council, and many other servants, whose places they supplied with rigid covenanters.

He was surrounded, and incessantly importuned by their clergy, who came to instruct him in religion; obliged to give constant attendance church he was to pray and admit the tyranny of his father, the idolatry of his mother, and his own malignant disposition.

They insisted upon his observing Sunday as the most rigorous fast of a Jewish Sabbath; they kept a strict watch upon his looks and gestures; and, if ever he chanced to smile during this religious mummery, he underwent a severe reprimand for his profanity. With respect to the external appearances of royalty, he had no occasion to complain.

He lived in great state and plenty, was well attended, and served with marks of deference and submission; but debarred all exercise of regal power, and restricted in every article of private satisfaction.

The marquis of Argyle at first strove to ingratiate himself with Charles, indifferently and by the most complaisant deportment, and such entertaining conversation as he thought would be agreeable to his majesty but, when the king hinted the desire of effecting an union between him and Hamilton, he appeared extremely averse to the idea of such a coalition, and gradually withdrew himself from all communication with his sovereign, whom he now suspected of a design to accomplish his destruction by means of his inveterate rival.

The English Parliament, alarmed at the treaty of Breda, as supposing that the king would employ an army of Scots to recover the crown of England, resolved to anticipate the danger, by carrying the war immediately into Scotland, whither, in all probability, they were invited by the marquis of Argyle; and for this purpose they recalled Cromwell from Ireland, which by this time was almost wholly subdued.

The marquis of Ormond was disabled from opposing him effectually, by the dissensions that prevailed among the Irish. Monk, after a long imprisonment, had been persuaded to engage in the service of the Parliament, and now acted as one of-their generals, under Cromwell. He concluded a peace with O Neal, which was authorized by a council of state; but the Parliament having refused to ratify it, as being too favorable to the Catholics, O'Neal began to treat with Ormond; and was on the point of joining that nobleman, when his purpose was prevented by death: then his troops dispersed of then- own accord.

Meanwhile Cromwell reduced Kilkenny, with many other places, and prosecuted his conquests with surprising rapidity. That the Irish might not have opportunities to compromise their differences, and unite against him, he, by proclamation, permitted their officers to ate' enlist as many soldiers as they could engage in foreign service, and assured them that they should depart unmolested. Above five and twenty thousand immediately took the advantage of this permission, and entered into the service of France; so that all opposition was subdued.

When he took his seat in the house, the speaker thanked him for the services he had done the commonwealth: then they proceeded to deliberate upon the war with Scotland. They desired to know if Fairfax would conduct that enterprise. He knew they did not much depend upon his attachment, and that this was no other than a bare compliment.

He therefor sent his commission to the commons, who gratified him with a pension of five thousand pounds, and appointed Oliver Cromwell general of the forces of the commonwealth.

As the royalists and Presbyterians exclaimed against the injustice of this war, the house appointed a committee to draw up a declaration, in which they supposed the Scots intended to rule the throne of England, though they had not as yet signified any such intention.

They had indeed begun to levy some troops; and they were no sooner informed of the English preparations, than they redoubled their diligence in assembling an army, the command of which they bestowed upon Lesley earl of Leven. Argyle, in modelling this army, excluded all officers and soldiers who were suspected of having a warm side to the royal cause. Commissions were granted to none but rigid Presbyterians, who were generally destitute of courage and discipline.

They were at that time directed by a committee of the kirk and state. The ministers encouraged them to be committed and to be with long prayers, and preached with equal bitterness against the vices of the court, and the impiety of Cromwell. They promised victory with as much confidence as they could have expressed, if they had been actually inspired.

With great difficulty they consented to the king's seeing the army; but perceiving the soldiers were pleased with the sight of their sovereign, they removed him to a greater distance, declaring that the soldiers were too much inclined to put their confidence in the arm of flesh, whereas their hope and dependence ought to be in the prayers and piety of the kirk.

Cromwell, in about mid-July, at the head of an army amounting to eighteen thousand men, began his march for the Scottish border, where he published his manifesto, and understood that the Scots were encamped, to the number of eight and twenty thousand men, well-armed and equipped, in the neighborhood of Edinburgh. They had ordered all the people to quit the country between Berwick and the capital, and remove their effects so that Cromwell advanced without opposition through a desolate country, attended by a fleet which supplied him with provision. He found the enemy so strongly entrenched between Leitch, Edinburgh, and Walketh that he could not attack them with any prospect of advantage, and thought proper to retreat towards Musfleburgh. Lesley detached a body of horse to fall upon his rear, commanded by Lambert, over whom they gained some advantage.

Next day a hot skirmish happened between two detachments; and the Scots were repulsed to their camp with considerable loss. Cromwell made another motion towards them, in hope of drawing them from their entrenchments; but all his efforts were ineffectual. After the two armies had remained in sight of each other for several weeks, Cromwell was so strained for want of provision and forage that he found himself under a necessity of retiring. He resolved to embark his infantry on board of the fleet, and return with his horse to Berwick. With this view he marched to Dunbar, where his navy lay at anchor; and by this time his army was diminished to about twelve thousand men. He was followed by the Scots, who encamped upon a hill, at the distance of a mile from Dunbar, in full confidence of putting an end to the war, by the destruction of the whole English army.

Cromwell was now reduced to such difficulty, that he could neither embark his troops, prosecute his march, nor remain in his present situation, without exposing his army to the most imminent danger of being defeated or starved.

General Lesley, sensible of his advantage, was resolved to keep his ground, watch the motions of the enemy; but, the clamors of the ministers who attended the camp, and boldly promised victory in the name of the Lord, excited such a spirit of impatience among the soldiers, that he was obliged to yield to the torrent, and put his army in motion to attack the English.

Cromwell who was a strict Puritan spent his time in preaching, praying, and seeking the Lord, from whom, he said, he received particular comforts and assurances, during the exercise of his devotion.

On the second day of September, perceiving the Scots in motion, he exclaimed, "The Lord has delivered them into our hands." and ordered his army to sing psalms, as if he had already been assured of the victory. Indeed, he had no great reason to doubt of his success against such an enemy. He then advanced towards them, and next morning before day-light, began the attack.

The Scottish cavalry on the right wing made a vigorous charge; but were soon repulsed, broken, and put to flight: the left wing abandoned the field without engaging. Three regiments of their infantry stood until they were cut in pieces; but all the rest fled with the utmost precipitation.

Above three thousand were slaughtered on the spot, and in the pursuit; and among these some ministers, in the very act of encouraging them with assurance of vie tory.

Seven or eight thousand were taken, together with seven and twenty pieces of cannon, all their baggage and ammunition ; while, on the other hand, the English did not lose above forty men in the engagement. Cromwell immediately took possession of Leith and Edinburgh; but, the castle held out till the latter end of December.

Scottish attitude towards King Charles now changed, had they admitted the King and the Cavaliers into service the devastation may not have been as bad.

This defeat was far from being disagreeable to the king, who resided at St. Johnston's. The Scottish Parliament. They had excluded the Hamiltonians, and all the royalists, from the army over which Cromwell had obtained the victory and they now saw the necessity of employing them for the preservation of the kingdom. They now, unlike before treated the king as a person of some importance to the commonweal. They resolved that all those who had been formerly excluded should, upon proof of their repentance, be admitted to offices and employments in the state and army.

While Charles was happy to have his friends again in his

company, he was irritated with the Scots and the conditions that were set upon his friends and supports. Great numbers of Charles' followers did public penance. So that they might have an opportunity to serve their country and their King. Charles soon saw his friends in a condition to exert themselves for his interest.

To this end, the King was obliged to publish a declaration, acknowledging the sin of his father in marrying into an idolatrous family; and that he was guilty of all the blood that had been shed in the civil war. He expressed a deep sense of his own pernicious education, and the prejudices he had imbibed against the cause of God; he confessed all the former part of his life, had been a course of enmity to the work of God; he professed his repentance for having granted a commission to Montrose, and protested he would adhere to this declaration to the end of his life.

It was not without the utmost reluctance that Charles complied with this expedient, which unfortunately did not produce the desired effect. The Scottish protesters believed, that this extraordinary step, by which he voluntarily 'stigmatized his own family, was no other than a cover to some design which he had hatched against them.

On this supposition, they engaged in a closer union among themselves; and declared they would have no further communication with the resolutions, than with Cromwell and the English.

Charles, extremely chagrined to see he had subjected himself to no purpose, and very much dissatisfied with his present situation, listened to a proposal of the royalists, who solicited him to join them at Dundee, where he would find a considerable body in arms. He escaped in the night from St. Johnston's; but, at the place of rendezvous found only a very small party in waiting; and, while he deliberated upon his next excursion, he was overtaken by Colonel Montgomery, whom Argyle had detached in pursuit of him with a troop of horse. The king was obliged to return, not a little mortified at his disappointment; but, this attempt to escape had a good effect in his favor. And the attitudes of the Scots changed.

The marquis of Argyle and the committee of the estates, were now alarmed with the apprehension, that the rigor with which he had been treated, might reduce him to take some desperate resolution, perhaps, that of joining the cavaliers, and involving the nation in a civil war. They now relaxed in their severity; and even admitted him to some small share in the administration. Now trying to please the

King.

Charles perceiving that nothing effectual could be done for his service without Argyle, who was at the head of the clergy by whom the majority of the nation was directed, endeavored to gain over that nobleman to his interest. He affected to treat him with uncommon affability and esteem; and even hinted a desire of espousing his daughter. The marquis kept aloof, because he knew the king's aversion to his principles; but, his son Burnet. Lord Lorn, who was captain of the guard, attached himself to commissions.

The ceremony of the Kings coronation was performed at Scone on the first day of January 1651 and, after that time, all persons were indiscriminately admitted into his majesty's presence.

King Charles II
The Battle of Worcester:

Levies were now set on foot, without distinction of parties and an army of eighteen thousand men was completed by the beginning of June, before Cromwell could take the field, so much was he retarded by want of forage.

Charles appointed David Lesley his lieutenant-general, and putting himself at the head of his troops, took post at Torwood, between Edinburgh and Stirling, in a very advantageous situation, having at his back a plentiful country, from which he could be conveniently supplied with provision. All the passes of the Forth were strongly guarded, and his camp surrounded with entrenchments, which secured him against any attack of the enemy.

Cromwell marched up, and offered him battle; but, the Scots had been rendered circumspect by the experience of the preceding year, and would not quit their defenses. After the two armies had faced each other about six weeks. Cromwell decided to change course and detached Colonel Overton with sixteen hundred men towards Edinburgh, and they passed the firth in boats provided for that purpose. He was immediately followed by Lambert with a more considerable body; and these two officers took post in the shire of Fife, while Cromwell favored their descent by advancing to the king's entrenchments, as if he had intended to carry them by assault.

The king no sooner understood that the English had trike possession of Fife, than he sent major-general Brown, with four thousand men, to give them battle, but, he being totally routed by

Lambert, Cromwell transported his whole army without further opposition. Though he had thus cut off the king's communication with Fife, from whence he had drawn his chief supplies of provision, this motion had left the frontiers of England exposed; and even frustrated.

Charles therefore, instead of following Cromwell, who now made himself master of Perth, resolved to seize this opportunity of penetrating into England, where he did not doubt of being joined by a great number of royalists and Presbyterians. In that hope he took the route to Carlisle with all possible dispatch, and had been several days on his march before Cromwell received the least intimation of his design.

This was the second capital error which Oliver had committed since he invaded Scotland; the first was, that of suffering himself to be cooped up at Dunbar, where nothing could have saved him from ruin but the egregious folly of the Scots, joined to their want of true courage and discipline.

When he received intelligence of the King's march into England, he wrote an account of it to the Parliament, assuring them he would soon be at the heels of Charles He was prevented from assembling, and he himself be reinforced at his arrival in England.

He detached Harrison and Lambert, with a strong body of horse, to harass the king in his march: he left Monk and five thousand men' in Scotland, with orders to reduce Stirling and Dundee. They were to march quickly in hope of overtaking the King before Charles reached London.

Charles had sent Colonel Massey before him, with a detachment, to receive those who should join the royal standard and he wrote to the earl of Derby to quit the Isle of Man, and meet him in Lancashire, where that nobleman had great interest; but, because of certain events did not answer his expectation. The rigid Presbyterians in his army had deserted in great numbers, from dislike to the service.

The militia of England overawed the royalists, so that they could not rise in the king's behalf. The committee of the kirk, which followed the army, ordered Massey to publish a declaration, importing, that the king was a zealous friend to the covenant; and that such as refused to sign it would not be received in his army. Though the king refused to publish this declaration, the purport of it was so well known, that many cavaliers were deterred from joining their sovereign. The English Presbyterians were extremely averse to the king's being established, until he should have previously confirmed the concessions made by his father in the treaty of Newport.

The earl of Derby having assembled twelve hundred men for the king's service in Lancashire, was encountered by colonel Lilburn, on his march with a reinforcement to Cromwell had defeated, after an obstinate engagement, in which lord Worthington lost his life.

The king's army, instead of being augmented, was daily diminished by desertion and disease; so that he laid aside his design of marching to London, and directed his route to Worcester, where he thought he should be able to refresh and recruit his fatigued army, without running great risk from the efforts of the enemy. He met with a cordial reception from the magistrates of the place, where he was solemnly proclaimed; and he quartered his troops in the neighborhood.

Meanwhile, Cromwell being strongly reinforced, called in his detachments, and advanced towards Worcester, with an army greatly superior in number to the royalists, who were encamped within a mile of the city, and waited the attack without flinching. Cromwell, resolving to make a diversion on the other side of the Severne, detached Lambert to pass the river at the bridge of Upton, guarded by Massey, who defended it with great vigor, until he was severely wounded them and "then the bridge was abandoned, and the enemy, under the command of Fleetwood. Thus, the king was obliged to weaken his army, by sending a detachment to the same side of the river.

On September 3, 1651, the anniversary of the battle at Dunbar, which some believe was planned by Cromwell as a 'good omen.' Cromwell attacked the royalists at both ends of the town; and the engagement lasted several hours, during which, the brigade commanded by the duke of Hamilton and general Middleton, fought with great gallantry, until Middleton was dangerously hurt, the duke mortally wounded, and the greatest part of his officers and soldiers disabled or slain. No other part of the royalists made the least resistance.

The cavalry were immediately driven back into the town, which was filled with confusion and dismay. In vain did the king endeavor to rally and lead them back to the charge. They fled at full gallop; and being pursued by the enemy's horse, were killed, taken, or dispersed Two thousand perished by the sword ; and four times that number being taken, were sold as slaves to the American planters.' The earls of Lauderdale, Rothes, Carnwath, Kelly, Derby, Cleveland, and General David Lesley, fell into the enemy's hands; and the duke of Hamilton died of his wounds, sincerely regretted by all good men, as a nobleman of unblemished worth and integrity.

The Escape of King Charles

The king retired from the field with Lesley, and a good body of horse; but, seeing them overwhelmed with consternation, and believing they could not possibly reach their own country, he withdrew himself from them in the night, with two or three servants, whom he likewise dismissed, after they had cut off his hair, that he might have a better chance for remaining unknown.

By command of the earl of Derby, Lesley then went onto Boscobel in Shropshire, where he was for several days entertained by four brothers of the name of Pendrell; three of these acted as scouts, while the fourth accompanied the king, who being disguised in the habit of a peasant, worked for some days at wood-cutting.

Charles made an attempt to retire into Wales under the conduct of his companion; the passes of the Severne were guarded in such a manner, that he returned to Boscobel, where he met with colonel Careless, who had, like himself, escaped from the battle of Worcester.

It was during his residence in this place, that they were obliged to climb a spreading oak, among the thick branches of which, they passed that day together, hiding from the enemy, beholding, and overhearing the conversation of several persons, who went thither on purpose to search for their unhappy sovereign, that they might deliver him into the hands of his enemies.

In the dusk of the evening, Careless conducted the king over hedges and ditches, for about eight miles, till they arrived at a cottage belonging to a poor Roman Catholic peasant, known to the colonel, who was himself of that religion. Their host being told that the stranger was a cavalier who had escaped from Worcester, conveyed him to a little barn almost filled with hay, among which the king enjoyed a profound steep, after the fatigue he had undergone in this last pilgrimage, which he had performed in his boots. But, before he went to rest, it was thought proper that Careless should retire, as the danger was the greater while they travelled together; and send some person in whom he could confide, to conduct the king to another place of security.

Meanwhile he was entertained with coarse bread and butter-milk, this was the best fare his landlord could provide for the King without incurring the suspicion of his neighbors.

After he had rested two nights upon the hay-mow, a man came from Careless with directions to guide him to another house, more out of the way of visitation, and, at the distance of twelve miles. Before he set out on this nocturnal excursion, he exchanged apparel with his host, who, in lieu of his boots, procured an old pair of shoes; but they were so uneasy to his feet, that, after he had travelled in them a few miles, he threw them away and walked in his stockings, and these were soon torn with the hedges over which he passed.

His feet were so wounded with thorns and sharp stones, and he was so exhausted with the fatigue of this dismal journey. Before morning he reached the place of his destination, where he was again lodged in a barn among straw, fed with the most homely fare, and supplied with shoes, that did not fit properly, and stockings. From thence he was conveyed to a third house; and thus, for some days, he passed from one to another, through the habitations of poor Roman Catholics, who concealed him with great fidelity.

He received great assistance from one Mr. Huddleston, a Benedictine monk, who provided him occasionally with a horse, and more decoct apparel than the wretched garb he- had hitherto worn.

This man effected an interview between his majesty and lord Wilmot, who was likewise concealed in that neighborhood. Wilmot introduced him to Mr. Lane, a worthy gentleman, in the county of Stafford, in whose house he was conveniently accommodated. There he read the proclamation, by which a price of a thousand pounds was set upon his head, and the penalty of high-treason denounced against those who should harbor or conceal the person of Charles Stuart.

He now deliberated with Mr. Lane about the means of escaping to France; and the son, who had been a colonel in his service, was admitted to the council. They agreed that, as the king wished to be in the western parts of the kingdom bordering upon the sea, he should ride before Mr. Lane's daughter to the neighborhood of Bristol, on a visit to one Mrs. Norton, a friend and kinswoman of this young lady.

The 'journey could not be performed in less than four or five days; and there was the necessity for passing through many market-towns, where he might run the risk of being recognized. Nevertheless he resolved to hazard the adventure. He was equipped with clothes and boots for the service; and, Mrs. Lane riding on the same horse behind him, was attended by a servant in livery; Charles was dressed the part. The Colonel accompanied them at a distance, with a hawk and spaniels, on presence of taking his diversion. In this manner they set out in the month of October; and, at the house in which they lodged the first night, they were met by Lord Wilmot, with whom they adjusted the stages, in such a manner that he was seldom seen in their company.

On the morning of the fourth day colonel Lane returned to his father's house and the king, with his conductress, arrived in safety at Mr. Norton's house. During this journey it was her constant practice, that when she reached their lodgings for the night, to introduce the king as a neighbor's son, in their employment who, at the desire of his father, rode before her that he might the sooner recover of a wound with which he had been afflicted: on this presence she always provided a convenient bedchamber, to which he retired, and thither she herself carried his supper. They every day met people whose persons he knew; and when he passed through Bristol, he could not help turning out of his way, from an emotion of curiosity, and riding round the place where the castle formerly stood. When they arrived at the house of Mr. Norton, the first person he saw was Dr. Gorges, one of his own chaplains, sitting at the door, amusing himself with seeing people play at bowls.

Mrs. Lane, after the compliments of salutation had passed between her and Mrs. Norton, desired that a chamber might be provided for William, who was newly recovered of an illness. This being immediately prepared, and the king, who had retired to the stable, on the pretense of tending his horse on his return to the house was conducted to his apartment. The butler, being sent to him with a mess of broth, no sooner beheld his countenance, than he fell on his knees ; and, while the tears' ran down his cheeks, exclaimed,

"I am rejoiced to see your majesty." Charles also recognized him, he had been falconer to Sir Thomas Jermyn, and he was well acquainted with the physiognomy of Charles, who enjoined him secrecy even from Ms. Norton and his wife. He assured him of his fidelity, and scrupulously kept his word.

After supper he was visited by Dr. Gorges, who now practiced medicine, and came to offer his assistance in quality of physician. The king retired to the dark side of the room, where the doctor felt his pulse, and then asked him several other questions concerning his health, bade him be of good cheer, as the fever had left him, and withdrew.

Having stayed some days in this place, he and lord Wilmot, who lodged in the neighborhood, repaired to the house of colonel Francis Wyndham, where he was cordially received, and introduced to that gentleman's. Mother, a venerable matron, who had lost three sons and a grandson in the service of his majesty's father. While he remained in this agreeable retreat, one Mr. Ellison, a friend of the colonel, bespoke a bark at Lyme in Dorsetshire, to convey two passengers into France.

The ship-master appointed a place in the neighborhood of that town, where they should come aboard. The king, Lord Wilmot, and the colonel, rode to a small inn near the beach, but no vessel appeared; and, after they had waited all night in vain, they returned to Ellison's house, which they had left the preceding day. This disappointment was owing to the fear of the ship-master's wife, who suspected her husband of having engaged in some dangerous design, and declared she would inform the magistrate against him, should he attempt to leave his house before morning. The king made a very providential escape from the little inn at which he had lodged: it chanced to be a solemn fast; and a fanatic weaver, who had served in the Parliament's army, was preaching against Charles Stuart in a chapel that fronted the house, where he actually sat among other strangers.

A farrier, employed to inspect the shoes of the horses belonging to some of the passengers, took the liberty to examine that on which the king had travelled from the house of Colonel Lane, in hope of finding further employment. He told the inn-keeper, that one of those horses had come from the North Country; a circumstance he pretended to know from the fashion of the shoes. Then he repaired to the chapel; and, after the sermon, communicated this particular to divers persons of his acquaintance ; at length it reached the ears of the preacher, who declared the rider could be no other than Charles Stuart.

He went immediately with a constable to the house; and, finding the strangers were gone, hired horses to go in pursuit of them. Charles returned to the house of colonel Wyndham, from whence he was conducted to a place of greater security, in the neighborhood of Salisbury, prepared for his reception. He passed through a regiment of horse, and Desmond walking down a hill, with several officers. While he stayed in the house of Clarendon. Sergeant Hyde, at Heale near Salisbury, a vessel was provided by means of Dr.

Hinchman, a pretend of that cathedral.

In Scotland Monk reduced Stirling, where he found the records of that kingdom, which he sent to London, from. whence they never returned. Then he besieged Dundee; which, after an obstinate resistance, he took by assault, massacred the garrison and inhabitants, and abandoned the town to pillage. Aberdeen, St. Andrew's, and many other

The Parliament now passed an act, abolishing the royalty of Scotland, and incorporating that country with the English commonwealth empowering it however to send a certain number of representatives to the British Parliament. Commissioners were sent thither to regulate this union, in. which the whole nation voluntarily acquiesced, except a few royalists who had retired to the mountains under the earl of Glencairn and lord Balcarras, and the clergy, who protested against the incorporation, because it would produce a subordination of the church to the state, in the things of Christ. All causes were determined by a mixture of English and Scottish judges. The people, secured in their property, exercised themselves in the arts of industry; and, under this usurpation, they enjoyed infinitely more plenty and satisfaction than ever was known to their ancestors.

Prince Rupert, with his fleet, being obliged to quit Kinsale, steered to Portugal, and anchored in the river Tagus. Thither he was pursued by Blake. Being prevented, by the remonstrance's of his Portuguese majesty, from attacking him in sight of Lisbon. The prince at length escaped, with help and directed his course to the West Indies, where his brother prince Maurice was shipwrecked in a hurricane. There he committed depredations on the maps of Spain and those of the republic; and, at last, returned to France, where he sold his prizes, together with the remains of his navy. Meanwhile Blake, in revenge for the partiality manifested by the king of Portugal, made prize of twelve Portuguese ships richly laden, and intimidated the monarch with menaces of further vengeance ; so that he was fain to make submissions to the republic, and they consented to a removal of the alliance between England and Portugal.

The conquest of Ireland was finished by Ireton the new deputy, who punished with great rigor all the prisoners who had been concerned in the massacre; and, among these, Sir Phelim Oneale suffered an ignominious death upon the gallows, which was a just judgment upon him for the unparalleled cruelties he had committed. After Limeric was reduced, Ireton died of the plague in that city: Cromwell expressed great sorrow, and the republicans were inconsolable at the death of this officer, who was a man of an inflexible, savage disposition, and an inveterate enemy to kingly government.

~ From the History of the Rebellion, Lord Clarendon

King Charles II returned to England and was crowned King.

The Commonwealth was gone forever and England's Monarchy was restored. These were times of great celebration. Music, plays, balls, masques, theatre was all reintroduced to England. Everything that had disappeared with The Lord Protector and his Puritan Laws. Several historians describe his court as one of "Great Immorality." There is no denying that. He had been through so much as well as his Cavaliers, they had something to finally celebrate.

Despite his son Montrose, being alive when Charles died, he left his crown to his brother James. James had Montrose executed and shortly after that James lost the Crown to William and Mary, his own daughter. England did not and does not want a Catholic King. James other than his religion was a great Statesman and man of war. He had spent much time at sea, had been the Lord Admiral after his cousin Rupert. Those stories to follow with the next book of England's Monarchy from The Commonwealth to the new Prince George, England's future.

Chapter Nine

Conclusion of the Succession of England's Kings

The Succession of Kings Conclusion: Summary

One King Eventually defeated all his rivals and united the Kingdom of Britain. King Egbert is the King that has been credited with laying the foundation of the British Monarchy. Although the rules that the Monarchy is governed by today was far in the future, he did follow a royal blood succession one that succession has survived thousands of years

There is no doubt that besides early Rome, England has had the strongest Monarchy in history. As with every family there are a few bad apples in the pile, some just bad and some really evil.

Amongst those though we have some Monarchs that have been recorded as "True King's" and despite the evil mongers, we have anointed Saints.

While I am not writing this book to dispute, or even bring doubt to the reign of England's Monarchy, and I am not a DNA specialist nor am I a lawyer of inherent rights. I did have some doubt where John of Gaunt was concerned.

William Malmsbury did raise some of his opinions in the legitimacy of the Succession:

Of all the Kings of England that succeeded the Conqueror, Henry the 7th had the least pretention to any title to the Crown.

" For though he were supposed to have been descended from John of Gaunt, Duke of Lancaster, yet it was the Dukes paramour, Katherine Swinford, whose issue by the Duke, though by act of Parliament they were legitimized to all other purposes, yet were not capacitated to succeed the Crown of England: but if the title of Lancaster had been preferable to that of York, and Henry had been of the legitimate line, yet could not have succeeded as heir, his Mother, under whom he claimed, being then alive and out-lived her son should have been the hereditary heir.[1]

Nor did the Kings marriage with Elizabeth, the Eldest daughter

---

[1] History of the Kings of England; William of Malmsbury's Manuscripts

of Edward the 4th, improve his Title to his succession, the marriage subsequent to it; and before it the Crown, by act of Parliament, was entailed upon Henry the 7th, and heirs of his body; and after marriage he never used her name in calling Parliament, or in any Proclamation or in the coin, or in passing any Act of Parliament; and as he reigned without her before marriage, so he did after her death, (for he outlived her)- Though she left two Sons, Arthur and Henry (After Henry the 8th) and two daughters, Elizabeth Queen of Scotland and Mary Queen of France.

It seems to me that Ferdinand, King of Castile and Aragon, had the same opinion that Richard the 3rd, and the Parliament had. That the Issue of Edward the 4th were not legitimate.

This is believed because Ferdinand would not consent to the marriage of his daughter Katherine with Arthur, Prince of Wales, as long as the Earl of Warwick (Presumed legitimate heir) lived. "there was a fine trick was found out to put the poor Prince to Death, for endeavoring to make his escape out of the Tower with Perkin Warbeck, and in him ended the masculine line of the Plantagenet's, who had governed the English Nation after Stephen, to Henry the 7th. A succession lasting 340 Years. So that from the Conqueror to Henry the 8th, only one of four of the Kings succeeded in a right line, as heirs to the conqueror." (Bede)

King Henry VIII.

As the Saxon Dynasty ended in Edward the Confessor and the Norman began in the Conqueror, so it seems to me that the Norman Dynasty ended in Richard the 3rd, and another of the British was erected in Henry the 7th, who was Son of Edmund of Hadham, the son of Owen Tudor, by Katherine, daughter of Charles the 6th of France. Wife of Henry the 5th of England, and mother of Henry the

6th.

Henry the 7th's Title to the Crown of France was better and much sturdier than his claim to the Crown of England. For his title to England was that of a Maternal Ancestor, Margaret, Countess of Richmond. SO he was no otherwise related to the Crown, than descended from John of Gaunt, by Katherine Swinford his mistress. Although the King had John 'legitimized' by Parliament. It is no different than Queen Elizabeth I, her mother Anne Boleyn married to Henry VIII while his first wife was still living. OF course this marriage was the main reason England separated itself from the Church of Rome. The war of religion and persecution of both Catholics and the Protestants followed. Perhaps that was a punishment? Some of England's persecuted would have said, absolutely! They were a bit superstitious back then too.

Though I do not find Henry the 7th, or any of his descendants ever assumed the surname Tudor- Many movies, books and historians have labeled that line with the name. The Tudors just so happened to be my favorite.

For some reason, from poor Lady Jane, to the six wives and unfortunate deaths of Anne Boleyn and Katherine Howard, the Tudors makes Great Hollywood. While some have followed history accurately some have not. We will avoid talking about the 'Virgin' Queen. Although I do like Elizabeth. She played war very well.

So it is quite obvious that the Crown of England, neither in the Saxon nor Norman race has been hereditary, by any means. Neither was the succession to the Crown elective, we never read that Parliament meddled with the succession of the Crown before Henry the Forth, even though the First Parliament of Edward the 3rd renounced their allegiance to Edward the 2nd, and are said to have chosen Edward the 3rd. yet they went no further.

Such an election was no more than a declaration of their submission, as when the council declared James the Second or even before that when the Parliament was called by Queen Mary, and declared her over Jane Gray. I assume they regret that.

But weather the Crown of England was hereditary on the Saxon and Norman line, it is evident it was NOT so in the British Lines.

Before we proceed in the succession of the British line, we should take a look at the genealogy of it.

I am not talking about the current Richard the 3rd DNA reports,

I am talking historical reports, compiled from sources hundreds of years ago.[2]

I am not going to go through the whole of this I am going to copy the genealogy that pertains mostly to Richard the 3rd and the genealogy reported in the manuscript that pertains to it, due to the fact that media and internet has made light of it, I will skip over the parts prior to John of Gaunt.

John of Gaunt, by Katherine Swinford, had issue John, created Earl of Somerset. Who had issue John, created Duke of Somerset, who had issue Margaret.

After the death of Henry the 5th, Katherine his wife, (Sister of Charles the 6th of France) Married Owen Tudor, a Welch Gentleman, who had issue- Edmund of Hadham, Created Earl of Richmond. Edmund married Margaret (You know her from the White Queen Mini-series) Margaret was the daughter and Heir of John Duke of Somerset, they had issue- Henry the 7th.

Henry the 8th succeeded his Father without any contradictions. The wars between the houses of York and Lancaster had destroyed the legitimate line of the Lancastrian line. Richard the 3rd after the murder of his bother Clarence, and death of Edward the 4th, and of course after he murdered his two nephews, Edward and Richard, (those being the sons of Edward the 4th, though one is now reported to have been a female) and Richard himself being Killed in the fight of Bosworth Fields, afterwards Henry the 7th putting Edward the Earl of Warwick (The Actual heir above Richard and the last of the line) to death, NONE of the Royal Line of the Plantagenet's survived.

If by chance one of the Princes survived, that could have possibly have been Perkin Warbeck, he was also put to death.

None of the Royal Line of the Plantagenet's were left to be competitors with King Henry the 8th. After his death he was succeeded by his son.

Edward the 6th, however, contrary to the will of his Father, which ordained his daughter Mary to succeed in case he died without issue, by his will disposed his succession to his cousin Jane.

The story of Mary, poor Lady Jane and her husband Dudley.

---

[2] current media of Richard III- University of Leicester

Historians have well covered the subject. However- This has been left unsaid....

By the Law of Inheritance in England Queen Mary could NOT inherit the crown from Edward. She was a half-sister (half-blood) to him. And the same for Queen Elizabeth. Elizabeth was illegitimate, being born in the life of Mary's Mother Katherine. Mary being only half-sister to the King Edward and not related by a complete blood line. However, Mary the Queen of Scots, the daughter of James the 5th of Scotland being of complete blood relation to Edward and descended from the eldest daughter of Henry the 7th could and was the rightful heir to the throne.

"For the opinion of the Judges, after King James came in, that the Succession of the Crown differs from that of the inheritance subjects in regard of Alien born, and those of half-blood may inherit the crown; it gratis dictum, and said to please the King; for there never was such usage in England, nor any such act of Parliament to warrant their opinion.

But admit the Crown of England were inheritable from Henry 7th, yet Mary and Elizabeth could not 'both" succeed.

Regardless of the hereditary succession of Mary I and Elizabeth, the crown ultimately ended up on the head of James IV of Scotland, Son of Mary Queen of Scots and a rightful heir.

The Stuarts however were very unfortunate in their Reigns. A time of great change in England that shaped the politics of history as we know it today. A time of uprising, and Civil Wars. It is my favorite Monarchy and one that I have spent a great deal of time writing in historical novels.

This book was somewhat of two things, neither were planned. I have done a TON of research for my Stuart Novels and in the process I tend to get side tracked on interesting stories that most of the time fascinate me but know that one, they will never find their way into or novel. Also, I thought that they should be in a novel but most have nothing to do with the Stuarts. I have kept little files, and never really had a plan for them- even though it was killing me not to share some of the stories!! Recently the media has made a lot of hype about the discovery of Richard III which prompted me to do some research, and find MORE wonderful stories. About the same time I was told by several people I have way to much back story in my

Novels. (I love the 'Telling of History")

So, to kill several birds with one stone, I decided to get over my 'fetish' of back story in a reference book, and at the same time have a reason so share some of the stories I loved and thought fascinating- but have never had a reason to write about.

I also need to mention that I did not go into great details when it came to periods of the Cousin's Wars and that of the Tudors. These periods have been written into history in great details, from authors to television series. I wanted to write about subjects that are not generally known. I did not want to cram into a reference book subjects that have been covered several times by many who specialize in that specific time period. There is not much that has not already been uncovered in those periods.

This is not a book that I had planned, it was a thought that started as an article and kept going. While my Novels are my top priority, even though they have been in production for six years, this was a fun and good learning experience for me. Nothing I ever thought I would do, and as difficult as it has turned out to be, still something that I am glad I kept with and completed. I honestly hope that everyone finds something that I have included in here that they did not know before. I love those ah ha moments! I tried to include stories I thought would be interesting and perhaps not generally known. I am positive that many history buffs have heard several, I still hope there is at least one or two in here you hadn't heard before.

About the Author

I started writing when I was in Junior High. I would spend hours writing down stories and sharing them with friends. I love research, spending hundreds of hours reading rare and original materials. History is absolutely fascinating to me and the characters in my books were and are as real to me as anyone alive today. They lived amazing and trying times hundreds of years ago! Their stories haven't been told, that is my inspiration.

I am the proud mother of three children. Maygen, Brandi and my son Tristin. They're amazingly wonderful children and my other inspiration. And one furry child Bear bear who sits with me for countless hours while I read and write.

The Stuart Novels quickly became a passion, not just telling a story bit rather telling 'their' story. The complete and accurate truth of the Stuart Reign is my main goal. Keyword is the truth. That is actually quite easy because it really needs no embellishment.

When people ask what exactly it is, historical? Romance? My answer is simply this: Everything is true, the times, the places, the people. It was so exciting I don't need to make anything up. All I really do is add some personality and dialog.

The Stuart's have been the neglected step child in England's Kings and Queens of the who's who list. They have great stories, some sad, some secret and some extremely unfortunate.

I hope to complete all of them this year. Scandal in a Stuart court is coming out March of 2015. Secrets of a Princess is in the Process. The Third book in the series will be about Rupert, the devilish Prince of the Rhine. I honestly cannot wait to start writing that one! For updates on the progress of the Stuart Novels visit thestuartnovels.com or Kelliklampe.com

--Kelli Rea Klampe

Contributor Biographies

I asked Jennifer Denman and Javaneh Fennelll who were amazing to write Bio's so you can get to know them an look for their future works. I cannot thank them enough for being Contributing Authors for this bok. to both write Bio's I said this in the beginning of the book and I will say it again. They were absolutely invaluable to the completion of this book. I never imagined what an undertaking it truly was when I started. Without them this would have taken a year. I am continuously working on the Stuarts so that just would not do. I am very grateful for their friendship and their contributions to this book!

Jennifer Denman

"And If I Laugh At Any Mortal Thing, Tis That I May Not Weep." Lord Byron.

That quote has followed me since high school. It is a quote that I have lived by then and it is a quote that I have lived by throughout my life. It bears an enormous meaning when you think about history, because history parallels life. It is the basis of my life and it is the basis of everyone's life.

My life began in as anyone's, I had a mother and a father and one brother, who is nearly three years older. My family was split apart due to divorce and we all went our separate ways. I, however, was fortunate enough to land in Maryland where I achieved an unusually excellent education from Glenelg High School that I graduated from in 1986, along with some of the most gifted alumni that I am still blessed to call my friends today. And they know who they are! In that school I was challenged to write in several different styles. The teacher printed and published in different categories, some of what I wrote, and I won awards locally and nationally. So that was where I began.

Twin boys were born to me on 3 December 2001. The happiest day of my life that turned into the scariest...and then regretted them. The proudest...then the most resented. Don't mess with my boys! I mean it!

Does the term Mother Hen mean anything to you? Ha! That's Me! Jennifer Denman Musick; the now, single mother of twins; The Duchess of Fly; The Facebook Famous; The Royalist; The Admin To The Fly on The Wall.

Just Follow me on Facebook! I'm on The Fly on The Wall (I know a lot of stuff!)

Javaneh Fennell:

As a young child, I imagined faraway lands full of princes rescuing princesses from tall towers. I had a great pension for story telling at a very early age. My fairy tale dreams morphed into a love of history thanks to my mom buying me a few fictional diary books about young Marie Antoinette, Elizabeth I and Cleopatra. I became obsessed with all things to do with historical women. Marie Antoinette sparked my interest and love affair of Paris. At the age of 13 my mother sent me on a trip to Europe. The world just exploded with opportunities on that trip. To say I was obsessed with Paris and history is a wild understatement. I spent many days reading fictional and non-fictional accounts of any bit of history I could get my hands on, especially if it was about Paris.

I eventually had to live life and finished up schooling to become a licensed massage therapist. I still practice massage and specialize in deep tissue and neuromuscular therapy but my true passion is writing. Ernest Hemingway and F. Scott Fitzgerald introduced me to a new world of writing. As Hemingway once said, "There is nothing to writing. All you do is sit down at a typewriter and bleed." This quote changed my life. I decided I wanted to be a writer and was told I needed to just call myself one. I began writing short stories then I began blogging those stories at javafennellthewordsmith.blogspot.com.

Thanks to my wonderful and adoring husband, Scott, I got the opportunity to vacation in Paris with him. I ate in Hemingway's spot at Les Deux Magots. I wrote stories in a windowsill looking out at the Eiffel Tower while the gorgeous sun set creating a lovely pink warmth to the atmosphere. I saw Monet's garden. I looked upon Marie Antoinette's writing desk and her grand bedroom in Versailles. It was a writer and history buffs dream! It was an incredible journey that will last forever in my memory.

I am a writer, forever and always, and this book is the start of a beautiful adventure into endless possibilities for me and my career as a writer.

--Javaneh Fennell

Bibliography

Primary Resources:

Bede's Ecclisiastical History of England, Venerable Bede

Ecclisiastical Memoir relating chiefly to religion, John Strype

The history of the reigns of Edward V and Richard III, Sir Thomas More

The first English life of King Henry V, Tito Livio dei Frulovisi

England and France in the fifteenth Century, Charles d'Orleans

An English Chronicle of the Reigns of Richard II, Henry IV, Henry V and Henry VI, Camden Society, 1816

The History of England; from the accession of James II, Thomas Babington, Macauley

History of The Anglo Saxons, Francis Palgrave, 1850, London

The History of the Anglo Saxons from the Earliest time to Norman conquest, Sharon Turner, Vol I, II and III, 1840 London

History of English Civilization, Vol I, Vol II, 1884, New York

A History of England, J.N. Larned, 1900, New York, Boston

Lives of Queens before the Norman Conquest, Mrs. Matthew Hall, 1859

The Chronicle of Henry of Huntington, Henry of Huntington

The History of the Kings of England, William of Malmsbury, 1142

The Life of Alfred the Great, John Asser, 893

History of the Life of Richard Coeur de lion, London, 1849

The Whole Works of King Alfred the Great, Alfred King of England Charters 856

Caxton's Chronicle, John Warwork/Warkworth

Richard II, Mouwbray Duke of Norfolk

Anglo-Saxon Chronicles, E.E.C Gomme, 1909, London

Lives of Queens Queens of England From The Norman Conquest, Agnes Strictland

Memoirs of Sir Thomas More, Arthur Cayley

A Royal rhetorician, King James I of Scotland

History of the Life of Edward the Black Prince, GPR James

A History of the English Puritans, William Martyn

Hamilton Memoirs, Everard Hamilton

Historical Memoirs in the life of Mary Queen of Scots, and Reign of King James IV, Abbotsford Club

Cathedral Antiquities, Historical and descriptive accounts, John

Britton

The Life and writings of Sir Thomas More, 1892, London, Burns & Oates

The cause of the Gunpowder Plot, James Caulfield

The Gun Powder Treason, King James of England

Eikon baslike: King Charles the First

Histories of England, Oldmixon

Hustory of England under the Duke of Buckingham, Samual Gardiner

Online Referances and Resources:

The BCW Project

The University Of Leicester

Project Gutenburg